THIS B...
DATE SHO...

Where to watch birds in

Cumbria, Lancashire & Cheshire

Second edition

Jonathan Guest and Malcolm Hutcheson
Illustrated by David Mead

D1390001

Christopher Helm
A & C Black · London

BF 9/97

07184132

Second edition 1997
First edition 1992

© 1997 Jonathan Guest and Malcolm Hutcheson
Line drawings by David Mead
Maps by John Mather

Christopher Helm (Publishers) Ltd, a subsidiary of
A & C Black, 35 Bedford Row, London WC1R 4JH

0-7136-4479-6

A CIP catalogue record for this book
is available from the British Library

All rights reserved. No part of this publication may be reproduced in any form
or by any means — graphic, electronic or mechanical, including photocopy-
ing, recording, taping or information storage and retrieval systems — without
the prior permission of the publishers.

Printed and bound by Redwood Books, Trowbridge, Wiltshire

CONTENTS

CHESHIRE AND WIRRAL

ACKNOWLEDGEMENTS

We would like to thank the following people for their help in providing information, records or comments and corrections on the first proof of this book:–

I. Armstrong (RSPB), Miss K.M. Atkinson, S. & G. Barber, M. Bailey (English Nature), P. Burton, M.F. Carrier, P. Carty (National Trust), Adam Davison (Mersey Valley Warden Service), A.F. Gould, R. Harrison, P. Hill (Witton Area Conservation Group), R. Irving, I. Kinley, Rev. H. Linn, P.J. Marsh, B. Martin (Woolston Eyes Conservation Group), D. Messenger, J. Miles (RSPB), D.G. Newell, D.J. Radford (RSPB), R. Rhodes (North West Water), N.J. Sale (National Trust), J. & M. Turner, C. Wells (RSPB), J. Wilson (RSPB) and G. Yates.

We also obtained useful information from various publications, as acknowledged in our Select Bibliography (p. 217).

Special thanks to Mrs Ann Hutcheson for her patience and typing skills in setting out part of the basic manuscript.

Finally, thanks to John Mather for his artwork setting up the maps and to the staff of A & C Black for their encouragement and professional guidance.

INTRODUCTION

The counties of Cumbria, Lancashire and Cheshire, together with Merseyside and Greater Manchester which are, for convenience, subsumed within the title of this book, make up Northwest England, running from the Welsh border and the Ellesmere moraine (limit of the last glaciation) in the south, to the Scottish border in the north. The region encompasses the mountainous Lake District, where the higher hills exceed 750 m (2500 ft) above sea level, and the western flank of the Pennine hills to the east, as well as the more fertile lowlands of the Fylde and the Lancashire-Cheshire Plain. The uplands are devoted largely to sheep-rearing, with some heather management for grouse. In the south of the region, the Cheshire moors have dwindled, large areas having been converted to grazing land, while further north there has been increasing emphasis on forestry.

Hill reservoirs in the southern Pennines, constructed within the last 200 years, have suffered from the acidifying pollution that accompanied the Industrial Revolution. Many of them are steep-sided, with sparse vegetation and a limited aquatic fauna. All of them attract birds from time to time, and might reward regular coverage as a local patch, but only a selection of the more productive are included in this book.

The waters of the Lake District vary from small, clear upland tarns to large, reed-fringed meres, the best of which are ornithological sites of high quality, with excellent scenery too. Many of the Cheshire meres, also glacial in origin, are difficult of access. The cluster around Marbury, near the Shropshire border, attracts many birds but, with the exception of Marbury itself, is best left to the attentions of local watchers who can arrange ready access with landowners. Cheshire and south Lancashire contain many subsidence 'flashes', stretches of water in hollows resulting from salt or coal extraction respectively. These, like the pools caused by extraction of sand, clay and gravel, are industrial sites of benefit to birds.

The Cheshire and Lancashire lowlands contain only small fragments of ancient woodland, with further relic oak woods dotted along the southern Pennines. A thriving coppicing industry survived into the twentieth century in the Lake District, where far more broadleaved woods survive. The lowland mosses of the region, which formerly housed large heath butterflies, have now all but vanished, and some of the few remnants are still exploited for gardeners' peat, but public attitudes are changing and protection for peatlands is improving.

The coastline is for the most part low-lying, with extensive sand dunes and beaches, and estuarine mudflats.

The region's climate is heavily influenced by its west coast position. Winter temperatures along the Cumbrian coast and the Cheshire-Lancashire plain are a couple of degrees warmer than on the east coast, with fewer frosts, increasing the importance of these areas for wintering birds. Rainfall is typically 75–100 mm (30–40 in) per year on the plain, with 150 mm (60 in) or more in the central Lake District and locally elsewhere in the hills, where snow often lies in winter.

FEATURES OF THE REGION'S BIRDLIFE

Virtually the whole coastline from the Dee to the Duddon is connected at low tide by a series of sandbanks which, with the mudflats of several large estuaries, provide winter and passage quarters for hundreds of thousands of waders. Wildfowl too are well represented, both in the estuaries and on inland waters. The Lancashire mosslands hold huge winter flocks of Pink-footed Geese, thousands of Pochards frequent waters along the Mersey valley, and over 100 Ruddy Ducks gather on certain waters. The Irish Sea has relatively narrow entrances at the north and south, causing many migrant seabirds to detour round the west of Ireland. Consequently, seawatching tends to be disappointing except in strong onshore winds, particularly in autumn. Furthermore the sandy coastline lacks rugged headlands, so breeding seabirds are scarce, although several colonies of terns exist, and a few gulleries, notably Europe's largest at South Walney.

Walney is the southernmost breeding site for Eiders on the west coast of Britain. Other northern species that occasionally enter the region are England's only breeding Black Guillemots and Golden Eagles. Moorland species such as Golden Plover, Merlin and Black Grouse are found on the Pennine moors, but are coming under increasing pressure from forestry, ramblers and the excessive grazing of moorlands, especially in the south of the region. Conversely, a number of birds with southerly distributions peter out in the northwest of the region. Reed Warblers have their northernmost outpost around Leighton Moss, but are vigorously colonising any newly suitable sites. Nuthatches and Lesser Spotted Woodpeckers, which were formerly seen only south of the Mersey, have spread northwards as nineteenth-century plantations have matured, and the twentieth-century neglect of broadleaved woods has allowed nesting cavities to develop in trees. Little Owls, although numerous in the south of the region, are scarce north of Hadrian's Wall.

This region's birdwatchers have to work harder than their east coast counterparts to find rarities. However, small numbers of Eurasian landbird rarities do find their way through to the western coastline in the days following arrivals on the east coast. The best chance of finding a rare bird lies in persistent scanning of wildfowl and wader flocks for transatlantic strays, hence what some see as disproportionate interest by the region's watchers in wetland species. As authors, we may be accused of perpetuating this emphasis in our choice of sites. This is partly because it is difficult to identify agricultural or moorland sites that can absorb visitors without harm to birds or annoyance to landowners. In general, however, the status of wetland species is far better understood than that of many landbirds. In giving details of passage movement through Macclesfield Forest, by way of example, we hope to raise interest in identifying east-west corridors for migrants through the Pennines and elsewhere.

Intensive agribusiness continues to march into the Pennine foothills, immune to concerns to reduce energy consumption which face every other industry. Gas drilling and leisure marinas add to the list of threats to estuaries. Numbers of migrant species such as Turtle Dove, Tree Pipit and Ring Ouzel are much reduced, even since the first edition of this book, yet in the same few years such predators as Peregrine, Merlin, Raven and Hobby have increased and spread in response to greater protection and reduced persecution.

HOW TO USE THIS BOOK

The sites included in this book are grouped into regions, each with a map to give a general idea of their position. From north to south these regional maps cover Solway and the Border Country, the Vale of Eden, the Lake District, Cumbrian Coast, South Cumbria, North Lancashire, South Lancashire (including Greater Manchester and North Merseyside) and Cheshire with Wirral.

The format standard to the rest of this series of guides has not been adopted rigidly, nevertheless for many sites the sub-headings of 'Habitat', 'Species', 'Access', 'Timing' and 'Calendar' have been employed. The 'Species' and 'Calendar' sections in particular were often found to overlap, and in such cases the 'Calendar' heading has been dropped.

Habitat

A brief description of the habitat is given. The availability of habitat types is in itself a guide to which species of birds are likely to appear. For example any site with exposed mud is likely to attract waders from time to time even where these species are not specifically mentioned as occurring at that site. Any special protection or other details of ownership and status are also given. In some cases, reference is made to other aspects of natural history for which a site is noted.

Species

For each site, an account is given of the species likely to be seen through the varying seasons of the year. Speciality birds are given particular attention. There are, however, several sites in the region which, by their nature and because they are constantly watched at passage seasons, attract a number of rarities annually. Rare birds are just that. Their occurrence cannot be predicted with confidence, and a mention of past occurrences in the text does not mean that those occurrences will be repeated, even though that possibility remains.

Access

For most sites, there is a map showing access routes. In all cases access from nearby towns or main roads is described. Where we are aware of restrictions on access, these are detailed. The region contains a number of valuable ornithological sites of industrial nature, whose accessibility depends on the consent of the owners. In many cases good relations have been built up over the years between birdwatchers and landowners or tenants. Changes in policy towards access by such landowners may occur overnight. It is vital that all visitors respect the authority and property of landowners, both to maintain good relations and good will towards the birds, and to spare us, the authors, from embarrassment.

Several of the sites in this book are accessible by permit only. Permit systems are established in order to avoid excessive disturbance at conservation sites, to provide a source of funding for conservation bodies, and in a few cases to meet the legal requirements (insurance etc.) of the landowners. Addresses are included from which permits can be obtained.

Timing

For coastal sites, visits may need to be timed to coincide with certain states of the tide. Country parks inland may be thronged with people and apparently birdless on sunny weekends. Wind direction and other weather conditions are critical at many sites. At some sites such factors matter little, but for those where they do, recommendations are made for the best times to visit.

Calendar

This section summarises in brief note form the possible highlights at each season. There is no guarantee that all the species listed will be present on any given date. At a few sites, where interest is seasonal, there may be entries for only a part of the year. This does not necessarily mean that the site is not worth visiting at other seasons. It may indicate a lack of available information.

THE MAPS

In addition to the regional maps which indicate the general position of sites, simple larger scale maps accompany most site descriptions. These are intended to help the visitor to locate the site with confidence. (Very often there will be birdwatchers present on site—northwestern birders are generally friendly and willing to share any information they may have.) Little topographical or vegetational detail is given. A key to the maps is provided below.

Key to Maps

	Large towns and urban areas	——	Main roads
		——	Minor roads
	Deciduous woodland	++++++	Railways
	Coniferous woodland	- - - -	Track (may be motorable)
	Sea	....	Footpath
	Lakes, reservoirs and ponds	≈≈≈	River or canal
		⌒⌒	Stream or dyke
●●	Small towns and villages	P	Parking area

ABBREVIATIONS USED IN THE TEXT

CWT	Cheshire Wildlife Trust or Cumbria Wildlife Trust	NNR	National Nature Reserve
		NT	National Trust
EH	English Heritage	SSSI	Site of Special Scientific
LNR	Local Nature Reserve		Interest
LWT	Lancashire Wildlife Trust	WWT	Wildfowl and Wetlands Trust

THE SOLWAY PLAIN

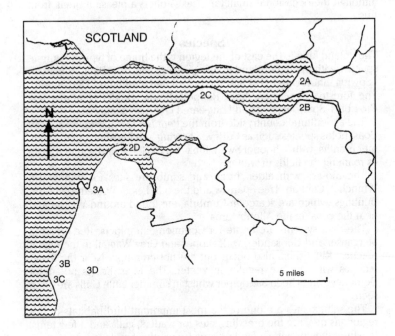

1   Longtown and Oakbank
    Gravel Pits
2A Rockcliffe Marsh
2B Burgh Marsh
2C Bowness-on-Solway
2D Grune Point and Moricambe
    Bay
3A Silloth Docks and Shore
3B Mawbray Banks
3C Dubmill Point
3D Tarns Dub

This area of Cumbria has not been closely studied by natural historians generally. It stretches from the slopes of the northern Pennines with their wide expanse of moorland, interspersed with large blocks of coniferous woodland, into the kinder territory of mixed cattle and sheep farms at the lower altitudes.

Moving westwards past Carlisle, into the Solway Plain, the lushness of the fields and hedgerows is punctuated by mixed woodland, remnant peat mosses, and raised bogs isolated by the advance of land reclamation. The whole area is drained by many rivers and streams. The River Esk, flowing from Scotland, is joined by the River Lyne and Liddle Water, which is for some of its length the border between England and Scotland. The River Eden having meandered through Carlisle, empties into the Solway headwater near the mouth of the Esk. Between the two is a vast expanse of saltmarsh—Rockcliffe Marsh. Further west the Rivers Wampool and Waver empty into Moricambe Bay, a very large intertidal area. From Silloth to Maryport the Outer Solway provides a coastal habitat complete with dune-slack systems and pebble-strewn shores. The farmland in this area is generally flat and uninspiring, although the occasional small tarn (lake) offers a pleasant break from this.

Species

The upland area to the east of the region is the home of typical Pennine species, with open moorland holding Skylark, Meadow Pipit, Wheatear, Lapwing, Short-eared Owl and the occasional Merlin and Hen Harrier. The forestry zones here hold Redpoll, Siskin, Goldcrest and a few Crossbills. Sparrowhawk and Long-eared Owl also occur.

The agricultural countryside from the Pennine foothills to the Solway Coast holds species such as Curlew, Lapwing and Redshank in the summer months, with Whooper Swan, Pink-footed Goose and winter thrushes roaming the fields in winter.

The mosses with alder, birch and scrub are sites for Willow Tit, Whinchat, Cuckoo, Tree Sparrow and the odd Lesser Whitethroat. Corn Buntings, which are scarce in Cumbria, are found around Wigton and near the coast in the Allonby area.

The river systems are home for Common Sandpipers, Red-breasted Merganser and Goosander, with Dipper and Grey Wagtail in the higher reaches. Kingfishers also occur but are not common. Near the lower reaches wildfowl are regular in winter. The River Esk is noted for Goldeneye and Green Sandpiper whilst in summer Little Gulls are often seen.

The saltmarshes are one of the most important bird habitats of this region, as they are the breeding sites for waders, gulls and a few terns. In winter they provide a feeding area for wildfowl and waders, particularly in the latter part of winter when thousands of Barnacle and Pink-footed Geese gather prior to their migration northwards. Wader passage is also strong here with large numbers of Grey Plover, Knot and Dunlin, for example. Grune Point on Moricambe Bay is a good migration watch-point for smaller migrants, which in recent years have included rarer species such as Golden Oriole, Hoopoe and Barred and Yellow-browed Warblers. Offshore, Great Shearwater, Storm and Leach's Petrels and three species of Skua have occasionally been 'storm-bound' here in adverse conditions.

Along the Solway Coast large parties of Scaup are found in winter along with Red-throated Diver and Great Crested Grebe in smaller numbers. Glaucous and Mediterranean Gulls both occur here from time to time. Among the tidewrack in the dune areas small flocks of Goldfinch and Twite are regular, the odd Snow Bunting and, more unusually, Shore Lark have occasionally appeared here.

1 LONGTOWN AND OAKBANK GRAVEL PITS

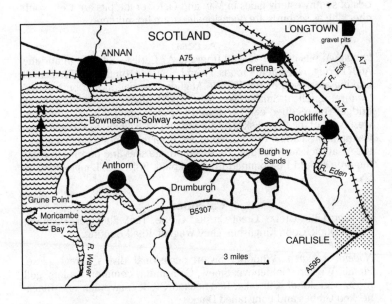

Habitat

The village of Longtown is situated 8 miles (13 km) north of Carlisle on the east bank of the River Esk. Beyond the river, on the opposite side, lie three flooded gravel pits, two being rather exposed, while the third, smaller one is surrounded by alder-fringed reedbed. A mile (1.6 km) to the north, at Oakbank Farm, are two larger gravel pits which are also exposed. The Carlisle and District Coarse Angling Association have the rights to the Longtown pits whereas Oakbank gravel pits are run by Oakbank Fisheries who have the fishing rights.

Species

The winter months and autumn and spring passage times are the best periods here. Although there is disturbance from fishing activities, the wildfowl tend to move between Longtown and Oakbank, with the River Esk the final refuge if constantly disturbed. It is an important site for wildfowl in winter with Whooper Swans and geese frequenting local fields. Smew, Great Crested Grebe and the odd diver occasionally appear. Rarer wildfowl have included grebes and the first Cumbrian record of Ruddy Duck in 1969. The cover of the reedbed at Longtown has held Bittern and the odd Reed Warbler, which is rare this far north. Spring passage brings large numbers of hirundines and a few Black Terns. The River Esk at this time is a popular place for Little Gull and Green Sandpipers. In autumn, large flocks of waders, including good numbers of Golden Plover and Curlew, gather on the surrounding fields. The gravel pits often hold the odd wader and passage tern. The reedbed in autumn has a large hirundine roost and the occasional

Water Rail, and sub-rarities have appeared at this time of year.

Timing
General visits are best made early in the day to avoid anglers. In winter a gull roost is worth checking at the latter part of the day. During periods of southwesterly gales in May and October the pits are well worth checking as seabirds are occasionally storm-bound here.

Access
Longtown pits can be viewed from the A7 Carlisle–Edinburgh and the A6071 Longtown–Gretna roads. From Longtown, on the A6071, a small parking area used by the Carlisle Angling Association can be reached by turning left at Smalstown (NY 367687) after crossing the railway bridge. The reedbed can be viewed from this point. Access along the west bank of the River Esk is by a footpath (NY 377689) to Kirkandrews. Oakbank pits can be viewed at one end from the minor road that leaves the A7 at Dickstree Cottage. These are private sites and permits to enter the area should be obtained from Oakbank Fisheries, Longtown, CA6 5NA.

Calendar
All year: Little Grebe, Great Crested Grebe, Teal, Shoveler, Pochard, Tufted Duck, Coot, Kingfisher, Grey Wagtail, Reed Bunting.

November–March: Whooper Swan, occasional divers, 'grey' geese, Pintail, Wigeon, Goldeneye, Smew, Goosander, common waders, gull roost, occasional Kittiwake, Red-necked Grebe, Slavonian and Black-necked Grebes and Long-tailed Duck.

March–May: Gadwall, Shelduck, Green and Common Sandpiper, Whimbrel, Little Gull, Black Tern, Grasshopper Warbler, Lesser Whitethroat, Whinchat and Redpoll. Sub-rarities have included Night Heron, Hobby and Mediterranean Gull.

June–July: Canada Goose, moulting Mute Swan, Ringed Plover, Green and Wood Sandpipers, Spotted Redshank and Little Gull. Two rarities, Spotted Sandpiper and Whiskered Tern, have also been recorded at this time.

August–October: Peregrine, Merlin, Dunlin, Ruff, Greenshank, Common and Arctic Tern, Chiffchaff, Sedge Warbler, Stonechat and large flocks of mixed finches, Tree Sparrow and Yellowhammer. Sub-rarities have included Ferruginous and Ruddy Duck, Osprey, Jack Snipe, Roseate Tern, Yellow-browed Warbler.

Habitat

The Solway is one of Britain's major estuaries and is of international importance for both wildfowl and waders. The English shore has extensive saltmarshes from Rockcliffe to Grune Point, all scheduled as Grade 1 SSSIs. The shoreline from Port Carlisle to Bowness and, thereafter, the Cardurnock Flatts are expanses of sand and boulder-strewn shingle. Grune Point on the south side of Moricambe Bay is a shingle promontory with a mixed scrub cover of gorse, thorn and bramble and is a well known Cumbrian migration point. At Silloth, the Solway becomes much wider and deeper and as a consequence is a site for sea-duck and other seabirds.

Species

The saltmarshes of the Inner Solway are well known for wintering geese particularly Barnacle and Pink-footed. They normally arrive in October and build up to around 10,000 birds in the case of Barnacle and 15,000 birds in the case of the Pink-footed, before departing in April to their breeding grounds. Other wildfowl for which the area is important include Cormorant, Whooper Swan, Shelduck, Scaup and Goldeneye. Waders too reach figures of national importance here including Oystercatcher, Golden Plover, Lapwing, Knot, Dunlin, Bar-tailed Godwit, Curlew, Redshank and Turnstone. Up to 100,000 gulls roost here in winter. Other wintering wlldfowl and waders include Greylag, Wigeon, Teal, Shoveler, Red-breasted Merganser, divers and grebes, Ringed and Grey Plovers, Black-tailed Godwit and Greenshank. Short-eared and Barn Owls, Hen Harrier, Merlin and Peregrine often prey on this abundance of shorebirds. Flocks of Goldfinch, Twite, Meadow Pipit and Skylark frequent the saltmarshes, with the occasional group of Snow Bunting being seen. Gravel beds on the River Eden, south of Rockcliffe—locally known as Carr Beds (NY 359607)—have produced some good rarities such as Greater Yellowlegs, Pectoral Sandpiper and

Scaup

White-winged Black Tern in the last five years, although access is rather difficult.

Bowness and Grune Point are favourite sites to visit in spring when migration is quite marked in the area. Recent years have shown May as a good month to see passage Skuas on the Inner Estuary, including Great, Arctic and Pomarine Skuas, as well as shearwaters, Fulmar, Gannet and terns. At Grune Point migrant warblers and hirundines abound, often with a sub-rarity such as Golden Oriole, Wryneck, Black Redstart or Red-backed Shrike being seen. The saltmarshes at this season are alive with the noise of breeding waders and it is also at this time that birds such as Little Egret and Spoonbill may appear, Black Tern and Little Gull often being seen at high tide. Passage Sanderling are at their most numerous in May. It is an important breeding site for wildfowl, waders, gulls and a few sea terns.

The first return migrants of autumn appear in July and, as passage increases, often include Whimbrel, Ruff, Little Stint, and Curlew Sandpiper. Black-tailed Godwit appear in numbers large enough to be of national importance on Cardurnock Flatts and around Bowness for a brief few weeks in August and September. October often brings stormy conditions and the chance of something rarer being 'storm-bound' in the natural funnel of the estuary. Great Shearwater, Storm and Leach's Petrels, Long-tailed Skua and Grey Phalarope have been seen in this month. Rare waders have also occurred, for example Pectoral and Buff-breasted Sandpipers, and in 1987 two Long-billed Dowitchers together at Anthorn in Moricambe Bay. Autumn passage of passerines can be obvious on Grune Point with large flocks or groups of warblers, finches and winter thrushes. Amongst them have occurred birds such as Firecrest, Yellow-browed Warbler, Ring Ouzel, Great Grey Shrike, Wryneck and Lapland Bunting. Gull and tern movements can be interesting at this time with stormy conditions bringing flocks of Kittiwake and Fulmar, Gannet, auks and other seabirds. Both Whiskered and White-winged Black Terns occurred out in the Inner Firth in 1987. As well as three species of skua being recorded in autumn, rarer gulls have occurred.

Timing

A large estuary such as this can be attractive to birdwatchers all the year round, but the best times are spring and autumn for waders and passerines and late winter for wildfowl, especially large concentrations of geese and birds of prey. An hour or so either side of full tide is the best time to see most of the shorebirds as they are pushed up on to their high-tide roost sited on the saltmarsh.

Access

2A ROCKCLIFFE MARSH

OS ref: NY 334648

This is an important site for breeding waders and as such is wardened throughout the summmer months by Cumbria Wildlife Trust. Access is limited and *strictly by permit*. In winter it is popular with wildfowlers. Take the A74(T) north from Carlisle, 4 miles (6.4 km) to Todhills and follow the minor road to Rockcliffe Village; turn right to Castletown House and Rockcliffe Cross 2 miles (3.2 km) from the village. Follow the lane

Barnacle Geese

half a mile (0.8 km) to the Esk Boathouse where you must leave your car. A track round the inner marsh runs along the top of the grass sea-protection embankment giving good views across the whole marsh.

2B BURGH MARSH

OS ref: NY 328608 and NY 294594

This large saltmarsh, owned by the National Trust, has two access points. Follow the B5307 in Carlisle to Bellevue where you take a minor road to the right to Kirkandrews and Burgh-by-sands. At the crossroads in the centre of the latter village turn right for the King Edward I monument. After approximately one mile (1.6 km) the road becomes a track: follow this on foot to the monument where there is a good vista of the northern part of the saltmarsh. A track to the north of this point leads to the estuary of the River Eden at Old Sandfield. The second access is at the west end of the village where the minor road to Drumburgh and Bowness follows the line of Hadrians Wall. There are good views along the tideline and the southern half of the saltmarsh 2 miles (3.2 km) west of Burgh-by-sands. Beware of high tides, which may cover the road. The winters of 1993 onwards have seen flocks of Barnacle Geese on this site with a Red-breasted Goose amongst them in the winter of 1994/95.

2C BOWNESS-ON-SOLWAY

OS ref: NY 224628

The minor road from Burgh-by-sands through Port Carlisle and Bowness-on-Solway to Cardurnock travels along the shoreline of the Inner Solway near Bowness for 3 miles (4.8 km) with good viewpoints along its length. The best viewpoints are at the car park just east of Bowness (NY 233628), the embankment of the old Solway viaduct at Herdhill Scar (NY 212628) and at Campfield Farm (NY 194610), now an RSPB reserve for studying Campfield Marsh. The passage of Pomarine

Skuas in May at this site has become a significant feature of the birding scene in Cumbria in recent years. Numbers can vary (e.g. 603 in 1992 and only 111 in 1994). They move in all weather conditions, but westerlies, with cloud and showers, are likely to produce more birds and keep them low. A new wader scrape here produced a Pectoral Sandpiper during September 1994.

2D GRUNE POINT AND MORICAMBE BAY

OS ref: NY 144569

Good views of this bay can be had on the eastern shore from the wireless station to the village of Anthorn. The western shore can be covered from Grune Point and Skinburness. To reach Grune Point take the B5302 from Carlisle to Silloth where a minor road northwards takes you to Skinburness Park near the Skinburness Hotel, where you can walk along the edge of Skinburness Marsh (NY 128559) to Grune Point or along the shoreline from the private road behind the Hotel. This makes a good circular tour of the area covering all the various habitats.

Calendar

All year: Cormorant, Oystercatcher, Redshank, Lapwing, Curlew, Snipe, Teal, Greylag, Grey Heron, gulls, Grey Wagtail, Stonechat, Reed Bunting.

November–March: Great Crested Grebe, Whooper Swan, Pink-footed Goose, Barnacle Goose, Pintail, Wigeon, Goldeneye, Scaup, Red-breasted Merganser, Eider (occasionally), Sanderling, Dunlin, Knot, Golden and Grey Plovers, Bar-tailed Godwit, Jack Snipe, Turnstone, Kittiwake, Guillemot, Short-eared Owl, Barn Owl, Hen Harrier, Merlin, Peregrine, Rock Pipit, Twite, Snow Bunting.

March–May: 'Grey' geese, Barnacle Geese, ten species of duck, Green and Common Sandpiper, Ruff, Black-tailed Godwit, Little Gull, terns, skuas (Arctic, Pomarine and Great), Black Tern, Wheatear, Whinchat, Black Redstart and hirundines. Sub-rarities have included Little Egret, White Stork, Garganey, Storm Petrel, Mediterranean Gull, Crane and Bluethroat.

June–July: Fulmar, Manx Shearwater (during gales), Gannet, terns, skuas, Wood Sandpiper, Whimbrel, Ruff, Lesser Whitethroat, Grasshopper Warbler.

August–November: Returning geese, ducks, swans and waders, Little Ringed Plover, Little Stint, Curlew Sandpiper, Grey Plover, Black-tailed Godwit, Spoonbill, terns, skuas, gulls. Excellent passage of passerines on Grune Point at this time. Sub-rarities have included Great Shearwater, Storm and Leach's Petrels, Pectoral and Buff-breasted Sandpipers, Long-billed Dowitcher, Long-tailed Skua, Wryneck, Golden Oriole, Red-backed Shrike, Yellow-browed and Barred Warblers, Firecrest and Lapland Buntings.

Habitat

This region of the Solway Firth has low, mixed coastline of sand dunes and shingle. It offers a panaromic view across to the Scottish side, Criffel being the dominant mountain. The sand dunes at South Silloth and Mawbray Banks (NT) are the two largest areas of dune slack on the English shore of the Solway and provide habitat for Natterjack Toads and a good dune flora as well as birds. Between Silloth and Allonby, at low tide, several large 'scars' come into view: these are banks of deposited large stones and shingle with small pools where many shorebirds feed. The landward side has little in the way of ornithological interest except Tarns Dub, east of the village of Holme St Cuthbert, and Salta Moss north of Allonby.

Species

The shore here holds several groups of waders and wildfowl not usually seen in the Inner Solway. In autumn and winter Mallard, Wigeon, Scaup, Goldeneye and Red-breasted Merganser predominate whilst Ringed Plover, Bar-tailed Godwit, Sanderling and Turnstone are in the majority among the waders. Wintering Great Crested Grebe are also a feature with up to 100 birds recorded recently. Red-necked and Slavonian Grebes have appeared as well as various auks and the odd Arctic and Great Skua. Gulls feature strongly, Kittiwake, Little, Mediterranean, Iceland and Glaucous Gulls often appearing in the winter months. Rock Pipit often feed on the tideline with the odd party of Twite or Goldfinch. During periods of heavy snow this coastline is often a narrow 'green' corridor and large flocks of Redwing, Fieldfare, Meadow Pipit and Skylark move in from the neighbouring countryside. It is an important breeding area for shorebirds such as Oystercatcher, Ringed Plover and the occasional pair of Little Tern. Stonechat, Whitethroat, Lesser Whitethroat and Corn Bunting also breed here, the latter is becoming a rare bird in Cumbria.

Timing

The best conditions for watching the wildfowl and waders of this area occur one or two hours before and after high water when the birds are closer to the shore. The Silloth outfall attracts large numbers of gulls, Scaup and Goldeneye. The highest tides of the year often push the waders off their roost sites into neighbouring fields. Many gulls will move inland to wash and roost at Tarns Dub, where the odd Iceland or Mediterranean may be found in the winter. Southwesterly gales can often be rewarding in bringing to the Outer Solway numbers of divers, auks, skuas and other seabirds. Spring and autumn passage of landbirds is often noteworthy and 'hard weather' movements in winter can be heavy.

Access

Access to the shore is good as the B5300 Maryport to Silloth road runs along the coast with car parks at regular intervals.

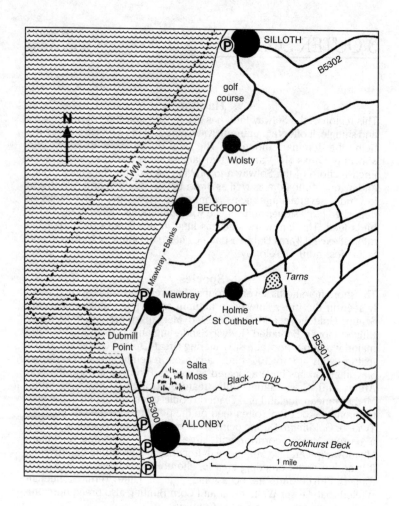

3A SILLOTH DOCKS AND SHORE

OS ref: NY 105535

Habitat and Species

The high and low water mark in Silloth Bay are close together. The promenade leading along the shoreline northeast of the town to the lighthouse and beyond to East Cote overlooks the whole of the Solway Firth. The town's public park has small groups of pines and ornamental shrubberies and is a good place to find landbird migrants amongst the high population of Collared Doves. In winter a wide selection of wildfowl, waders and gulls can be seen in the Bay, including good numbers of Great Crested Grebe, Goldeneye, Scaup and Red-breasted Merganser. Waders can best be seen at low tide as the sandbanks and scars in the Firth are exposed. Good numbers of Oystercatcher, Knot, Dunlin, Sanderling, Bar-tailed Godwit and Curlew occur. The outfall attracts many gulls at high tide with the odd Mediterranean Gull having been recorded. Arctic Skua sometimes 'harry' those birds. Seabirds are often recorded in the Bay, with Red-throated Diver, Gannet, Shag and auks being the most regular. The docks have two large grain warehouses and a large flock of Collared Dove and 'feral' pigeons reside here. The grain also attracts Chaffinch, Greenfinch, Brambling and Yellowhammer, which in turn attract the regular Sparrowhawk and the occasional Merlin and Peregrine. Stonechat and Twite have also been recorded here. A large flock of gulls is also present in the docks, sometimes including Glaucous Gull. Scaup, Common Scoter, Goldeneye, Red-breasted Merganser and Shag have been recorded in the docks, which form an excellent vantage point for observers.

Access

From the centre of Silloth, both the Docks and the promenade car park are well signposted.

3B MAWBRAY BANKS

OS ref: NY 083475

This is a mile (1.6 km) long fixed sand-dune system with some gorse and scrub cover. The shore consists of pebbles and mussel beds. Waders on the shore include Oystercatcher, Ringed Plover, Redshank, Turnstone, Sanderling, Bar-tailed Godwit, Curlew and the odd Purple Sandpiper. Mallard and Wigeon are the most common wildfowl, with occasional grebes, Shelduck, Scaup, Goldeneye and Red-breasted Merganser. Passage waders include Greenshank, Common Sandpiper, Knot and Dunlin whilst in summer the commoner gulls share the site with sea terns. The dunes are habitat for Skylark, Meadow Pipit and Short-eared Owl during migration. Large flocks of Starling roam the dune slacks in autumn and are often joined by Redwing and Fieldfare in bad weather conditions. Spring migration in the dunes is the site for 'chats'—Stonechat, Whinchat and Wheatear—with Kestrel and Sparrowhawk looking for small bird prey. Barn Owl are seen in the area. Pink-footed Geese sometimes use the coastal fields, especially in cold conditions, and small finch flocks with Reed Bunting, Yellowhammer and the odd Corn Bunting are found. Stock Doves replace Woodpigeon in this area. Mawbray Banks was the site for a wintering Hoopoe in 1988/89.

Access

The B5300 traverses the site and access to the shore is from Mawbray down a track at the road junction for The Tarns (NY 083469).

3C DUBMILL POINT

OS ref: NY 076458

The shoreline at Dubmill Point is dominated by Dubmill Scar, a large mussel bed and shingle bank where large groups of waders assemble at high tide. As well as the commoner waders this is the gathering ground for Curlew, Bar-tailed Godwit, Knot and Sanderling at peak tide time. Numbers of Bar-tailed Godwits may exceed a hundred. Grey Plover, Greenshank, Whimbrel and Spotted Redshank can be found here at migration time. Red-throated Diver, Great Crested Grebe, Whooper Swan, Eider and Common Scoter are regular wildfowl visitors and Glaucous Gull have been recorded with the gulls. The short turf along the shoreline is, as well as a roosting point for gulls, a feeding area for a sizeable flock of Twite in winter. Wheatear use this area during migration periods, large numbers having been recorded. (The first British record of Isabelline Wheatear was found in Victorian days near Allonby.) With them are Skylark, Meadow Pipit and Wagtail. On the landward side of Dubmill Point lies Salta Moss: this wetland area attracts Short-eared and Barn Owls with the odd Hen Harrier or Peregrine. Stonechat, Whinchat, Grey Wagtail, Reed Bunting, Redpoll and Siskin can also be found here. The point where Crookhurst Beck runs into the sea at Allonby is the favourite site for roosting gulls. Flocks of Ringed Plover, Turnstone, Redshank, Knot and Sanderling gather here at high tide to feed and to wash in fresh water.

Access

Access to Allonby is relatively easy as there are several coastal car parks in and near the town. Dubmill Point itself is a bit more difficult and is best approached along the road or shore from Allonby.

3D TARNS DUB

OS ref: NY 115474

This small inland lake or 'dub', some 3 miles (4.8 km) from the coast, is a regular roost site for gulls. They also use it as a site to wash, preen and rest whilst on passage. More unusual species may occur among the large flocks of Herring, Lesser Black-backed, Common and Black-headed Gulls. The lake is deep and reed-fringed, with alders growing on one side, and at the west end there is a large area of bog and associated marsh plants. Apart from the gulls, the lake attracts wildfowl such as Tufted Duck, Pochard and Goldeneye, with Teal in the marshy fringes. Barn Owl, Short-eared Owl, Hen Harrier and Merlin have all been seen quartering the marsh and surrounding fields. Sedge and Grasshopper Warblers frequent the marsh in summer and Redpoll are attracted to the alders.

More unusual species recorded here include Iceland and Glaucous Gulls, Kittiwake and the occasional tern, Jack Snipe and Water Rail; a Crane has been recorded nearby at Wolsty.

Access

To view Tarn Dub take the minor road to The Tarns from Mawbray: half a mile (0.8 km) past Holme St Cuthbert, Tarns Dub can be viewed from the road. Views of the site can also be had from the B5301 Silloth to Aspatria Road (NY 118474).

VALE OF EDEN

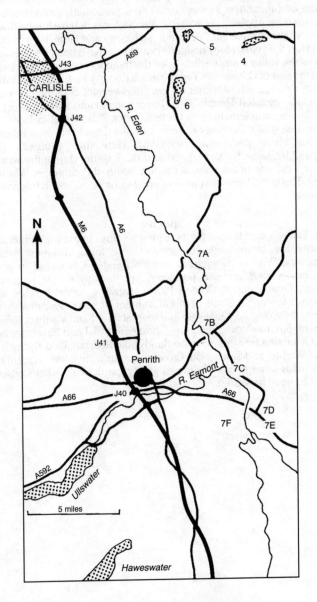

4   Geltsdale Tarn and Tindale Tarn
5   Talkin Tarn
6   Castle Carrock Reservoir
7A   Lazonby

7B   Langwathby
7C   Culgaith Area
7D   Acorn Bank
7E   Kirkby Thore
7F   Whinfell Forest, Cliburn

This sheltered, agriculturally rich valley lies on the western side of the northern Pennines. This protects the area from cold east winds in winter. It stretches for 40 miles (64 km) from Carlisle nearly to the source of the River Eden beyond Kirkby Stephen. The river is the area's dominant feature as it meanders its way north and is particularly interesting as it deepens from Appleby northwards. Although it is rich pastureland with a percentage of mixed arable farming it has, by and large, kept its character over the years. Many hedgerows and trees have been retained and only as the valley nears Carlisle does the trend for larger fields appear.

To the east of Carlisle lies Talkin Tarn, a Country Park run by Cumbria County Council, whilst higher up, on the lower slopes of the Pennines, is the more isolated Tindale Tarn. The moorland and forestry sweep of Geltsdale is complemented by Castle Carrock Reservoir at its foot.

The area where the River Eamont joins the Eden is the most interesting for birds, particularly wildfowl. Here, near Culgaith and Langwathby, large flocks of geese and duck gather during the winter. On the west side of the Vale, at Cliburn, south of Penrith, lies Whinfell Forest. This is the largest expanse of coniferous woodland in this part of Cumbria.

Species

Eden Valley is best known for its visiting wildfowl in the winter months. Notable are large flocks of 'grey' Geese and Whooper Swans. Cormorant, Wigeon, Goldeneye and Goosander also gather in good numbers. Waders are also prominent, particularly during migration periods. Oystercatcher, Golden Plover, Lapwing, Curlew, Snipe and Redshank forming the bulk of this movement. The river system also has Dipper, Grey Wagtail, Kingfisher and several large Sand Martin colonies. Buzzard, Sparrowhawk, Peregrine, Short-eared Owl and Raven are regular. Of the smaller birds, the woodlands hold Redstart, Pied Flycatcher, Wood Warbler and Siskin, with Crossbill occurring in a few areas. In the open fields large flocks of finches gather, particularly where oilseed rape has been harvested.

4 GELTSDALE (RSPB) AND TINDALE TARN

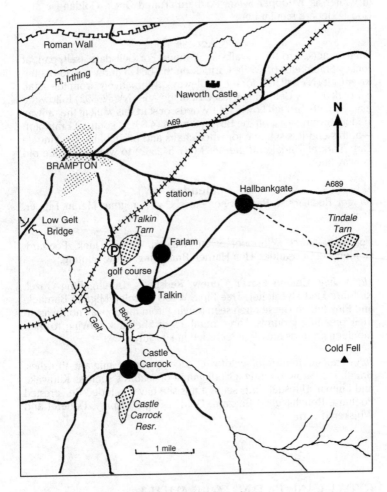

Habitat and Species

This moorland reserve, in the Northern Pennines, has a wild spectacular landscape which can be awe-inspiring, giving one a feeling of great isolation. The fells of the Kings Forest of Geltsdale are mainly covered with moorland grasses with smaller areas of heather cover. Many parts are boggy, with small streams, and some of the highest regions are bare and stone-covered. This makes for good breeding habitat for Red Grouse, Golden Plover, Curlew, Raven and Ring Ouzel.

Passage migrants at these levels include Hen Harrier, Short-eared Owl, Peregrine, Merlin, Dunlin, Twite and Snow Bunting. On the lower pastures Lapwing, Skylark, Wheatear and Meadow Pipit breed. Sparrowhawk, Kestrel, Common and Jack Snipe, Redshank, Whinchat,

Linnet and Yellowhammer are also found here. Along the path which passes through woodland of oak and beech, by the steep-sided Rivers Gelt and Irthing are breeding Dipper, Grey Wagtail and Common Sandpiper, with Redstart, Pied Flycatcher, Wood Warbler and Tree Pipit in the woods. Tindale Tarn, a typical moorland lake, is well worth a visit in winter as Whooper Swan, Pochard, Tufted Duck, Goldeneye and Goosander are regular here.

Access

There is access to three walks at all times. For Geltsdale itself, park at Jockey Shield east of Castle Carrock on the B6413 and walk across the River Gelt (NY 542562) for the bridleways. Alternatively, from the small car park at Low Gelt Bridge, just east of the A69 (NY 520592) follow the marked path through Lower Gelt Woods, or start this walk at the railway viaduct turning west off the B6413, 3 miles (4.8 km) south of Brampton —at this end it is suitable for wheelchairs and pushchairs. For Tindale Tarn, park at Tindale off the A689 (NY 542562) to walk along the old railway line.

Calendar

All year: Red Grouse, Raven, Short-eared Owl, Peregrine, Merlin, Dipper, Twite.

November–March: Whooper Swan, Wigeon, Tufted Duck, Pochard, Goldeneye, Goosander, Hen Harrier, Brambling, Snow Bunting.

March–July: Golden Plover, Curlew, Redshank, Dunlin, Ring Ouzel, Redstart, Pied Flycatcher, Tree Pipit, Wood Warbler. Migrant Barnacle and Pink-footed Geese often seen moving from the Solway northeast to their breeding grounds. Large numbers of Shelduck moving to their moulting grounds are often recorded in late July.

July–October: Return of wildfowl, large flocks of migrant thrushes, Brambling, Snow Bunting. Overflighting of seabirds such as Kittiwake and Fulmar. Unusual birds seen at this site have included Red-crested Pochard, Rough-legged Buzzard, Golden Eagle, Osprey, Dotterel and Whiskered Tern.

5 TALKIN TARN (CUMBRIA COUNTY COUNCIL)

OS Map 86
NY 545588 (see map p. 25)

Habitat and Species

This is a large lake used for recreational purposes as part of a Country Park under the auspices of Cumbria County Council. However, it is a well known site for wildfowl, passage waders and terns. In winter, wildfowl include Greylag Goose, Wigeon, Pochard, Tufted Duck, Goldeneye, Goosander and Red-breasted Merganser. Almost anything may turn up with Whooper Swan, Black-necked Grebe and Smew appearing in recent years. Breeding birds include Tufted Duck, Canada Goose, Common Sandpiper and Grey Wagtail while the surrounding woodland holds breeding Redstart, Wood Warbler and Tree Pipit. Passage waders and terns have appeared in spring and autumn and have included Avocet, Green and Wood Sandpiper, Greenshank, Black-tailed Godwit, Dunlin and Turnstone. Black Tern and Little Gull have also appeared at this time of year. The mature beech and oak around the shoreline hold a good range of woodland birds.

Access

The main car park is signposted to the left from the B6413, 3 miles (4.8 km) south of Brampton, immediately you have crossed the level-cross-ing (NY 540592). Footpaths from the car park give good access to all of the lake and most of the woodland area. Timing is important as the Country Park is popular at the weekends for canoeists and windsurfers.

6 CASTLE CARROCK RESERVOIR (NORTH WEST WATER)

OS Map 86
NY 544545
(see map on p. 25)

Habitat and Species

This reservoir is situated to the south of the village of Castle Carrock on the lower slopes of the Northern Pennines. It is planted on three sides with a mixture of conifer, larch and oak. The western edge has several areas of tall grasses and reed giving food and cover to some birds.

In winter it holds a wide selection of waterfowl including Greylag Goose, Whooper Swan, Wigeon, Teal, Pochard, Tufted Duck, Goldeneye, Red-breasted Merganser and Goosander. Rarer wildfowl such as Black-necked Grebe, Long-tailed Duck, Smew and Common Scoter have been seen from time to time. Coot also gather in large num-bers here in winter and there is a noteworthy gull roost of around 1,000 Black-headed and Common Gulls. Wader species increase during spring and autumn migration and can include Ringed Plover, Golden Plover, Dunlin, Snipe, Greenshank and Green Sandpiper; less frequent-ly are Sanderling, Ruff, Jack Snipe and Whimbrel. Common Terns appear occasionally along with the odd Black Tern and Little Gull.

The conifer woodland holds Goldfinch, Redpoll, Siskin and parties of tits and Goldcrest. Birds of prey to be seen include Buzzard, Sparrow Hawk, Peregrine, Merlin, Kestrel and Tawny Owl. Long-eared Owl have been recorded too. Osprey have occurred but Barn Owl are now scarce here as elsewhere in the county.

Access

From Castle Carrock take the B6413 south towards Croglin, turn first left on a minor road to Tottergill. Excellent views can be had of most of the reservoir (NY 543540) on a footpath to Tottergill.

Habitat

The central area, between Armathwaite and Appleby, is the most interesting part of the Eden Valley for birdwatchers. It is a mixed farming locality with large flat fields in the regions east of Penrith. Where the River Eamont joins the River Eden near Culgaith, large numbers of geese and other wildfowl occur during the winter months. Being on the lee of the highest part of the Pennines adds interest as migrant birds often travel the length of the valley between the Solway and the East Coast, over Stainmore. Forestry is being developed in this area with new stands of deciduous and coniferous woodland. Of particular interest is Whinfell Forest at Cliburn, which is mature conifer woodland managed with rotational planting and felling.

Species

This is a rich area for water-associated birds. Wildfowl such as Canada Goose and Goosander breed here as do Grey Heron, Common Sandpiper, Redshank, Oystercatcher and the odd pair of Ringed Plover, Dipper and Grey Wagtail. There are several large colonies of Sand Martin. During the winter months the wildfowl species increase, with Cormorant, Greylag Goose, Whooper Swan, Wigeon, Teal and Goldeneye. Lapwing, Golden Plover and Curlew gather in riverside fields. The arable fields, particularly where oilseed rape has been harvested, hold very large finch flocks of up to 1,000 birds. These comprise Greenfinch, Chaffinch, Brambling and Linnet, with a few Goldfinch, Tree Sparrow, Yellowhammer and Reed Bunting. Small flocks of Stock Dove can also be found here. The finch flocks attract birds of prey down from the bleaker parts of the Pennines and Sparrowhawk, Merlin and Peregrine can all be seen when the finches are present. The deciduous woodland is home for both Green and Great Spotted

Whooper Swans

Woodpeckers, and Little and Tawny Owls. Breeding birds include Tree Pipit, Redstart, Spotted Flycatcher, Wood and Garden Warblers and Blackcap. Smaller numbers of Willow Tit, Siskin, Pied Flycatcher and Chiffchaff also occur. In the birch and willow woodland that is regularly found in areas of raised peat bog, flocks of Siskin, Goldfinch and Redpoll (including some Mealy Redpoll) are seen in winter. The conifer woods are less popular with birds but Coal Tit, Siskin, a few Crossbill and Long-eared Owl are at home here. Of the migrant species, gulls and waders are often seen flighting west or east along the river. Geese and winter thrushes also migrate along this route, as do hirundines and other small passerines in summer. Unusual birds also appear from time to time: Black-throated Diver, Little Auk, Bean Goose, Smew, Red Kite, Grey Phalarope, Glaucous Gull, Firecrest and Yellow-browed Warbler have been recorded in the winter months, while in summer Night Heron, Black and White Storks, Avocet, Wood Sandpiper, Osprey, Wryneck and Red-backed Shrike have occurred.

7A LAZONBY

OS Map 86
NY 53/54

Species and Access

The village of Lazonby lies 8 miles (13 km) north of Penrith. Take the A6 to Carlisle and at Plumpton take the B6413 to Lazonby. Pass through the village to the majestic red sandstone Eden Bridge where there is a car park by the river (NY 562404). The parkland to the east of the river and fields to the west often hold large flocks of Greylag and Canada Geese in winter. Whooper Swan occur along with Goldeneye and Goosander. Common Sandpiper, Dipper, Sand Martin, Kingfisher and Grey Wagtail are some of the summer residents.

7B LANGWATHBY

OS Map 90/91
NY 53

Species and Access

Take the A686 to Alston from Penrith and after 5 miles (8 km) Langwathby is reached. The fields west of the metal girder bridge over the River Eden (NY 565338) attract a large flock of Whooper Swan in winter with Bewick's Swan in small numbers occasionally. These fields sometimes flood, which attracts good numbers of Mallard, Teal and Wigeon. Summer months bring Green Sandpiper, Grey Heron, Goldfinch and Redpoll.

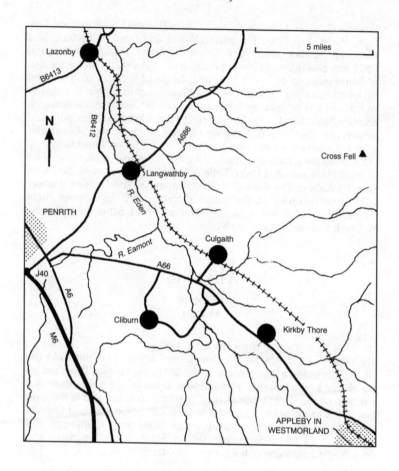

7C CULGAITH AREA

OS Map 91
NY 53 and 63

Species and Access

Where the River Eamont joins the River Eden (NY 587310) there is an area of arable farming with large flat fields. This is one of the most attractive areas for birds in the whole Eden Valley. Good views of the area can be had from the hillside by the B6412 Langwathby to Culgaith road (NY 588312). The river at this point also attracts good numbers of wildfowl; there is a Cormorant roost too. Merlin and Peregrine often hunt here and the fields attract finches, pigeons and Stock Doves. Less common birds that have been seen here include Black-throated Diver, Bean, White-fronted and Barnacle Geese, Red Kite, Mealy Redpoll and Corn Bunting. If the goose flocks are not present they may well be at Aigill Sike, north of the village of Culgaith (NY 615317).

7D ACORN BANK (NT)

OS Map 91
NY 62

Species and Access

Acorn Bank is a red sandstone manor house set in mature oak woodland. It stands beside the River Crowdundle, a tributary of the River Eden, dividing the old counties of Westmorland and Cumberland.

The house is owned by the National Trust, and besides its well known Herb Garden has woodland and riverside walks where a good range of birds can be seen. The woodland areas hold Green and Great Spotted Woodpecker, breeding Pied Flycatcher (scarce in the Eden Valley), Redstart, Tree Pipit, Chiffchaff, Siskin and Redpoll. The river attracts Grey Heron, Goosander, Dipper, Kingfisher and Grey Wagtail.

In the winter months, seed heads in the garden attract finches, including Brambling, whilst the fruiting trees and shrubs are often visited by winter thrushes and occasionally the elusive Waxwing. Overhead, 'grey' geese and Whooper Swans are often seen moving between various feeding areas in the Eden Valley. Closer observations at this site in recent years have produced records of Osprey overflying and Firecrest in an autumn tit flock.

The National Trust opens the garden and some of the walks during the open season (April–October), but the house is not open to the public. A public footpath does give access through the grounds along the River Crowdundle to the nearby village of Newbiggin.

A mile north of Temple Sowerby on the A66 take the B6412 to Culgaith at Eden Bridge (NY 605280), turn right at the bridge over the River Crowdundle and follow it to the entrance gates of Acorn Bank estate. A car park is at the main house (in the open season) where the public footpath dissects the property.

7E KIRKBY THORE

OS Map 91
NY 62

Species and Access

This is another area of large fields at a river junction. Here the Trout Beck joins the River Eden to the west of the village. The area may be viewed from two sites, one at a layby on the A66 on the site of the old railway station (NY 642240), the other north along the A66 from the village, taking the first lane left. From the railway bridge to the bend in the lane good views of the area can be obtained. Whooper Swan, 'grey' geese, Wigeon, Short-eared Owl and Peregrine are among the species seen here.

7F WHINFELL FOREST, CLIBURN

OS Map 91
NY 52

Species and Access

North of the village of Cliburn lies Whinfell Forest, a large part of which is a major forestry plantation with mature and semi-mature Sitka spruce and Scots pine. Surrounding the main forest area are several woods of Oak, Birch and Sycamore. The trackbed of the old Penrith to Darlington railway divides the forest from Cliburn Moss, which is a mature Scots pine woodland with raised bog heathland flora and all the wildlife associated with such a site. The forest holds plentiful birdlife: apart from the more common woodland species you may also find Sparrowhawk, Buzzard, Woodcock, Tawny and Long-eared Owl, Tree Pipit, Whinchat, Willow Tit, Siskin, Redpoll and occasional Crossbill.

Access to the area is limited as large parts of the forest are private. However, a minor road to Cliburn leaves the A66, 2 miles (3.2 km) northwest of Temple Sowerby (NY 595286) and passes through the eastern side of the forest. From this minor road a footpath through the forest starts at NY 587268, leading to Sawmill Cottages and eventually to the A66. Further along the minor road (NY 585264), another track leads to South Whinfell and Cliburn Moss, the latter being situated along the Penrith to Cliburn road. Planning permission has been granted in 1995 to develop part of this area as a holiday complex and may alter access in the future.

THE LAKE DISTRICT

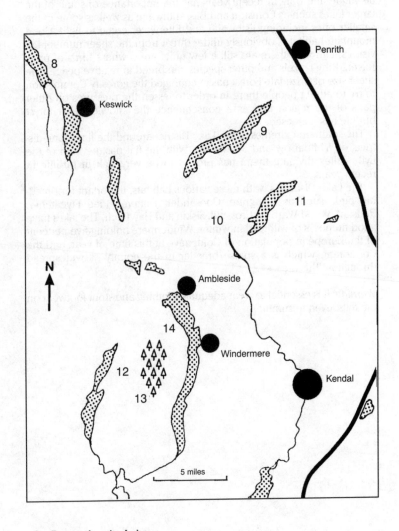

8 Bassenthwaite Lake
9 Ullswater
10 Brothers Water and Dovedale
11 Haweswater and Wet Sleddale Reservoirs
12 Coniston Water
13 Grizedale Forest
14 Lake Windermere and Esthwaite Water

The Lake District has always been a popular area for tourists, attracting many people to venture onto the mountains and lakes and into the forests. Records of good bird sites in the area have in the past been a little vague and only in recent years has the importance of some of the larger lakes such as Coniston and Bassenthwaite as well as some of the smaller ones including Esthwaite and Elterwater come to light. Good mountain habitat is obviously under threat from the sheer numbers of visitors, although there are still a few quiet areas where birds of prey, Raven, Ring Ouzels and other species can breed in relative peace. The sheer size of Grizedale Forest has encouraged the Forestry Commission to try to attract people there in order to lessen the pressures on other parts of the region and as a consequence the knowledge of forest birdlife has increased.

The southern extremes of the Lake District around the limestone districts of Whitbarrow and Scout Scar, with the flat pasture land of the Lyth Valley dividing them, has proved to be very rich in birdlife in recent years.

The Lake District is, with these various habitats, important for breeding birds such as Peregrine, Goosander, Dotterel, Pied Flycatcher, Redstart, Wood Warbler, Crossbill, Siskin and Hawfinch. The lakes have good numbers of wildfowl in winter, Windermere holding five per cent of the European population of Goldeneye at this time of year, and the Cormorant, which is a sparse breeder in the county, is widespread throughout this area.

Warning: It is essential to wear adequate clothing and stout footwear on the fells, even in summer.

Habitat

Bassenthwaite Lake is an SSSI, and as it is the fourth largest of the lakes, any disturbance is kept to a minimum. The large catchment area at the south end of the lake, with its fluctuating water level and shallow nature has produced an area of fen known as Braithwaite Bog. This mix of mire, reedbed and alder and birch scrub is very scarce now in the Lake District. Access is minimal, and as a consequence a good range of birds can be found here, particularly breeding waterbirds. At this end of the lake there are several shingle banks and islands which are roost and breeding sites for wildfowl, waders and gulls.

The western shore of the lake is dominated by steep-sloping fellsides, which are clothed for a large part by the mixed mature woodlands of Wythop Wood. Along this shore runs the A66 trunk road providing good views along its length. The eastern shore with its dominant Skiddaw skyline is less accessible. Here scattered shallow bays and inlets hold a good aquatic flora and are favourite areas for dabbling ducks. A footpath round the wooded headland at Bowness Bay to Scarness provides the best access to this shore. The local sailing club restricts its activities to the northern end of the lake.

Species

The reedbeds and fen at the southern end of the lake are an important breeding site for waterfowl, some waders and Sedge and Grasshopper Warblers and Yellow Wagtail, a bird that is scarce in the Lake District. During the winter months the number of wildfowl using the lake can reach 2,000. Cormorant, Whooper Swan, Wigeon, Goldeneye and Pochard join the resident grebes, Greylag Goose, Red-breasted Merganser and Goosander. Common Scoter, Scaup and Long-tailed Duck, along with a few Ruddy Duck, are irregular visitors. Over Braithwaite Bog hunt Sparrowhawk, Buzzard, Peregrine, Merlin and Short-eared Owl. Hen Harrier, Barn Owl and Great Grey Shrike visit from time to time, while in the reedbeds Water Rail are frequent and the

Buzzards

Bittern is an occasional visitor. Unusual species and rarities appear from time to time, including Red-throated Diver, Osprey, Great Skua, Roller, Hoopoe and Water Pipit.

Timing
Spring and autumn migration periods and the winter months are the best times to visit. Early in the day most wildfowl are visible but they tend to move to the centre of the lake in the middle of the day and are easily disturbed by the activities of the sailing club, especially at weekends.

Access
A lakeside footpath on the western shore gives excellent views of the lake from Dubwath (NY 202309) to Blackstock Point. Over the stream and along a further 100 yards (90 m) from the latter point is the public hide (NY 225265) overlooking the southern end of the lake and Braithwaite Bog.

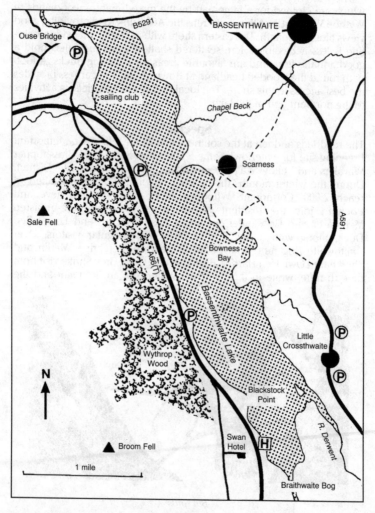

Habitat and Species

The second largest lake in the region is very beautiful and unspoilt. It is a little over 8 miles (13 km) long and is at least 180 ft (55 m) deep off Glencoyne. It winds its way around steep-sloping fells and mountains which mellow to a typical placid, reed-fringed lake at its outflow at Pooley Bridge. Ullswater is accessible around two-thirds of its shore and has a varied habitat from shingle shore and shallow bays to steep-sided wooded slopes and the odd area of reedbed. The area at Skelly Nab is named after a white fish unique to Ullswater—the 'Schelly' or freshwater herring. Huge quantities of this fish were caught at one time in a net laid across the lake at this point. During the winter the lake has an enormous gull roost with up to 25,000 birds, mainly Common and Black-headed Gulls with smaller groups of the larger gulls. In winter wildfowl numbers increase with the arrival of Cormorant, Greylag Goose, Whooper Swan, Wigeon, Pochard, Tufted Duck, Goldeneye and Goosander. Great-crested Grebe are scarce but Common Scoter, Scaup and Long-tailed Duck are sometimes seen. Breeding waterbirds include Red-breasted Merganser, Coot, Redshank, Common Sandpiper, Dipper and Grey Wagtail. The oak woods of Glencoyne, Gowbarrow and Sandwick hold Buzzard, Sparrowhawk, Tawny Owl, Woodpeckers, Nuthatch, Redstart, Pied Flycatcher, Wood Warbler, Siskin and Redpoll. Of the more unusual species, Great Northern Diver, Bewick's Swan, Barnacle Goose, Smew, Goshawk, Osprey, Hoopoe, Wryneck and Red-backed Shrike have been recorded here.

Timing

Ulllswater is popular with tourists and holidaymakers, so it is advisable to avoid a visit in peak holiday season and on bank holidays. Visits to the shoreline are most rewarding in the morning during migration seasons and in the late afternoon during the winter for the large gull roost assembly. Spring, when most of the trees have no leaves is best for passage migrants in the woodland areas.

Access

The A592 traverses the whole length of the western shore. There are parking areas along the length of this road with larger long-stay car parks at Glenridding, Glencoyne Wood, Aira Force and Pooley Bridge. Information centres at Glenridding and Pooley Bridge will provide local details and reports on conditions on the paths around the lake and on to the nearby mountains.

10 BROTHERS WATER AND DOVEDALE (NT)

Habitat and Species

Brothers Water lies at the foot of the Kirkstone Pass near the village of Hartsop. It is one of the smallest lakes, low-lying with bog and reedbed to the south and wet pasture to the north. Low Wood rises steeply from its western shore. Dovedale Beck feeds Brothers Water from the south-west and from its source flows rapidly down through Dovedale. Resident birds of the lake include Little Grebe, Heron, Tufted Duck and Goosander. Snipe frequent the boggy shores along with Dipper and Reed Bunting. In winter, Greylag Goose, Wigeon, Pochard, Goldeneye and Red-breasted Merganser enlarge the wildfowl population while in the reedbeds roam small parties of tits, Siskin and Redpoll. The summer migrant visitors include Oystercatcher, Redshank, Common Sandpiper, Yellow Wagtail and Sedge Warbler. Along the wooded shoreline and up on to the higher ground of Dovedale are the resident pairs of Buzzard and Raven. In the woods are Woodcock, Woodpeckers, Treecreeper, Nuthatch and finches; these are joined in winter by Redwing and Fieldfare and by Redstart, Pied and Spotted Flycatchers, Tree Pipit and warblers in summer.

Peregrines

Higher up the valley into Dovedale the boulder-strewn scree slopes have scattered specimen trees of oak, rowan, ash and hawthorn with juniper and gorse scrub. Sparrowhawk and Peregrine hunt here and migrant species such as Wheatear, Ring Ouzel and Whinchat occur in summer. Recently recorded scarce birds include Black-necked Grebe, Whooper Swan, Osprey, Gadwall, Shoveler and Ferruginous Duck.

Access

Brothers Water lies 3 miles (4.8 km) north of Kirkstone Pass on the A592. Beyond the lake (NY 402134) is a car park with access to a footpath along the western shore, leading to Dovedale and beyond to the

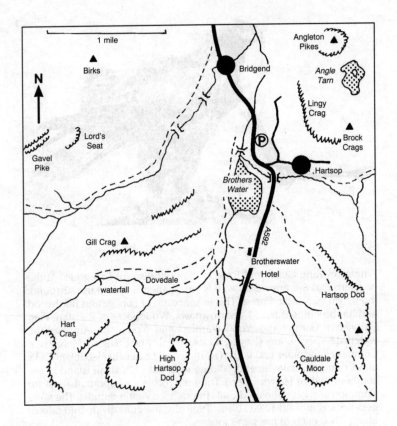

fells and Fairfield Summit. Near the waterfalls in Dovedale is a view-point near a prominent tree (NY 382117). Look out here for Raven, Peregrine and Ring Ouzel in the screes. Avoid visiting in peak holiday periods as the track is very popular with tourists, fellwalkers and ramblers.

11 HAWESWATER AND WET SLEDDALE RESERVOIRS

OS Map 90
NY 41, NY 51

Habitat and Species

The reservoir of Haweswater is situated in a horseshoe of the fells of the High Street mountain range. It is 3 miles (4.8 km) long and half a mile (0.8 km) wide and is best known for England's only breeding pair of Golden Eagles. They frequent a site near the head of the valley, which is wardened by the RSPB at an observation post throughout the spring and summer. The rugged surrounding fells have breeding Kestrel,

Golden Eagles

Wheatear, Ring Ouzel and Raven. Look out also for Peregrine. At the northern end the huge dam wall is landscaped well into the surrounding length of Naddle Forest. This is a mixture of conifer and hardwood and has breeding Buzzard, Sparrowhawk, Woodpeckers, Redstart, Pied Flycatcher, Garden and Wood Warblers and Woodcock. Amongst the waterside species are Greylag Goose, Teal, Red-breasted Merganser, Common Sandpiper and gulls. (Herring and Lesser Black-backed Gulls and Cormorant have recently started to breed on a small island to the southern end of Haweswater.) The reservoir is an important roost for Common and Black-headed Gulls through the winter months. The numbers peak at around 12,000 birds. Typically, the gulls divide into rafts of about 2,000 each of the same species.

Wet Sleddale reservoir is at the head of a small valley running southwestwards from Shap Summit. The wet meadows at the inflow to the reservoir are excellent habitat for Teal, Snipe, Curlew and Redshank. It is an important site for wildfowl, particularly Greylag and Canada Geese and Goosander. Passage migrants at both of these sites have included a few rare birds and include all three divers, Gannet, Bewick's and Whooper Swans, Wigeon, Pintail, Shoveler, Pochard, Tufted Duck, Scaup, Long-tailed Duck, Common Scoter, Goldeneye, Hen Harrier, Merlin, Ringed and Golden Plovers, Sanderling, Dunlin, Ruff, Whimbrel, Spotted Redshank, Turnstone, Kittiwake, Common and Arctic Terns, Short-eared Owl, Yellow Wagtail, Waxwing, Nuthatch, Twite, Crossbill, Hawfinch and Snow Bunting. Rarer migrants in the past decade include Slavonian Grebe, Red Kite, Osprey, Goshawk, Rough-legged Buzzard, Water Pipit, Firecrest, Golden Oriole and Red-backed Shrike. This area also has a rich variety of mountain flowers on the fells and red squirrels frequent the forest.

Access

Wet Sleddale is reached from the A6 a mile (1.6 km) south of Shap village where a minor road (NY 567128) to Wet Sleddale leads to the car park by the dam wall (NY 555114). A footpath leads into the Shap Fells from this car park, giving good views of the reservoir and the wet meadows beyond. From the A6 in Shap Village take the minor road to

Haweswater and Bampton Grange. Turn left over the bridge past the church in Bampton Grange (NY 522180) for Burnbanks. Here the road winds round the dam (NY 510162) and along the western shore for 3 miles (4.8 km) past Mardale Hotel to the car parking area at the head of the reservoir (NY 469108). Good views of the reservoir and fellside are obtained along the length of the road. Motorway access to both sites is from junction 39 on the M6 turning right along the A6 for Penrith.

Timing

Minor roads in both areas are single-track with passing places and are very narrow at some points. Avoid bank holidays as Haweswater is popular with holidaymakers and potential 'eagle-spotters'. The best time to see Golden Eagle here is late summer and autumn when the young are on the wing and disturbance to the breeding birds is reduced.

| 12 CONISTON WATER | OS Map 96/97 SD 28/29 and 39 |

Habitat

This lake is popular with visitors to the Lake District. For birdwatchers the best habitat is at either end of this 5.5-mile long (9.7 km) lake as the water here is sheltered and has areas of reedbed on its fringe for cover. The south end around High Nibthwaite is perhaps the best locality on the lake as access is difficult and the area is, as a consequence, less disturbed. The eastern shore is well wooded, the oak wood here covering the fellside over the top to Grizedale Forest. Also on this shore, about halfway along its length, is a small islet covered with Scots pine known as Fir Island. This is the main Cormorant roost site for the lake. The southern part of the western shore has easy access as the A5084 runs along its length. Beyond this is Torver Back Common, a popular area for resident and migrant birds of the open countryside. The rest of this shore is occupied by Torver Common Wood and Coniston Hall and its large camp site.

Species

This is a good lake for wildfowl, particularly in winter when numbers of Teal, Wigeon, Tufted Duck, Pochard, Goldeneye and Goosander join the resident population of Little Grebe, Canada and Greylag Geese and Red-breasted Merganser. The lake is also popular with gulls, with a Black-headed and Common Gull roost reaching around 5,000 birds at its peak. Torver Back Common and the woods around Coniston Hall are a good area to see early passage migrants such as Wheatear, Redstart, warblers and Tree Pipit. These woods, as well as the woods around Coniston and Monk Coniston, hold Nuthatch, woodpeckers (including the elusive Lesser Spotted Woodpecker), Jay, Redpoll, Siskin, Crossbill and the locally common Hawfinch.

A walk from Coniston up into the Coniston Fells can be productive as birds of higher altitudes such as Peregrine, Short-eared Owl, Ring Ouzel,

Stonechat, Raven and Twite may be found. A Chough appeared in the area around Dow Crags in 1985, probably one of the stragglers from the Manx population that occasionally turn up in Cumbria. More unusual species have been seen on the lake from time to time including all three Divers, Red-necked and Slavonian Grebe and Ring-necked Duck. Osprey has been seen on migration here.

Timing

Early morning is the time to see migrant passerines on Torver Back Common. Early in the day is also the best time to locate wildfowl, even in the winter months, as the lake is popular with yachts and windsurfing enthusiasts all year round. The south end is the most undisturbed area. Avoid visiting at bank holiday periods and midsummer weekends. Woodland specialities such as Lesser Spotted Woodpecker and Hawfinch appear more frequently in spring and early summer.

Access

Western shore: There are car parks at the southern end of the A5084 at Brown Howe (SD 290910) and at Waterhead at the north end, a mile from Coniston just off the B5285 (SD 315978). A footpath up through the arboretum at Monk Coniston Hall leads over the fell 3 miles (4.8 km) to Tarn Hows.

Eastern shore: Many car parks along the length of this shoreline, many in the woodland area. Best views of Nibthwaite area are from the car park (NT) at southern end (SD 297910). A track on to Coniston Fells and the summit of the Old Man of Coniston starts at the mountain rescue post in Coniston (SD 300976).

Calendar

All year: Little Grebe, Cormorant, Grey Heron, Greylag and Canada Geese, Teal, Tufted Duck, Red-breasted Merganser, Sparrowhawk, Buzzard, Peregrine, Snipe, Woodcock, gulls, woodpeckers, Grey Wagtail, Dipper, Nuthatch, Jay, Raven, Siskin, Twite, Redpoll, Crossbill and Hawfinch.

November–March: Great Crested Grebe, Wigeon, Shoveler, Pochard, Goldeneye, Goosander, Water Rail, Jack Snipe, winter thrushes, Brambling and flocks of mixed finches. Unusual species and rarities recorded in recent times include all three divers, Red-necked and Slavonian Grebe, Ring-necked Duck, Scaup, Long-tailed Duck, with Hen Harrier, Merlin, Chough, Waxwing and Snow Bunting at higher levels on the fells.

April–October: Shelduck, Oystercatcher, Ringed Plover, Dunlin, Curlew, Redshank, Common Sandpiper, Common Tern, Tree Pipit, Redstart, Ring Ouzel, warblers, Spotted and Pied Flycatcher, storm-blown seabirds, e.g. Fulmar, Gannet, Shag and Kittiwake. Recent unusual summer visitors include Osprey, Arctic Tern and Golden Oriole.

13 GRIZEDALE FOREST (FORESTRY COMMISSION)

OS Map 89/96
SD 39

Habitat

Grizedale Forest lies between Coniston Water in the west and Esthwaite Water in the east. It covers around 8000 acres (3240 hectares) from Hawkshead south to the village of Satterthwaite. Although large expanses of conifers clothe most of the higher ground in the area, the native oakwoods have been preserved for hardwood timber production covering around 750 acres (300 hectares). This is a relatively new forestry area and the Forestry Commission have applied a multi-purpose policy for the forest's use, encouraging wildlife conservation and recreation as well as general timber production practices. The large upland coniferous areas are now important for deer, fox, badger and red squirrel as well as many species of birds. An unsuccessful attempt was made to reintroduce Capercaille to the area in the early 1970s.

There are several nature trails through the forest, all starting at the wildlife centre. The longest trail, of 9.5 miles (15.2 km), is called the Silurian Way, named after the underlying rock formation. Through the centre of the forest runs a strip of rich agricultural farmland along the course of the Grizedale Beck. There are also several man-made lakes within the forest in created clearings. These attract wildfowl and some waders as well as providing a source of water for deer and other animals, while insects such as dragonflies and butterflies are found in good numbers.

Species

The area is a stronghold for breeding Crossbill, Nuthatch and Hawfinch, all of which are uncommon birds in Cumbria. The coniferous woodland also has breeding Redpoll, Siskin and the odd pair of Long-eared Owls. In the established oakwoods, woodpeckers, Redstart, Pied

Crossbill

Flycatcher, Tree Pipit, Wood Warbler and Chiffchaff join the commoner species such as Spotted Flycatcher, Coal and Marsh Tits, Treecreeper and various finches. Woodcock are fairly common in this area but Nightjar, once regular, has all but disappeared. In the open boggy clearings by the various tarns, Teal, Tufted Duck, Pochard, Goldeneye and Red-breasted Merganser occur from time to time, while Snipe, Curlew and Redshank appear in the boggy sites. Birds of prey also feature strongly in the forest, including Sparrowhawk, Buzzard, Peregrine and Barn, Little and Tawny Owls, with the odd sighting of Goshawk and Honey Buzzard.

Timing

The more unusual woodland species, for example Lesser Spotted Woodpecker, Crossbill and Hawfinch are most likely to be seen on a regular basis in early spring from February to April. Early morning is the best time to visit to see most of the woodland birds, although an evening visit will give a better chance of finding Nightjar and Woodcock.

Access

The main access route to Grizedale Forest centres on the minor road through the area from Hawkshead to Satterthwaite. From Hawkshead take the road to Newby Bridge and a mile (1.6 km) south of the village (SD 354976) turn right up the hill to Grizedale and Satterthwaite. Three miles along this road is the village of Grizedale and the Grizedale Forest Visitor Centre. Here there is parking, an information centre with guides to the various nature trails, hides and other access within the forest. A campsite is also situated here. Care must be taken when walking in the forest as it is easy to get lost, even with a local map. Extraction roads are constantly being added to and extended, which can cause confusion, obscuring the right of way and reducing visibility of landmarks. A compass is necessary for freestyle wanderers.

Calendar

All year: Grey Heron, Gadwall, Teal, Sparrowhawk, Buzzard, Peregrine, Snipe, Barn Owl, Long eared Owl, Woodcock, woodpeckers, Grey Wagtail, Dipper, Goldcrest, Nuthatch, Treecreeper, Jay, Siskin, Redpoll, Crossbill, Hawfinch.

November–March: Tufted Duck, Goldeneye, Red-breasted Merganser, Water Rail, Jack Snipe, Short-eared Owl, Waxwing, Stonechat, winter thrushes, Raven, Brambling.

April–October: Shelduck, Oystercatcher, Curlew, Redshank, Common Sandpiper, Nightjar, Tree Pipit, Yellow Wagtail, Redstart, Whinchat, Wood Warbler, Spotted and Pied Flycatchers. In the last 20 years less common visitors have included Honey Buzzard, Red Kite, Hen Harrier, Goshawk, Rough-legged Buzzard, Osprey, Hobby, Turtle Dove, Wryneck, Water Pipit, Firecrest, Golden Oriole and Great Grey Shrike.

14 LAKE WINDERMERE AND ESTHWAITE WATER

Habitat

Windermere, which is 10.5 miles (17 km) long, is the largest lake in England. It is also one of the most beautiful, with the head of the lake to the north lying amongst the craggy volcanic mountain ring of the central Lake District. The shoreline of the southern half is well wooded in hardwood, giving spectacular autumn colour at the end of the year. The lake appears to be in two halves, but is in fact divided by a group of islands of which Belle Isle is the largest. Although the lake is very popular with holidaymakers and tourists, they are mainly attracted to the towns of Bowness-on-Windermere and Ambleside. You can still find peace in the area in the summer months either in the woodlands of Claife Heights on the western shore or on the high pastures of the opposite side which offer magnificient views. On the western shore there are several secluded bays with reedbeds, and these, together with the various islands, give sanctuary to a wide range of waterfowl during the winter months. Goldeneye in particular can be found in good numbers on Windermere. Information of current natural history activities around the area of the lake can be obtained at the National Park Centre at Brockhole.

Esthwaite Water with its large reedbeds is a better known site for wildfowl and often attracts more unusual species.

Species

The winter months and migration times attract numbers of wildfowl, gulls and other waterbirds to the lake. Because the lake lies from south to north it is used as a regular flight lane by passage geese and is often host to storm-bound seabirds from nearby Morecambe Bay. Pink-footed Geese use this flight lane regularly as part of their movements between the Ribble estuary and the Solway during the winter. With the lake varying in depth throughout its length, wildfowl often choose regular sites in which to feed. Diving ducks are to be found at either end of the lake at Fell Foot and Waterhead, and in the shelter around the islands near the ferry. These areas often attract more unusual species such as divers, grebes, Scaup, Smew, Long-tailed Duck and Common Scoter along with small groups of Whooper Swan. Numbers of Cormorant seem to be slowly increasing over the years and now it has become a winter stronghold for the bird in the Lake District. The local feral population of Greylag Geese is occasionally joined by other species and the large gull roost between Belle Isle and Millerground has also gained Little Gull, Common and Black Tern.

The summer months attract occasional breeding pairs of Shelduck with Red-breasted Merganser, Tufted Duck and Mallard. Goldeneye are often found throughout the summer. Of the shoreline birds, the reed attracts Sedge Warblers and Reed Bunting in summer and Water Rail in winter.

Common Sandpiper are summer visitors to the open shoreline and are joined by passage Dunlin, Redshank and Greenshank from time to time. Odd migrant waders such as Sanderling, Turnstone and Purple

Nuthatch

Sandpiper have been recorded during or after bad weather conditions. Seabirds too are particularly evident after autumn gales and have included Storm and Leach's Petrels, Gannet, Fulmar, Shag, Grey Phalarope, Kittiwake, terns, Guillemot and Little Auk.

The oak woods on the western shore hold breeding Nuthatch, Redstart, Pied and Spotted Flycatchers, Tree Pipits, Wood Warbler and Hawfinch, while the conifer stands on Claife Heights have Redpoll, Siskin and Crossbill. Buzzard, Sparrowhawk and Peregrine are to be seen here and rarer raptors such as Honey Buzzard, Goshawk, Montagu's Harrier, Hobby and Osprey have all been reported. In 1977 a pair of Fieldfare bred in this area.

The lake is also well known for other forms of wildlife as the wood-lands have deer, badgers and red squirrel whilst in the deep waters char and pike attract fishermen from a wide area.

Esthwaite Water is a breeding site for Great Crested Grebe, which is scarce in the county, while in winter rarer wildfowl such as Red and Black-necked Grebes, Long-tailed Duck, Scaup, Common Scoter and Ring-necked Duck have all been recorded in recent years. Bittern have been found in winter in the reedbeds, which are also a favourite haunt for Water Rails.

Timing

Winter and early spring is the best time to watch the lake and walk the local woods and fellsides. The deep water areas at Fell Foot and between the Ferry and Belle Isle are favourite locations for divers, grebes and diving duck. The large gull roost is at its peak in midwinter and can be viewed from either shore. During spells of keen frost the lake freezes over, and the restricted deep-water areas then focus the numbers of wildfowl and gulls. After autumn and winter storms, look out for weak and lost seabirds.

Access

On the eastern shore the A592 and A591 follow the length of the lake: there are numerous car parks or viewpoints along its length.

Noteworthy among these is Fell Foot Country Park (SD 380870) run by the National Trust. The car park here is open all year, offering good views of the southern reedbeds and tail of the lake. Cockshot Point (SD 397965) is a vantage point for viewing the area near the ferry and around the islands. Brockhole (NY 390001), the National Park Centre, is only open from April to October. Waterhead, Ambleside (NY 375032) is useful for viewing the head of the lake.

On the western shore, Wray Castle (NT) (NY 375001) offers an area of oak wood and shoreline paths with all-year access. Take the A593 from Ambleside and at Clappersgate take the B5286 to Hawkshead. After 1.5 miles (2.4 km) take a minor road left to High Wray and after a further mile (1.6 km) the imposing arched gateway to Wray Castle is on the left. Drive through the arch and down to the Castle. The car park and start of the various paths are at the north side of the Castle.

There are numerous walks through the woods on Claife Heights, several passing tarns on the summit which can hold wildfowl in winter (Moss Eccles Tarn has a Black-headed Gullery in early summer). The recognised approach to Claife Heights is from Harrowslack (SD 387965), which is half a mile (0.8 km) along a minor road from the B5285 at Ferry House. At this point there are several routes over the Heights, or alternatively you can take the Claife Shore Walk of 1.5 miles (2.4 km) with its views to Belle Isle and beyond.

Esthwaite Water may be viewed along its length from the B5285 Hawkshead to Ferry Road. A car park (SD 364953) gives views of the reedbeds at the southern end of the lake.

Calendar

All year: Great Crested Grebe, Cormorant, Grey Heron, Greylag Goose, Tufted Duck, Red-breasted Merganser, Buzzard, Peregrine, Woodcock, gulls, woodpeckers, wagtails, Dipper, Goldcrest, Willow Tit, Nuthatch, Raven, Crossbill, Siskin, Hawfinch, Reed Bunting.

November–March: Red-necked Grebe, Wigeon, Pochard, Long-tailed Duck, Goldeneye, Goosander, Water Rail, Kingfisher, winter thrushes, Brambling.

April–October: Shelduck, Gadwall, Common Scoter, Oystercatcher, Dunlin, Curlew, Redshank, Common Sandpiper, Little Gull, terns, Tree Pipit, Yellow Wagtail, Redstart, warblers (including Reed and Grasshopper Warblers), Pied Flycatcher. Unusual and storm-bound birds have in the last ten years included divers, Slavonian Grebe, Fulmar, Storm and Leach's Petrels, Gannet, Shag, Bittern, Red-crested Pochard, Ring-necked Duck, Ruddy Duck, Montagu's Harrier, Goshawk, Osprey, Sanderling, Purple Sandpiper, Whimbrel, Greenshank, Turnstone, Grey Phalarope, Kittiwake, Little Auk, Golden Oriole and Nutcracker.

THE CUMBRIAN COAST

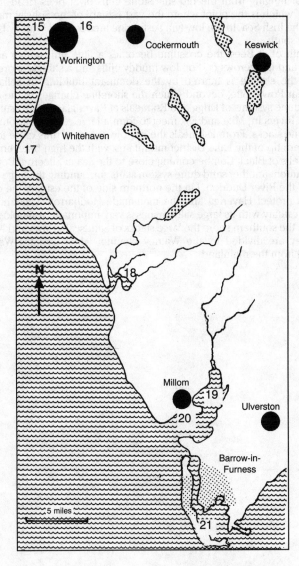

15	Workington Harbour	19C	Angerton Marsh
16	Siddick Pond	19D	Askam/Dunnerholme
17	St Bees Head	19E	Sandscale Haws
18	Ravenglass and District	19F	Borwick Rails
19	Duddon Estuary	20	Hodbarrow
19A	Lady Hall	21	Walney Island
19B	Green Road Station		

The coastline of Cumbria from Workington to Barrow-in-Furness is not generally associated with natural beauty. More often it is regarded as a polluted part of Britain's coast affected by the nuclear, chemical and coal industries which feature here. However, it has a great range of habitat ranging from the red sandstone cliffs of St Bees Head in the north, which is the point where the vast estuary of the Solway merges with the Irish Sea, to the low-lying estuarine area around Walney Island in the south.

South of St Bees, the coastline becomes a little uninspiring as the fields and hedgerows end on low muddy cliffs and a shingle shoreline. Here the skyline is marred by the dominant building of Sellafield Nuclear Power Site, beyond which the shoreline changes to the large sand-dune systems of Drigg and Eskmeals at Ravenglass. Here estuaries of the Rivers Irt, Mite and Esk meet to form a large estuary surrounded by dune slacks. From Eskmeals the narrow coastline runs close to the southern tip of the Lake District mountains, with the high bracken covered fells of Black Combe coming close to the sea at Silecroft. Beyond Kirksanton, another sand-dune system starts surrounding the large estuary of the River Duddon. On the northern side of the estuary the dune slacks protect Haverigg and the man-made Hodbarrow Lagoon. The inner estuary with its large saltmarshes is very important ornithologically. On the southern shore the large slacks of Sandscale Haws and North Walney are divided by the Walney channel which isolates Walney Island from the mainland.

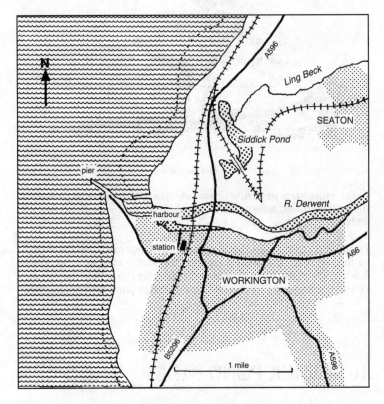

Habitat and Species

The harbour at Workington lies at the mouth of the River Derwent. Although the docks are still active with coasters, fishing boats and a small marina, the surrounding area has lost all the large foundries and slag banks associated with the steel industry and has been landscaped. Access to the old pier on the southern side of the harbour gives good views over the whole area as well as along the local coastline and out to sea. From the shelter of the old light station at the end of the pier one can watch Purple Sandpiper and Rock Pipits feeding amongst the concrete block breakwater. Farther out, more regular divers, sea-duck, auks, gulls and terns can be found with occasional visits from Manx Shearwater, Storm Petrel, Shag, Arctic and Great Skuas, Mediterranean, Little and Glaucous Gulls. Along the shoreline, waders such Ringed Plover, Dunlin, Knot and Sanderling are to be found, while the newly landscaped area attracts passage Wheatear, Stonechat, Whinchat, Meadow Pipits and occasionally Black Redstart. The northern shoreline at low tide exposes shingle and sandbanks where Curlew, Godwits, Knot, Dunlin and Turnstone feed and the larger gulls come to roost. Look out for Glaucous Gulls here in winter.

Glaucous Gull

The inner harbour itself is always worth a look for gulls, especially at the outfall. It was here a first-summer Ross's Gull was found in June 1994.

Access

From Workington Railway Station take the minor road over the railway to the harbour. This road meanders round the railway yards to the Marina, where it follows the estuary of the River Derwent to the pier and coastguard lookout (NY 985298). The pier is popular with sea anglers.

16 SIDDICK POND (ADC)

OS Map 89
NY 93, NY 02 and NY 03
(see map on p. 51)

Habitat

Siddick Pond lies between the northern bank of the River Derwent and the village of Siddick. It is an area of open water and reedbed surrounded on the northern shore by an old colliery waste tip while a railway embankment bounds the western and southern fringes. To the east a large timber yard of the local Board Mill and the main Carlisle to Workington road form the boundary. The pond lies in an ancient channel of the River Derwent and is shallow in nature being between 9 and 10 feet (about 3 m) deep at the deepest point. A culvert under the railway lets the water flow to another smaller pond. The whole area is fed by a small stream known as Ling Beck.

A major feature of the site is that its fringe is predominantly reedbed mingled with patches of rush, sedge and areas of waterlily. In summer the water level falls, exposing areas of mud popular with passage waders. The embankments behind the reedbeds are covered with bramble, gorse and hawthorn, while at the southern end a small thicket of willow gives shelter to passerines and birds of prey

Species

During the winter months a wide selection of waterfowl is normally present including Whooper Swan, Wigeon, Teal, Shoveler, Pochard, Tufted Duck and Goldeneye, with Great Crested Grebe, Shelduck, Gadwall, Pintail, Long-tailed Duck, Goosander and Red-breasted Merganser appearing from time to time. During periods of winter gales or prolonged frost conditions rarer species such as Red-throated Diver, Black-necked Grebe, Bewick's Swan, Scaup, Common Scoter and Smew have been recorded. Gull's use the pond all year to bathe and preen, with Cormorant also being a regular visitor. The reedbed is a roost for Starling in winter and they are predated by Sparrowhawk, Tawny Owl and occasionally Merlin, Barn Owl and Long and Short-eared Owls. Bittern and Water Rail have also been recorded at this time of year.

During spring and autumn passage waders, for example, Little Stint, Curlew Sandpiper, Dunlin, Ruff, Jack Snipe, godwits, Greenshank and sandpipers have been found along with Goldeneye, Black Tern, hirundines (which gather in large numbers), wagtails, warblers including Grasshopper and Reed (which is scarce in the north), Lesser Whitethroat and other passerines. In 1981 and 1990 an irruption movement of Bearded Tits was recorded here and in 1982 a singing Savi's Warbler was found. Rarities and sub-rarities seen here in recent years include Leach's Petrel, Little Egret, Spoonbill, Ruddy Duck, Marsh Harrier, Long-tailed Skua, Red-necked Phalarope, Barred and Yellow-browed Warblers, Firecrest and Little Bunting. Breeding species include Little Grebe, Tufted Duck and Reed Warbler.

Access

A hide is now open with access and a key obtainable from the security gate of the Thames Board Mill (the hide is on their property) on the A596. The railway track bed has been taken up and is to become a cycleway and footpath during 1996. Obviously, good viewing will be had from this vantage point.

Calendar

All year: Little Grebe, Cormorant, Grey Heron, Teal, Shoveler, Tufted Duck, Water Rail, Barn Owl, Reed Bunting.

November–March: Whooper Swan, Wigeon, Pochard, Goldeneye, Red-breasted Merganser in cold weather, Goosander, possibly Bewick's Swan and Red-throated Diver, Sparrowhawk, Merlin, Peregrine, the occasional Hen Harrier, Long and Short-eared Owls, Snipe, Jack Snipe, gulls including possibly Glaucous and Kittiwake, Kingfisher, Grey Wagtail, Stonechat, winter thrushes, Blackcap, Starling roost, finch roost, mainly Chaffinch, Greenfinch with a few Brambling, Goldfinch and Linnet.

April–July: Garganey, lingering winter wildfowl, the odd passage Osprey and Marsh Harrier, migrant waders, a few terns including Common, Arctic, Little, Sandwich and Black, landbird migrants including pipits, swifts, hirundines, Grasshopper, Sedge and Reed warblers.

August–October: Returning winter wildfowl and migrant raptors. Waders include Little Stint, Curlew Sandpiper, Ruff, Greenshank, large hirundine roost, Pied Flycatcher, warblers, Wagtail roost.

Habitat

The magnificient red sandstone cliffs at St Bees Head dominate the Cumbrian coastline. The North Head with its lighthouse is the highest point. A coastal path follows the cliff-top from St Bees to Workington. Inland from the cliffs are large fields and drystone walls with little cover for birds. The only feature along the cliff path is Fleswick Bay, which is halfway between North Head and South Head. This is a small sheltered bay behind which a steep-sided valley extends inland with good gorse and bramble cover and a small stream tumbling down to the shore. The farm at Tranflat Hall is behind the North Head and is part of the RSPB recording area.

Species

The cliffs of St Bees hold around 5,000 breeding seabirds, the largest colony on the west coast of England. The bulk of this colony is made up of Guillemot, Razorbill and Kittiwake, with a few pairs of Puffin and Black Guillemot. This is the only breeding site in England for the latter species. Several thousand pairs of Herring and Lesser Black-backed Gulls breed, as do a few Greater Black-backed Gulls. Surprisingly, neither Cormorant nor Shag breed here regularly.

During spring and autumn migration seabird passage and passerine passage over the cliffs are notable. Divers, grebes, sea-ducks, 'grey' geese, skuas and terns are all noted here. Midsummer sees a regular movement of Manx Shearwater, Fulmar and Gannet while in autumn there is a good possibility of seeing Storm and Leach's Petrels.

Passerine passage along the cliffs can be heavy in early spring with good numbers of Skylark, pipits, chats and warblers. Hirundine and Swift movements can be noteworthy from time to time. All the small birds attract birds of prey such as Sparrowhawk, occasional Merlin and Peregrine. Little Owls breed in the area. Late autumn movements of corvids, for example Carrion Crow, Rook and Jackdaw have been

Black Guillemots

known to include the odd Chough or Hooded Crow, probably from the not so distant Manx population. Raven is a breeding species here.

In winter the sea still holds interesting species such as Red-throated Diver, Great Crested Grebe, Eider, Common Scoter and the odd over-wintering auk. The feral pigeons on the cliffs keep Peregrine in the vicinity while the cliff-top fields hold flocks of winter thrushes, Skylark, pipits, Starling and mixed finch flocks. Corn Bunting and the occasional Black Redstart or Stonechat occur in these flocks.

Bottle-nosed dolphins and seals add to the wildlife interest of this stretch of coast.

Timing

Breeding seabirds are present from March to mid July. Although most activity occurs early in the day, many of the auks sit on the sea near the cliffs. Black Guillemot and Puffin tend to feed away from the bulk of the other birds and are often nearest to the cliffs. A visit early in the day is best when looking for spring and autumn migrants particularly in the 'valley' of Fleswick Bay and the fields and low hedgerows behind the North Head around Tarnflat Hall.

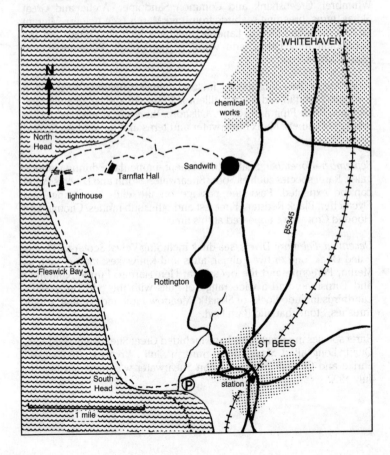

Access

From the north follow the A595(T) from Whitehaven to the outer edge of the built up area of Mirehouse, approximately 2 miles (3.2 km), where a minor road to the right to Sandwith village crosses the valley and the B5345. In Sandwith leave your vehicle near the Post Office and walk along the private road to St Bees Head, starting at NX 965147. It is approximately 2 miles (3.2 km) to the lighthouse and the cliff path via Tarnflat Hall. Although it is an uphill walk it is fairly easy. From the lighthouse take the cliff path south to St Bees. The best views of the breeding cliffs are between the lighthouse and Fleswick Bay.

From the south you will find the start of the cliff path in the car park in St Bees at NX 961118. Stout footwear is recommended.

Calendar

All year: Fulmar, Cormorant, gulls, Grey Partridge, Kittiwake, Stock Dove, Little Owl, Rock Pipit, Stonechat, Raven, Corn Bunting.

March–May: Divers, Manx Shearwater, Gannet, Common Scoter, Eider, Red-breasted Merganser, Pink-footed Geese, waders including godwits, Whimbrel, Greenshank and Common Sandpiper, Arctic and Great Skuas, terns, breeding seabirds from mid March (see below). Migrant raptors including Merlin. Landbird migrants including chats and the occasional Ring Ouzel, and warblers, particularly Whitethroat and Lesser Whitethroat.

June–August: Breeding species include Fulmar, Guillemot, Razorbill, a few pairs of Puffin and Black Guillemot, Kittiwake and larger gulls, feral pigeons, Rock Pipit and Raven. Offshore, there are occasional movements of Gannets, Manx Shearwater and terns and the odd Arctic and Great Skua.

September–November: Seabird movement, particularly during westerly gales. Rarer species such as Sooty Shearwater, Storm and Leach's Petrel can be expected. Passerine passage on the cliffs can bring Pied Flycatcher, Black Redstart, Firecrest and other sub-rarities. Chough and Hooded Crow have appeared at this time.

December–February: Divers, sea-duck including Velvet Scoter and Long-tailed Duck, one or two Fulmar, auks and Kittiwakes, raptors such as Merlin, Peregrine and the occasional Hen Harrier, Purple Sandpiper and Turnstone, and a wide range of gulls with the odd Great Skua. Landbirds include flocks of Skylark, Meadow Pipit and Starling, winter thrushes, Stonechat and Barn Owl.

Rarer species in recent years have included Great Shearwater, Red Kite, Quail, Long-tailed Skua, Mediterranean Gull, Wryneck, Red-backed Shrike and Chough. Mediterranean Shearwater was recorded here in July 1992.

Habitat and Species

The historic village of Ravenglass is situated on an estuary where the Rivers Irt, Mite and Esk meet then flow into the sea through a channel in a large sand-dune system. The north shore is protected by the dunes of Drigg, once the largest Black-headed Gull colony in Europe, and the south shore by the dunes of Eskmeals Nature Reserve. The three inner estuaries provide shelter and feeding habitat for a large number of wild-fowl, waders, gulls and terns. During the winter the Greylag Geese, which are resident here, increase their numbers to over 100 birds, with Shelduck, Wigeon and Teal gathering in good numbers too. Smaller numbers of Whooper Swan, Pintail, Common Scoter, Goldeneye and Red-breasted Merganser also occur. Waders at this time include Ringed and Grey Plover, Knot, Dunlin, Snipe, Curlew, Redshank, the odd Greenshank and Turnstone.

The gull colony on the Drigg reserve dwindled away in the 1980s and the Tern colony there disappeared in 1977.

In spring, a small flock of Common Scoter gather off the Eskmeals dune system, as do numbers of Red-throated Diver, Cormorant and auks. Amongst the dunes grow good patches of sea buckthorn whose fruit attracts winter thrushes, finches and other passage migrants. Eskmeals Dunes are also a site of importance for a wide range of fauna and flora as well as a thriving natterjack toad colony. Down the coast 3 miles (4.8 km) south of Eskmeals reserve and the MOD gun range is a small headland with a coastguard station at Selker. In the last few years this has become a local seawatch point, particularly in spring and autumn. A good range of passage seabirds has been recorded during periods of October gales in which numbers of Manx and Sooty Shearwater, Storm and Leach's Petrel, Gannets, auks, gulls and skuas have been observed.

Access

The central confluence of the three estuaries can be seen quite well from the village of Ravenglass with viewpoints of the upper reaches of the River Irt, accessible from Drigg Station down a track off the minor road (SD 064983). The upper area of the River Mite can be seen from the A598 at Thornflatt Hill (SD 092971) and the minor road at the Esk railway viaduct (SD 086943) gives good viewpoints along the inner Esk estuary.

Eskmeals Dunes Nature Reserve is also acccessible at the latter grid reference by the Esk viaduct: permits are obtainable from the CWT Warden. Wear suitable footwear as the area is very muddy.

For the Drigg Dunes Nature Reserve, take the B5344 at Holmrook for Seascale and the village of Drigg, take the minor road left to Drigg Station and to the coast 2 miles (3.2 km) beyond. Permits are required from Cumbria County Council, and care must be taken to observe the war-den's instructions as to access on this site as it is in an MOD danger area.

At Tarn Bay, Bootle, the car park on the coast south of Eskmeals gun range (SD 080907) is excellent for passage seabirds and coastal wild-fowl, waders and gulls.

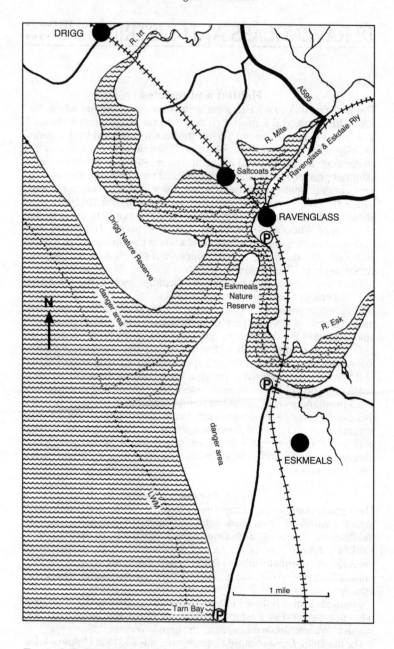

To reach Selker Coastguard Station, take the minor road westwards to Bootle Station off the A595 in the village of Bootle. At the station turn left along a minor road which becomes a track to Broadwater Farm. Continue past the farm to the Coastguard Station where the sea can be watched from the hill top.

Calendar

All year: Cormorant, Grey Heron, Greylag Geese, Shelduck, Teal, Red-breasted Merganser, Sparrowhawk, Buzzard, Peregrine, Oystercatcher, Ringed Plover, Dunlin, Snipe, Curlew, Redshank, gulls, Barn Owl, Little Owl, Stonechat.

March–May: Divers, Manx Shearwater, Gannet, Common Scoter, over-flighting Pink-footed Geese, godwits, Whimbrel, Greenshank, Sanderling, Common Sandpiper, Arctic Skua, terns, some migrant raptors, landbird migrants including hirundines, chats and warblers.

June–August: Breeding waders, gulls and terns. Offshore movements of Shearwaters, Gannets, auks, terns and occasional skua.

September–November: Seabird movement brought by autumn's south-westerly gales include shearwaters, petrels, auks, gulls, terns and skuas. Passage waders and returning winter wildfowl are also to be seen, as are migrant Short-eared Owl and small passerines.

December–February: Divers, sea-ducks, Whooper Swan, 'grey' geese, Wigeon, Goldeneye, Goosander, waders, gulls. Landbirds include flocks of Skylark, Meadow Pipit and Starlings with smaller numbers of winter thrushes and finches. Occasional small parties of Twite and Snow Bunting.

A ringing programme at Eskmeal Nature Reserve has trapped Barred Warbler and Nightingale during the early 1990s, both rare in Cumbria.

Of the scarcer species seen over the estuaries in recent years birds of prey figure high. Red-necked and Slavonian Grebes, Spoonbill, Red Kite, Rough-legged Buzzard, Goshawk, Marsh Harrier, Osprey, Stone Curlew. Red-necked Phalarope, Black Tern and Hoopoe have all been recorded.

19 DUDDON ESTUARY

OS Map 96
SD 18, 28, 17, 27

Habitat

The Duddon Estuary or Duddon Sands is a long wide area of saltmarsh, sands and channels running from Duddon Bridge south 8 miles (13 km) to Sandscale Haws on the south shore of the estuary and Haverigg Point on the north. Several large grassland saltmarshes on the inner estuary provide winter feeding sites for 'grey' geese whilst the shoreline hosts a good range of waders. South of the town of Millom is the RSPB Reserve at Hodbarrow. This is an area of scrub and marsh around a large fresh-water lagoon.

The outer estuary is dominated by the dune systems of Haverigg to the north and the very impressive sand systems of Sandscale Haws to the south. Behind the Sandscale Haws systems are areas of wet slack which have a rich flora as well as good breeding sites for wetland species. Haverigg Point is good for seawatching. Both these dune systems are SSSIs, having a wealth of fauna and flora.

Species

During the winter the Duddon Estuary attracts a wide range of both wildfowl and waders. The large saltmarsh areas of Millom Marsh and Angerton Marsh attract good numbers of grazing Greylag Goose along with smaller numbers of Pink-footed Goose. Teal, Wigeon and Shelduck are regular and Pintail have increased in numbers in recent years. The waters of the central estuary hold Goldeneye and Red-breasted Merganser with the occasional small party of Great Crested Grebe, Red-throated Diver, Eider, Common Scoter and Scaup. There are several large high-water wader roosts in the estuary with Oystercatcher, Ringed Plover, Curlew, Redshank, Dunlin and a few Turnstone frequenting Millom Marsh, Borwick Rails, Angerton, Dunnerholme Point and Askam. The upper reaches around Lady Hall regularly hold a few Green Sandpiper and Greenshank while, around Askam and Sandscale Haws, there are good numbers of Knot, Grey Plover, Bar-tailed Godwit and Sanderling. Odd numbers of Ruff, Snipe, Black-tailed Godwit and Spotted Redshank also occur around Borwick Rails and Dunnerholme Point. Black-headed and Common Gulls appear in large flocks along with the larger gulls. The odd Glaucous and Iceland Gulls have also been recorded. Sparrowhawk, Merlin and Peregrine regularly hunt the estuary for prey, which also attracts the occasional Hen Harrier. Cormorant and Grey Heron are a regular feature in winter with Kingfisher sometimes even on the upper reaches. Other smaller birds include Rock Pipit and Reed Bunting feeding on the tideline while on the outer estuary, along the dune systems, tideline Twite, Snow Bunting and in recent years, the odd Lapland Bunting have been found.

Spring sees the departing wildfowl and waders replaced by small numbers of Whimbrel, Greenshank and Common Sandpiper whilst the flock of Golden Plover on Kirksanton Haws increases, sometimes adding the odd Dotterel to its number. Sandwich, Common, Arctic and Little Terns return to feed in the estuary, which in turn brings in Arctic Skuas to predate them. The odd Black Tern and Little Gull are seen and Gannet also come to feed in the shallow waters of the outer estuary, as do small groups of Common Scoter. Wheatear and Yellow Wagtail can be found on the open saltmarsh while the boundary hedgerows and reed-fringed ditches hold passage Redstart, Whinchat, Stonechat, Sedge Warbler, the odd Grasshopper Warbler, Whitethroat, Lesser Whitethroat, Willow Warbler, Goldcrest and Spotted Flycatcher. Of the breeding birds seen in summer, Shelduck, Oystercatcher, Curlew and Redshank are the most noteworthy.

Autumn passage brings the return of the wintering wildfowl and waders and often more unusual species, for example Little Stint and Curlew Sandpiper, while in the outer estuary the flocks of feeding terns and Kittiwake attract Arctic and Great Skua.

Rare passage birds and weather-bound coastal migrants include Leach's Petrel, Little Egret, Spoonbill, American Wigeon, Osprey, Kentish Plover, Mediterannean Gull and Nightingale, many of which were recorded in and around the area of Hodbarrow.

Timing

The estuary is best viewed in the hour before, and during, high tide, when the feeding waders and wildfowl emerge out of the vast expanse of sand- and mudflat onto the high-tide roost sites. Sea-duck and other seabirds are often drawn in with the tide. Early morning is recommended in spring and autumn for passage migrants.

Access

See under individual sites for road access. Access is possible by rail to Green Road Station, Foxfield and Kirkby for Angerton Marsh and to Millom for Borwick Rails, using the regular Barrow–Workington–Carlisle service.

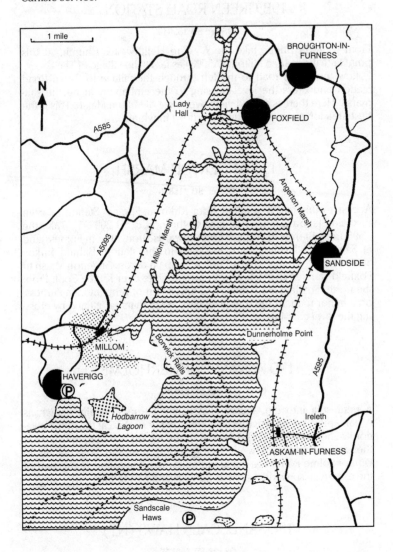

19A LADY HALL

OS ref: SD 193859

From Broughton-in-Furness take the A595 west over Duddon Bridge to Holme (SD 196874) where a minor road turns to the left and Lady Hall. At Lady Hall a track to the saltmarsh ends near the railway viaduct. A good site for Greenshank and Green Sandpiper throughout the year.

19B GREEN ROAD STATION

OS ref: SD 189840

From Duddon Bridge take the A595 to Hallthwaites Church. At this point take the road to Millom (A5093) as far as the village of The Green. Follow the minor road to the left through the village to Green Road Station and cross the level-crossing to the embankment on the salt-marsh. Here there is a good view over most of Millom Marsh. This is the best area for grazing geese and wildfowl in winter.

19C ANGERTON MARSH

OS ref: SD 215835

Access to this marsh is either from Kirkby-in-Furness Station or from Foxfield Station 2 miles (3.2 km) to the north (SD 209855). Take the A595 from Barrow-in-Furness north towards Broughton-in-Furness and at Sandside take the minor road left to the station. Behind Kirkby Station runs a stream, Kirkby Pool. A footpath across Angerton Marsh to Foxfield starts at the station with a footbridge over Kirkby Pool. From the north, Foxfield is 1.5 miles (2.4 km) south of Broughton-in-Furness, on a minor road. At the station, access to the marsh is gained by crossing the level-crossing.

19D ASKAM/DUNNERHOLME

OS ref: SD 210785

A peninsula into the estuary at Askam-in-Furness, locally known as Askam 'pier' can be reached by taking the minor road at the railway station to the golf course. The 'pier' is to the left on reaching the shore at the golf course. Follow the shore north past the golf course to Dunnerholme Point. Sea-duck and auks are often found in this part of the estuary, also waders such as godwits and Sanderling.

19E SANDSCALE HAWS (NT)

OS ref: SD 200757

This large dune system at the mouth of the estuary is an SSSI owned by the National Trust. It is very rich in fauna and flora. The flooded mines to the east of the dune slacks are a good wetland habitat to add waterfowl to the range of birds found on the site.

Heading south on the A590 take the new Dalton by-pass road to Barrow. Just after the third roundabout take the minor road on the right over the railway to Roanhead. Follow the road past the flooded mines to Roanhead Farm where there is car park behind the dunes.

19F BORWICK RAILS

OS ref: SD 190795

This is the old harbour area of Millom, most of which has been infilled. It is a good watchpoint for resident and passage wildfowl, waders, gulls and terns, providing views of most of the estuary and Millom Marsh, and is especially rewarding on a good rising tide. The road from Millom station past the town square ends after a mile (1.6 km) at Borwick Rails.

20 HODBARROW

OS Map 96
SD 175785
(See map on p. 61)

Habitat and Species

This RSPB Reserve is important on two counts: firstly as a passage site for wildfowl and waders, particularly for the large moulting flock of Red-breasted Merganser, and secondly as a breeding Sandwich Tern colony with a few pairs of Common, Arctic and Little Terns in most years.

Although part of this former industrial site is now a holiday complex with caravans and water-sport facilities, the main part of the area has become a first rate reserve. The lagoon and smaller pools are an important habitat, and the surrounding derelict landscape, which has

Red-breasted Mergansers

become overgrown, is a good refuge for passage migrants on this site at the mouth of the Duddon Estuary. The various lime waste tips are important for flora and the whole reserve has a good insect and mammal population. It is also a natterjack toad site. Resident bird species include Great Crested Grebe, Tufted Duck, Red-breasted Merganser, Sparrowhawk, Peregrine, waders, gulls, Stock Dove, Barn Owl, Lesser Whitethroat and Grasshopper Warbler.

During the winter this site can host divers, grebes, Whooper Swan, Wigeon, Teal, Pochard, Scaup, Long-tailed Duck, Goldeneye, raptors and gulls (including Glaucous). Regular waders include Golden Plover, Sanderling, Dunlin, godwits, Greenshank, Spotted Redshank and Turnstone. During storm conditions, the site is a refuge to sea-duck and other seabirds. Amongst the migrant passerines have been White Wagtail, Black Redstart, Ring Ouzel and Pied Flycatcher.

In autumn the moult flock of Red-breasted Merganser can number 250 birds. Other migrants at this time can include Garganey, Little Stint, Curlew Sandpiper, Ruff, skuas, Little Gull and Black Tern. Rarer species recorded in the last few years have included Temminck's Stint, White-rumped Sandpiper, Richard's Pipit and Icterine Warbler.

Timing

A visit coinciding with a high tide on the Duddon is best, particularly an early morning visit as the site is popular during the day with dog walkers and strollers from nearby Millom.

Access

Take the A5093 from Broughton to Millom. Turn left over the railway along Devonshire Road into the centre, then on Mainsgate Road take the right-hand turning signposted Hodbarrow Nature Reserve. Follow this road and park between the lagoon and access to the rubbish tip (closed). Alternatively, you can approach on foot from Haverigg via the entrance to the caravan site. There are also bus and rail services to Millom.

21 WALNEY ISLAND

OS Map 96
SD 16, 17, 26

Habitat

Walney Island is situated at the southwest corner of Cumbria and is the westernmost point of Morecambe Bay. The central part of the island is the residential area serving the shipyards across the Walney channel. The north and south ends of the island are the key bird sites. At the north end is a large dune-slack system forming the final part of the Duddon estuary. The Walney channel running to the east of the island has a muddy shoreline here and is attractive to waders. Walney aerodrome has an area of scrub known as 'Willow Woods' which attracts migrant passerines. On the coastal dune slack there are a few freshwater pools. The south end of the island is most important for birds. It is a

nature reserve of Cumbria Wildlife Trust and an active bird ringing station and observatory. The terrain is a mixture of intertidal mudflats, saltmarsh and dune systems with flooded gravel workings. It is home to one
of the largest gull colonies in Europe and is a key seawatch point in the
area.

Species

This is the most productive site in the county for passage seabirds with
up to 20 Red-throated Divers in the area during the winter period, along
with a few other diver species and Great Crested Grebes. Other Grebe
species are also to be found, the most regular being Red-necked.
Seabird passage usually starts in March and lasts through to October,
the peak being in August and September. Good numbers of Fulmar,
Gannet, Manx Shearwater, auks and Kittiwake can be seen. During the
'high' autumn migration, rarer species of shearwater and Storm and
Leach's Petrels have been found. Also notable are passage Common
Scoter which also bring odd Velvet Scoter and Long-tailed Duck. All
four skuas have been recorded, Arctic and Great being the most regu-
lar. Other wildfowl peak in winter with around 500 Shelduck, 1,000
Wigeon, and 500 Teal. Pink-footed Geese are recorded flighting over on
passage during the winter. Other winter wildfowl include Whooper
Swan, Greylag and a few Brent Geese, Pintail, Shoveler, Tufted Duck,
Scaup, Goldeneye, Red-breasted Merganser and the odd Garganey on
spring passage.

Eider

Of the birds of prey, Sparrowhawk, Kestrel, Merlin and Peregrine
have been recorded throughout the year with Marsh Harrier, Osprey,
Long and Short-eared Owls. Barn, Little and Tawny Owls are resident.

Walney is an important wader site with a winter peak of 12,000
Oystercatcher, 10,000 Knot and 3,000 Dunlin. Other waders to be found
in number include Ringed, Golden and Grey Plover, Lapwing, Curlew,
Redshank and Turnstone. Smaller numbers of Sanderling, Purple
Sandpiper, Snipe, godwits, Greenshank and sandpipers are also pre-
sent.

The south end of Walney is well known for its large breeding colony
of large gulls, numbering some 20,000 Herring and 30,000 Lesser Black-
backed Gulls during recent breeding seasons. Around 60 pairs of Great
Black-backed Gulls also breed.

Numbers of spring and autumn passage passerines through Walney
are not outstanding but it has proved to be excellent in the variety of
species recorded. Occasional 'falls' of chats, pipits and warblers have

occurred, with Meadow Pipit movement being particularly strong in early spring and autumn. Among the rarer passerines recorded on passage are Hoopoe, Wryneck, Richard's and Tawny Pipits, Icterine, Melodious, Subalpine, Barred and Yellow-browed Warblers, Firecrest, Red-breasted Flycatcher, Lapland and Snow Buntings.

Access

In North Walney, coastal waders and wildfowl may be viewed at Earnse Point car park (SD 170700). For access to the North End dunes and North End Marsh in Walney channel take the shoreline track from this point north past Walney Aerodrome. Do not enter or cross the airfield at any point. Alternatively, access to Willow Woods and Walney channel can be gained by turning right off Walney Bridge along the channel

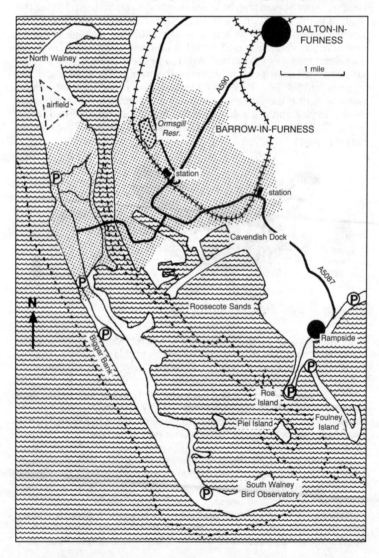

promenade following the signs to the Aerodrome at North Scale. At the aerodrome boundary leave the car and follow the footpath across the fields to Willow Woods and Walney channel.

The car park at the end of the coast road at Biggar Bank (SD 183664) is excellent for observing coastal movement of wildfowl and waders as well as being a good seabird watchpoint.

To reach Walney Bird Observatory (SD 220620), turn left on crossing Walney Bridge and continue for half a mile (0.8 km) towards Tummer Hill. Turn left at Tummer Hill Marsh or beyond the housing estate along the coast road to the village of Biggar. Go past the village and the refuse tip to the South End Caravan Site, where you drive along a track past South End Farm to South Walney Nature Reserve. A modest admission charge is levied, but this allows the use of four excellent well placed hides for watching local bird movement and seawatching.

Timing

The best time to visit Walney Island is during autumn migration from August to late October, although visits during the spring and winter can often be very rewarding. Early morning is the best time for passerine passage, particularly if light winds from the south or east predominate. Seawatching is best during September and October; following a south-west 'blow', there is a good possibility of seeing Leach's Petrel, shearwaters and skuas. May and September are the best months for seeing wader flocks gathering at South Walney and there is the chance of spotting an unusual one on the gravel-pit pools on the reserve.

Calendar

All year: Shelduck, Eider, Red-breasted Merganser, Peregrine, Oystercatcher, Ringed Plover, Dunlin, Snipe, Greenshank, Turnstone, large gulls, Barn and Little Owls, Meadow Pipit, Skylark and Linnet.

April–July: Breeding visitors include Sandwich, Common, Arctic and Little Terns, Yellow Wagtail, Stonechat, Whinchat, Sedge Warbler, Lesser Whitethroat, Spotted Flycatcher. Spring passage birds include all three divers, Great Crested Grebe, Fulmar, Manx Shearwater, Gannet, 'grey' Geese, the occasional Garganey, Common Scoter, Goldeneye, the odd Marsh or Hen Harrier, Osprey, Merlin, Golden and Grey Plovers, Knot, Sanderling, Black and Bar-tailed Godwits, Whimbrel, sandpipers, Arctic and Great Skuas, auks, Turtle Dove, Black Redstart, warblers and other small passerines.

August–October: Passage birds include Sooty Shearwater, Storm and Leach's Petrel, Shag, Whooper Swan, 'grey' Geese, Wigeon, Pintail, Shoveler, Scaup, Velvet Scoter, Merlin, the occasional Hobby, and waders. Also likely are Little Stint, Curlew Sandpiper, Ruff and Spotted Redshanks, skuas, various gulls including Little Gull, Black Tern, Short-eared Owl, Swift, hirundines, wagtails, chats, winter thrushes, warblers (with possibly Melodious and Yellow-browed), flycatchers, passage corvids, finches including Twite and Snow Bunting.

November–March: Red-throated is the commonest diver with small numbers of Black-throated and Great Northern. Other interesting winter species include Red-necked and Slavonian Grebes, Brent Goose, Wigeon, Teal, Pintail, Pochard, Tufted Duck, Scaup, Long-tailed Duck,

Goldeneye, Merlin, Peregrine, Water Rail, waders including Jack Snipe, Woodcock in severe weather, Greenshank, large gulls (including Glaucous), Short-eared Owl, Rock Pipit, winter thrushes, corvids, Brambling, Twite, the odd Lapland and Snow Buntings.

Rarities on Walney Island in recent years have included Black Stork, Cory's and Great Shearwater, King Eider, Common Crane, White-rumped, Baird's and Buff-breasted Sandpiper, Greater Sand Plover, Wilson's Phalarope, Ring-billed Gull, Richard's and Tawny Pipits, Desert Wheatear, Paddyfield and Dartford Warblers, Subalpine, Pallas's and Bonelli's Warblers, Red-breasted Flycatcher, Woodchat Shrike, Nutcracker and White-throated Sparrow.

Reference
Walney Bird Observatory Report is an annual report covering the whole of the island. Contact address: Bill Makin, Coastguard Cottages, South Walney Nature Reserve, Walney Island, Barrow-in-Furness, Cumbria, LA14 3YQ.

SOUTH CUMBRIA

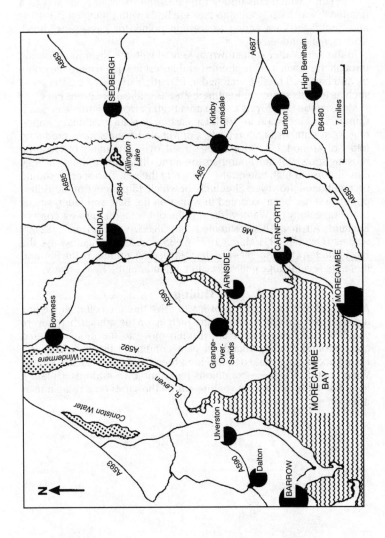

The South Lakeland Fells act as a northern boundary to this region. From them flows the Lune, Kent and Leven which form large estuaries on the northern shore of Morecambe Bay.

The Lune, which cuts through the beautiful Howgill Fells, acts as a notable flyway for migrant and passage birds, with Killington Reservoir and Sunbiggin Tarn acting as feeding points for passage wildfowl, waders, gulls and terns.

In the Kent Valley is the town of Kendal with the River Kent passing through the town. It is the shortest and fastest flowing river in the country and has good birdlife attached to it, particularly in the quieter areas such as near its source in Kentmere and its outflow in Levens Park.

Morecambe Bay covers a wide area from Barrow-in-Furness in South Cumbria to Fleetwood in North Lancashire. It is internationally important for a number of shorebirds. Coordinated counts have produced totals of around 140,000 waders spread over a number of favourite roosting spots. Wildfowl numbers are more difficult to estimate as they can disperse at high tide on the surface of the sea. Two species should be mentioned, however: Shelduck, of which 15 per cent of the British population has been recorded in winter on the Bay; and Eider, whose breeding colony on Walney Island is the only one on the west coast of England. All in all it is estimated that 38,000 wildfowl and 192,000 waders (October 1994/March 1995 WeBS Core Count figures) use the Bay in winter. Other species use the vast feeding grounds of the Bay and there are several large gull roosts, in particular in the Kent estuary.

Timing

Any tide of 30 feet (9.2 m) or over will drive the birds off their feeding areas on to the traditional roost sites high up on the saltmarsh. In severe winter weather many Knot and Dunlin move to the more sheltered areas around Walney Island. In gale conditions the Shelduck and Pintail flocks congregate behind Humphrey Head into the Kent estuary. Watch out during these conditions for windblown seabirds. Obtain a local tide table and do not venture out on the sands on a rising tide as it is swift and dangerous.

22 SUNBIGGIN TARN

Habitat

Sunbiggin Tarn lies at 1000 feet (300 m) in a basin of undulating moorland and is surrounded by large areas of exposed Westmorland limestone pavement and outcrops. The southern and western sides of the basin are low-lying, forming large *Phragmites* reedbeds from which the tarn drains into the Rais Beck, a tributary of the River Lune. Sunbiggin Tarn covers about 10 acres (4 hectares) and is connected to a smaller and shallower piece of water known as Cow Dub. Between the two is a large area of floating bog and reedbed, which is the breeding site for one of the county's major Black-headed Gull colonies, holding 4–5,000 pairs. This gullery has been in existence since the late 1880s and has in recent years expanded to all sides of the tarn. To the west of the tarn the outflow stream runs into a calcareous bog known as Tarn Sike, which is now a reserve managed by Cumbria Wildlife Trust. Here flourishes local flora, for example birdseye primrose, marsh cinquefoil and moonwort fern, all Westmorland flora specialities.

Species

The winter months provide interest with a wealth of waterfowl at Sunbiggin. Whooper Swan, Cormorant, Teal, Wigeon, Gadwall, Tufted Duck, Pochard, Goldeneye, Red-breasted Merganser and Goosander can be found. Water Rail occasionally frequent the reedbeds, as do Snipe and the odd Jack Snipe. Short-eared Owl, Buzzard, Merlin and Peregrine haunt the area for prey and Raven often gather in small groups looking for carrion. Few small land birds are present at this time but Skylark, Meadow Pipit, the odd Stonechat and small flocks of Goldfinch, Linnet or Twite may occur. Spring and autumn passage brings mainly migrant waders, with waterfowl and terns sometimes appearing. In spring the noise and spectacle of the gathering large flocks of Black-headed Gulls at their breeding site may mask the presence of passage birds such as Black-necked Grebe, Shelduck, Scaup, Pintail, Shoveler, Common Scoter and Long-tailed Duck. Hen Harrier and Osprey have appeared at this season. Flocks of Golden Plover and Curlew gathering on the neighbouring fellsides, where Red Grouse breed, have diminished in recent years but Ringed Plover, Oystercatcher, Dunlin, Ruff, Greenshank and Common Sandpiper are regular while Snipe, Redshank, some Curlew and the odd Dunlin stay to breed. Less common passage waders recorded in the last few years include Dotterel, Grey Plover, Sanderling, Little Stint, Pectoral Sandpiper, Turnstone and Red-necked Phalarope. Passage terns include Common, Arctic, Little and Black, while Kittiwake and Fulmar have been observed in stormy weather conditions and Little Gull may appear in midsummer. Hirundines gather in large numbers to roost in the reedbeds in autumn while numbers of breeding Sedge Warbler vary from year to year. Passage landbirds have included Klngfisher, Dipper, Redstart, Whinchat and Grasshopper Warbler. Among rarities recorded here are Bittern, Ring-necked Duck, Rough-legged Buzzard, Red Kite and Osprey. Breeding waterfowl include Gadwall, Teal, Tufted Duck and occasionally Shoveler and Wigeon.

Timing

The tarn is the centre of a local shooting and fishing syndicate so observations here are best made in the close season. During passage migration early morning or late afternoon, when birds use the site to feed or roost, are the appropriate times to visit. September gales or the occasional spring storm may bring something more unusual.

Access

Good views can be had from the minor road overlooking the tarn. Take the Orton road at the junction of the M6 and the A685 north of Kendal. Leave Orton on the B6261 and after half a mile (0.8 km) take the minor road to Raisbeck and Sunbiggin. The tarn is 4 miles (6.4 km) onto the moor along the road to Little Asby from Raisbeck. Tarn Sike can be viewed from the track which leaves the road at the cattle grid (NY 666074). A high viewpoint on the moorland (NY 674077) looks over the reedbeds and the Cow Dub.

Calendar

All year: Teal, Gadwall, Wigeon, Tufted Duck, Sparrowhawk, Buzzard, Peregrine, Red Grouse, Coot, Snipe, Gulls and Raven.

November–March: Cormorant, Whooper Swan, Shoveler, Pochard, Goldeneye, Red-breasted Merganser and Goosander, possible Pintail, Scaup and Long-tailed Duck, Merlin, Short-eared Owl, winter thrushes and Stonechat.

June–August: Little Grebe, Shoveler, the odd Common Scoter, Ruff, Black-tailed Godwit, Wood Sandpiper, Little Gull, Common Tern, Kingfisher, hirundines, Sedge Warbler and Twite.

April–May and July–October: Black-necked Grebe, Grey Heron, Shelduck, Hen Harrier, Osprey, Merlin, Ringed Plover, Dotterel, Golden Plover, Sanderling, Little Stint, Whimbrel, Spotted Redshank, Greenshank, Green and Common Sandpipers, Turnstone and Black Tern.

23 THE LUNE VALLEY

OS Map 91
NY 60

The River Lune has its source on Ravenstonedale Common high on the Westmorland Fells. It flows steadily westwards through a wide valley until it gets to Tebay. Here it swings south through the scenic gap between the Shap Fells and Howgill Fells where the motorway and railway follow its course. It is fairly swift-flowing through this area until it reaches the lowlands south of Sedbergh. Here it takes on a lazier pace as it meanders along a wide aluvial valley past Kirkby Lonsdale, into Lancashire and on to its estuary on Morecambe Bay.

It acts as a natural flight lane for passage migrants travelling from west to east or in reverse direction, often bringing coastal species to the inland waters of Sunbiggin Tarn and Killington Reservoir which lie near to its course.

23A TEBAY DISTRICT

OS ref: NY 625055

Habitat and Species

To the north of Tebay, the river flows through an area of large fields where species such as Oystercatcher, Redshank, Curlew and Common Sandpiper gather and occasionally breed. The riverbank is well exposed here making good sites for Sand Martins and the occasional Kingfisher. Other species to be seen here include Dipper, Grey Wagtail and Whinchat.

During times of migration, flocks of Swifts and hirundines are notable here and the large fields often hold Golden Plover and other waders. Great Grey Shrike have been seen here twice in the 1980s. South of Tebay the river turns south flowing swiftly down through the scenic area beside the M6 and railway. Here wooded hillsides and adjacent valleys provide breeding sites for Goosander, Buzzard, Wheatear, Wood Warbler, Redstart and Pied Flycatcher.

Also regularly seen here are Grey Heron, Red-breasted Merganser, Peregrine, Sparrowhawk and Raven with parties of Siskin, Goldfinch and Redpolls.

Access

Leave the M6 at Junction 38 and take the B6260 to Orton where good views of the river can be had at old Tebay (NY 618068). For the area south of Tebay take the A685 for Kendal from the M6 where you will pass through the village, over the river, railway and motorway. Travel on past the foot of Jeffrey's Mount to where the road crosses the Borrow Beck (NY 605025). Either walk from this point to the right into the wooded valley of Borrowdale or left along the minor road under the viaduct towards Carlingill and the river.

23B KILLINGTON RESERVOIR

OS ref: SD 595910

Habitat and Species

The reservoir is set among the Westmorland Fells and is the focal point from the Killington Service area on the southbound carriageway of the M6 motorway.

It was built and used as a supply for the Leeds and Lancaster canal system, situated at 600 feet (180 m) above the Lune Valley to the south between Sedbergh and Kendal. Today its focus is more recreational with both a sailing club and fishing activities.

As an upland grassland/moorland site the main area of bird interest is the north bay and wooded island. Here, local agreement restricts sailing from this part of the reservoir. On the island Canada Geese breed amongst a Black-headed Gull colony whilst in the conifers and oaks there is a rookery. Regular waterfowl include Great Crested Grebe, Cormorant, Teal, Wigeon, Tufted Duck, Pochard, Red-breasted Merganser and Goosander. Irregular passage wildfowl have included diver and grebe species, Whooper Swan, Common Scoter, Scaup, Long-tailed Duck, and over the past three years, a wintering Ring-necked Duck.

In spring/summer, Oystercatcher, Redshank, Curlew, Dunlin and Common Sandpiper are regular with Grey Heron, Buzzard, Kestrel, various gulls, hirundines, chats, Spotted Flycatcher and Raven.

A wide range of passage migrants has been seen including Long-tailed Duck, Hen Harrier, Merlin, various waders, Little Gull, Kittiwake, Long- and Short-eared Owls. A number of rarities also recorded here include Leach's Petrel, Common Crane, Velvet Scoter, Grey Phalarope, Hobby, Mediterranean Gull, Caspian Tern, Long-tailed Skua and Golden Oriole.

Access

Take the A684 for Sedbergh at junction 37 on the M6. Take the first minor road to the right for Killington and Old Hutton and after half a mile (0.8 km) the road reaches the east end of the reservoir at (SD 598912). Good viewing can be had from this point and along the road to the sailing club. Good views of the north end of the reservoir can be had from Killington services car park.

23C BARBONDALE

OS ref: SD 665835

Habitat and Species

Behind the attractive village of Barbon lies a scenic upland valley amongst the high fells known as Barbondale. At the foot of the valley, Barbon Manor is surrounded by larch and oak woodland where one can see Buzzard, Sparrowhawk, Coal Tit, Redstart, Siskin and Redpoll. Farther up, the road follows the Barbon Beck and riverside species such as Dipper, Grey Wagtail, Snipe and Heron can be seen. At the top of the valley the road is surrounded by imposing steep fellside. The highest on the left is Calf Top and is the home of Wheatear and Ring Ouzel, while Raven, Merlin and Peregrine often frequent the top ridge.

The valley acts as a migration route during spring and autumn with Common Sandpiper, Cuckoo, pipits, hirundines and chats often seen, with Hen Harrier, Short-eared Owl and winter thrushes possible between November and March.

Access

At junction 36 on the M6 take the A65 to Kirkby Lonsdale. Here, on crossing the River Lune at Devil's Bridge (SD 615782), turn left on the A683 to Sedbergh. The village of Barbon is on the right after 3 miles (4.8 km). There are several access lanes—mostly single tracked. The best route is the minor road to the village (SD 622826), which follows the Barbon Beck. In the village follow the route to Dent which passes right through Barbondale; Barbon Manor is approximately 1 mile (1.6 km) up the valley from the village.

24 THE KENT VALLEY

The River Kent is unique not only in that it is England's shortest river but also in that it is the country's fastest flowing. There are several good bird haunts along its length, the most notable being the slow moving upper reaches with alder- and willow-lined banks and small meadows between Staveley, Bowston and Burneside. On the northern outskirts of Kendal, the River Kent is joined by the River Mint, forming a large pool with long shingle banks. This area is locally known as Sandy Bottoms. At the southern end of Kendal the river passes Kendal Sewage Works at a pace before slowing down again in the wooded bends at Watercrook with its stands of alder. The river narrows and surges over limestone outcrops as it falls dramatically through Low Sizergh. Notable of the falls here is Force Fall, a local salmon leap. On passing under the A591, the river is subdued once more as it meanders through Levens Park. Here there are shallow gravel banks and limestone outcrops hanging with ivy and other scrub. Beyond Levens Hall at Sampool the river is joined by the River Gilpin. These are the upper reaches of the Kent estuary, with sand and gravel banks and some reedbeds, where the river becomes tidal.

Species

Typical river birds such as Common Sandpiper, Kingfisher, Sand Martin, Grey Wagtail and Dipper breed along the river's length. Added to these are a few pairs of Red-breasted Merganser, Goosander, Oystercatcher, Redshank and Yellow Wagtail. There is a small heronry near Staveley and the Cormorant is a frequent winter visitor. Also in winter the deep water areas around Kendal hold Little Grebe, Pochard, Tufted Duck, Goldeneye and occasionally Smew, waders such as Ringed Plover, Dunlin, Snipe and Green Sandpiper occur and there have been records of Little Ringed Plover, Jack Snipe and Wood Sandpiper. Gulls regularly move in good numbers along the length of the river with Kittiwake, Mediterranean Gull and Common Tern sometimes appearing.

The wooded and scrub areas along the river have breeding pairs of Little Owl, woodpeckers (with the odd pair of Lesser Spotted) and Nuthatch, also Sedge and Garden Warblers, Whitethroat and Chiffchaff. Buzzard, Sparrowhawk and Peregrine often hunt along the river. In winter, Merlin may visit from the fells. Ravens are seen moving between the Lake District and Howgill Fells and Greylag and Pink-footed Goose use the valley as a north–south flight lane. A flock of post-breeding Greylag gathers on the saltmarsh near Sampool from August onwards. Whooper Swan sometimes appear here too, as do wintering Green Sandpiper.

In the alders and birch at Burneside, Watercrook, Low Sizergh and Levens Park can be found wandering flocks of Siskin and Redpoll. Small mixed flocks of tits sometimes include wintering Blackcap and Chiffchaff and the occasional Nuthatch. Goldfinch and Brambling are also regular winter visitors.

In spring and autumn there is a regular steady migration through the valley with the open sites of Sandy Bottoms, Watercrook, Sampool and Kendal Sewage Works being particularly attractive. Often large numbers of hirundines, Swift, gulls, Starlings, corvids, winter thrushes and finches use the valley on passage movements. Oddities have appeared from time to time including Night Heron, Temminck's Stint, Pectoral Sandpiper, Bee-eater and Wryneck.

Timing and General Access

Cold weather movements in winter, particularly when the surrounding fells are snow-covered often finds the lower reaches of the river clear due to the influence of Morecambe Bay. Early morning is the best time to visit during the periods of migration.

The main trunk routes along the River Kent are the A591 from the M6 to Kendal and beyond to Staveley. The A590 Levens Bridge to Gilpin Bridge and the A6 at Levens Bridge.

24A KENDAL

OS ref: SD 48

The fact that the River Kent is its central feature makes the town of Kendal attractive to birdwatchers. Two sites, Watercrook, where the river slowly bends around a Roman Fort on one bank and Kendal Sewage Works on the other, and Sandy Bottoms to the north of the town, an open site where the River Mint joins with the River Kent, are the favourite locations for birds. Breeding birds include Common Sandpiper, Kingfisher, Dipper, Grey Wagtail and Sand Martin. In winter, Little Grebe, Tufted Duck, Goldeneye, Red-breasted Merganser, Goosander, Redshank, gulls, Blackcap, Siskin and Brambling appear regularly. Oddities have included Black-throated Diver, Night Heron, occasional Smew, Water Rail, Kittiwake, Blue-headed Wagtail and Black Redstart. Access is relatively simple as a footpath follows the river on its western side right through Kendal. For Watercrook take the foot-path at Helsington Garage on the A6 (SD 508907) through Scroggs Wood to the river. A footpath to Burneside along the river starts amongst the houses at Kentrigg (SD 515944) .

24B HELSINGTON BARROWS (NT)

OS Ref: SD 49090, SD 49

This is a popular area of open high ground in limestone country south-west of Kendal. It is well clothed with trees and shrubs, particularly oak, larch, yew and juniper, which having matured are allowed to regener-ate.

Regular breeding species include Curlew, Green Woodpecker, Redstart, Tree Pipit, Cuckoo, Goldcrest and Treecreeper. Passage birds include warblers and both species of flycatcher and often feeding par-ties of Redpoll and Siskin and occasionally Crossbills. The yews attract many winter thrushes with Waxwing and Great Grey Shrike also having been recorded here.

Access is from the minor road from Kendal to Brigsteer (SD 494899). Early visits in the day are to be recommended as the area is popular with walkers.

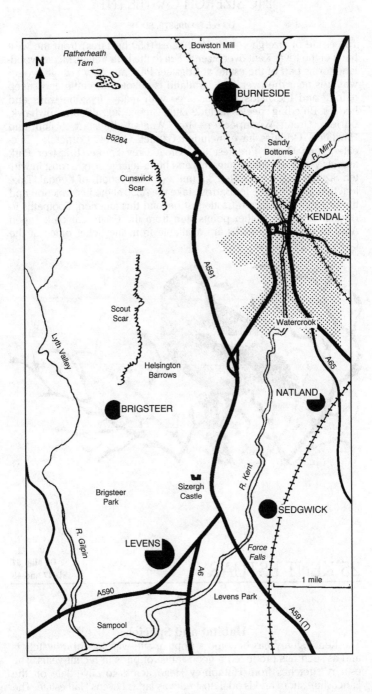

24C SIZERGH CASTLE (NT)

OS ref: SD 498879, SD 48

The estate of Sizergh covers 1600 acres (650 hectares) from the west bank of the River Kent over Sizergh Fell to the Lyth Valley. Mixed woodland forms part of the estate at Brigsteer Park and Low Sizergh Wood, which is near the river. The farmland is devoted to cattle and sheep rearing and the fields are not large with many drystone walls and hedges. Breeding species include Little Grebe, Buzzard, Sparrowhawk, Curlew, Green Woodpecker, Grey Wagtail, Redstart, Siskin and Hawfinch. Oddities have included Gannet, Osprey, Corncrake, Bee-eater, Ring Ouzel, Firecrest and Great Grey Shrike. Brigsteer Park attracts very early spring migrants and holds a large corvid roost in winter. Sizergh Castle is located 3.5 miles (5.6 km) south of Kendal. Take junction 36 off the M6 for Barrow, take the A590 at the first junction and the first right for Sizergh Castle just beyond this junction. Footpaths to Brigsteer Park and other points start from the Castle car park (open April to October). Details are available from the ticket office at the Castle on open days.

Hawfinch

25 KENT ESTUARY

OS Map 97
SD 47 and 48

Habitat and Species

The Kent Estuary has become a popular site with local birdwatchers and as such has produced a good range of birds in recent years. The estuary stretches from Humphrey Head across to Silverdale on the Lancashire shore and is tidal upstream as far as Levens Hall estate. The towns of Grange-over-Sands and Arnside are on the west and east shores respectively and a railway viaduct divides the area in two.

Beyond the viaduct the upper estuary has some important saltmarshes at Brogden, Arnside Marsh, Foulshaw and Halforth Farm. Near the latter point the River Gilpin joins the River Kent and is a site for Greylag Geese in winter. This area has had the odd interesting wader on passage. The 'grey' Geese use the mosses at Foulshaw and Brogden and have in recent years been joined by a few Pink-footed, White-fronted, Bean and Barnacle Geese. Waders visiting the shore here include Ringed and Golden Plover, Dunlin, Ruff, godwits, Whimbrel, Curlew, Spotted Redshank, Greenshank and sandpipers. These birds quite often move around the upper estuary, visiting Arnside Marsh or over the viaduct to Meathop Moss when disturbed. In the upper estuary, post-breeding Lapwings gather in autumn in a large flock often exceeding 1,500 birds. At this time there is also a very large gull roost of some 8,000 birds, mainly Common and Black-headed Gulls, with just a few larger gulls. Little, Mediterranean and Glaucous Gull along with Kittiwake and Great Skua have been found occasionally at this roost.

The river around the viaduct and Arnside Marsh is more disturbed and deeper round the viaduct piers, and diving duck with the odd grebe or seabird can be found feeding here. During autumn high-tide periods, pools formed on Arnside Marsh can attract waders such as Sanderling, Little Stint, Curlew Sandpiper and Wood Sandpiper. The county's first record of Baird's Sandpiper, an American vagrant, was made here.

The shore opposite Arnside is Meathop Marsh. This saltmarsh runs from the viaduct to Holme Island at Grange-over-Sands. Good numbers of Greylag Goose, Pintail, Teal, Wigeon and Red-breasted Merganser feed and roost here with Oystercatcher, Redshank and Curlew. The shoreline from Holme Island to Humphrey Head includes the promenades at Grange-over-Sands and Kents Bank. By the causeway to Holme Island is an area of *Spartina* grass, which attracts Redshank, Snipe, the odd Jack Snipe and, in winter, mixed finch flocks with Reed Buntings. The mudflats around Grange are known for a high population of Pintail and Shelduck. Wildfowl counts here often exceed a thousand for each species. The channel at Kents Bank railway station is particularly favoured by these ducks, especially in stormy conditions as it is sheltered by Humphrey Head. This area often attracts grebes, the odd diver, Goldeneye, Long-tailed Duck, Scaup and Common Scoter, Storm Petrel, Manx Shearwater, Fulmar, Gannet and Kittiwake have been seen during autumn gales.

Records of Hoopoe, Greenish and Subalpine Warbler in recent years suggest that searching for migrant passerines could pay dividends.

Access

A good part of this estuary has easy access as good views can be had from the promenades at Kents Bank, Grange-over-Sands, Sandside and Arnside.

For Brogden and Foulshaw marshes, take the A590 from the M6 Motorway at Junction 36 and follow the road for Barrow past Levens Bridge to the Derby Arms, Witherslack (SD 443828). At this point take the minor road to Ulpha. After 2 miles (3.2 km) a footpath (SD 450812) for Sampool Bridge leads down to the estuary at Crag Wood. Look across the fields from the sluice for geese and in the channel and estuary beyond for waders.

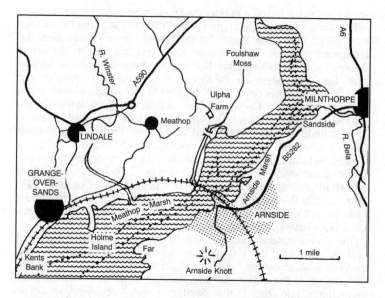

Halforth Farm is reached from the A6 at Heversham taking the lane left (SD 485840) past College Green to the farm. Park in the yard, courtesy of the farmer, and view from the gateway on the embankment.

Timing

Autumn and winter are the best periods to visit, particularly in or after stormy conditions as the estuary is a sheltered site. Choose a period on or around high tide as the wildfowl, waders and gulls come in off Morecambe Bay with the tide. Remember that certain tides here have a strong bore, the water rushing in on large waves similar to the Severn Bore.

Warning: Never venture out on the sands as there are areas of dangerous quicksand.

26 FLOOKBURGH MARSHES

OS Maps 96 and 97
SD 37
(See map on p. 83)

Habitat and Species

The vast expanse of tidal sand and mudflats between the Leven Estuary and the limestone headland of Humphrey Head are best viewed when there is a good high tide bringing the waders and wildfowl up on the equally vast saltmarshes of East and West Plains.

The West Plain is the largest saltmarsh, stretching for 3 miles (4.8 km) between Cowpren Point on the Leven Estuary to the Ponderosa Holiday

Complex at East Plain Farm. It is one of the most important high-tide roost sites for waders on Morecambe Bay and in peak migration period can hold 12,000 Oystercatcher, 15,000 Dunlin and 3,000 Curlew. According to tide, weather and disturbance, many of these birds will also use East Plain or, just to the east, Out Marsh. This was formerly a roost for large flocks of Knot and Bar-tailed Godwit but in recent years numbers have dwindled.

Flookburgh marshes also hold good numbers of Shelduck with a few Wigeon and Pintail, Ringed and Grey Plovers. Golden Plover gather on Cark Airfield behind East Plain Farm. Birds of prey regularly hunt here including Peregrine, Merlin, Sparrowhawk, the odd Hen Harrier and Short-eared Owl. West Plain has a Cormorant roost of over 200 birds and a large gull roost of all species; 'grey' Geese also visit. More unusual species on the marshes have included Leach's Petrel, Spoonbill, Crane, Dotterel and Glaucous Gull. Humphrey Head is now a Nature Reserve run by the Cumbria Wildlife Trust. It is a good site for passage migrants and in the last few years visible migration along the headland of hirundines, pipits, chats, warblers and finches is noteworthy. Irregular migrants have included Red-backed Shrike, Firecrest and Barred Warbler.

Access

Access to the saltmarshes is a little difficult. West Plain can be viewed from Cowpren Point, which is reached by walking, either along the shore from Sand Gate Farm (see Site 27) round Lenibrick Point or from the embankment of the Ponderosa Holiday Complex. To reach this take the minor road to Cark Airfield from the square at Flookburgh. Park by West Plain Farm at the end of the straight road by the airfield and walk towards the sea along the grass embankment. This has now become part of the Cumbrian Coastal Path. For the Out Marsh (East Plain) take the B5277 for Grange-over-Sands from Flookburgh. After 1.5 miles (2.4 km) turn right for Humphrey Head, follow the minor road over the railway crossing, turning left at the junction for the headland. This road leads to the shore under the limestone cliffs. A short walk along the shore to the west brings you to Out Marsh.

Timing

This area is obviously best visited during peak high tides in spring and autumn. Obtain a tide-table from a fishing tackle shop in Kendal, Grange, Ulverston or Barrow and visit just before high tide.

Warning: Do not venture on to the mudflats. Keep to the grass saltflats as there is quicksand and the rising tide comes in very quickly. There have been fatalities here through carelessness.

27 LEVEN ESTUARY

Habitat and Species

This large river estuary is divided in two by a railway viaduct. The Greenodd Sands and upper estuary to the north of the viaduct have good numbers of wildfowl in winter, with Teal, Wigeon, a few Pintail, Shelduck and Goldeneye, the latter gathering in flocks of 50 or more in late spring near Greenodd. Occasional 'grey' Geese use this area. It is also the haunt of waders such as Golden Plover, Dunlin, Curlew, Redshank and a few Greenshank. South of the viaduct the vast expanse of sand and mud is some 3.5 miles (5.6 km) across at its widest point between Bardsea on the west shore and Sandgate Marsh opposite. In its midst runs the Ulverston channel and a small limestone outcrop, Chapel Island. Wildfowl gather in large numbers here, particularly Mallard, Pintail, Wigeon, the odd Shoveler, a few Scaup, Goldeneye and Red-breasted Merganser. Red-throated Divers, grebes, Whooper Swan, 'grey' Geese including Bean and White-fronted, Barnacle Geese, Eider and Long-tailed Duck visit from time to time.

Chapel Island supports a strong high tide wader roost with Oystercatcher, Ringed Plover, Dunlin, Curlew and Redshank. Another Redshank roost on the old slag banks at South Ulverston occasionally has Spotted Redshank, Greenshanks and Turnstone present. This is also a good site for early and late migrants and passerines.

Sand Gate Marsh holds a Gull roost, mainly of the large gulls, and is always worth a look. Peregrine, Merlin, the odd Hen Harrier and Short-eared Owl often hunt the estuary marshes. Among the more unusual species recorded are Red-necked and Slavonian Grebes, Storm Petrel, White Stork, American Wigeon, Stone Curlew, Collared Pratincole and Golden Oriole.

Access

The west shore has easy access from Ulverston, which has both rail and bus services. For Canal Foot take the minor road parallel to the Ulverston Canal to the large Glaxo Chemical Works. Follow the road past the works entrance to the Bay Horse Inn at Canal Foot. The canal at this point in recent winters has had Red-necked Grebe, Chiffchaff and Waxwings. Access to the South Ulverston slag banks is from the rear of the Glaxo works car park (SD 307775). A shoreline footpath between Conishead Priory, Wadhead Scar (locally known as Priory Point) and Bardsea can be reached by two minor roads off the A5087. Good views of the wildfowl and wader roosts around Chapel Island can be had from the shore here. Bardsea Country Park is an SSSI, which includes Sea Wood, and oak woodland on the shore of Morecambe Bay. Access is easy here as the A5087 runs through the site with many parking areas.

North of the viaduct, parking areas off the A590 at Greenodd and near Arrod Foot (SD 308809) give good views across the Greenodd Sands. On the eastern shore of the estuary, views of the upper reaches can be had at Low Frith. Take the A590(T) to Haverthwaite and the B5378 towards Cark and Grange-over-Sands. After 4.5 miles (7.2 km), having passed through the woodland of Holker Moss, take the minor road to Old Park and Low Frith (SD 355780). This straight avenue of walnut

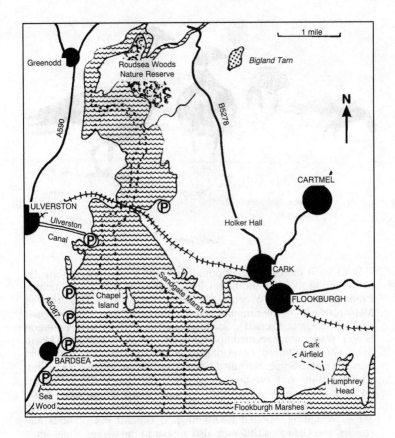

trees leads to Old Park Farm and beyond to Park Head car park. A short walk will give good views of the estuary from the viaduct to Low Frith. For Sand Gate Marsh continue further along the B5278 through Cark village to the square at Flookburgh, turn right and follow the road out of the village to the shore at Sand Gate Farm.

28 FOULNEY ISLAND (CWT)

OS Map 96
SD 26
(See map on p. 66)

Habitat and Species

This small shingle island is connected to the mainland by a granite block walkway. It is a nature reserve owned by Cumbria Wildlife Trust, who warden the large tern colony present here in the summer months. It extends along the eastern side of the Walney channel out into Morecambe Bay and is an excellent watchpoint for wildfowl, waders, seabirds and passerines.

Brent Geese

In winter it shares the Eider population with Walney Island (Site 21) according to weather and tide. Other wildfowl at this season include Brent Geese, Teal, Wigeon, Shelduck, Goldeneye, Red-breasted Merganser with smaller numbers of Red-throated Diver, grebe species (including Great Crested), Scaup, Long-tailed Duck and Common Scoter. Wader numbers are important here too. At the Rampside Marsh area, with its saltmarsh cover of grasses and sea lavender, good numbers of Dunlin, Snipe, Bar-tailed Godwit, Curlew and Redshank gather, whilst further out on the island are Ringed and Grey Plovers, Oystercatcher and Turnstone. Passage waders include Knot, Sanderling, Black-tailed Godwit, Little Stint, Curlew Sandpiper, Jack Snipe, Whimbrel, Spotted Redshank and Greenshank. Various auk species and Glaucous Gull may also appear in the winter, while small groups of Brambling, Twite and sometimes Snow Bunting forage on the tideline. Merlin and Short-eared Owl often cover the long grasses in the middle of the island. During the breeding season Black-headed Gull and four tern species occupy the nesting area at the tip of the island. At this time Roseate and Black Tern can appear along with Little Gull, Arctic and Great Skua. Spring and autumn passage have produced a crop of unusual species including Hobby, Temminck's Stint, Mediterranean Gull, Ring-billed Gull, Pomarine Skua, Shore Lark and Bluethroat. A Bridled Tern appeared in the tern colony for three days in early June 1994.

Access

Take the A5087 from Barrow-in-Furness to Ulverston as far as the village of Rampside. At the roundabout follow the route marked Rampside through the village and on to the causeway to Roa Island. Halfway along this causeway (SD 234657) you can park at the start of the track out to the island. The best time to visit is an hour or so before high tide, ideally during calm conditions as it has become a popular site for wind-surfing.

29 CAVENDISH DOCK, BARROW

Habitat and Species

This is an important site for wildfowl as the redundant dock is used by the local power station for a warm water outflow, thus keeping the water ice-free in winter. It is a local moult site for Mute Swans with a peak of 150 birds in July and August. Concentrations of wildfowl are notable throughout the winter period with good numbers of grebes (Great Crested and Little), Wigeon, Pochard, Tufted Duck, Goldeneye and Red-breasted Merganser. Coot numbers also increase at this time of year. A central barrier across the dock provides a roost platform for Redshank and Cormorant, the latter often numbering up to 200 birds. Gulls in large numbers use the dock to wash and preen and occasionally to feed.

On the east side of the dock is an area of *Phragmites*. This wet area attracts small passerines and some waders during spring and autumn. It also holds a few breeding pairs of Sedge and Reed Warblers. Beyond the seawall of the dock are Roosecote Sands, which expand southwards to the Westfield Gas terminal and beyond to Roa Island. This area has concentrations of wildfowl, for example, Eider, Wigeon and Shelduck, with flocks of Greylag Geese sometimes appearing in bad weather. Good numbers of waders are to be found here, with Ringed, Golden and Grey Plovers, Dunlin, Redshank, Bar-tailed Godwit and Curlew reaching good figures. Peregrine, Merlin and Short-eared Owl regularly harass the sometimes very large wader flocks.

The area around Cavendish Dock has recorded sightings of a fair number of unusual species including Red-necked, Slavonian and Black-necked Grebes, Red-crested Pochard, Ferruginous Duck, Temminck's Stint, Pectoral Sandpiper, Avocet, Lesser Yellowlegs, White-winged Black Tern. Water Pipit, Woodlark and Lapland Bunting.

Access

From Barrow Town Hall take the A5087 to Ulverston beyond the roundabout. At the first bend, by St George the Martyr Church, turn right down Cavendish Dock Road. Follow this over the railway, through Buccleugh Dock to the British Nuclear Fuels terminal where Cavendish Dock is visible on the left. Alternatively follow the A5087 a further half mile (0.8 km) under the railway bridge to the Catholic Church on the right, turn right down St Luke's Avenue, across the road junction under the railway bridge and park. Cavendish Dock is over the embankment on the right. There is a footpath right around the dock area.

NORTH LANCASHIRE

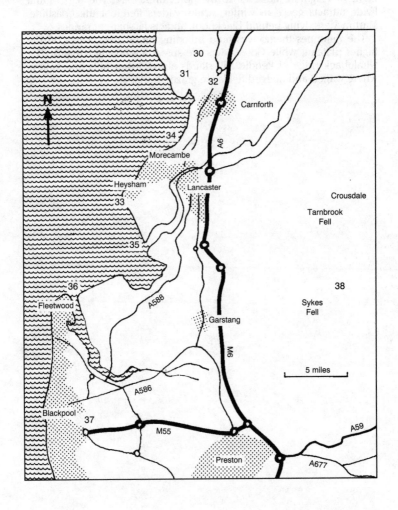

30 Leighton Moss
31 Carnforth Marsh and Hest
   Bank
32 Dockacres Gravel Pits
33 Heysham Bird Observatory
   and Nature Reserve
34 Morecambe Promenade

35 Lune Estuary
36 Wyre Estuary
37 Marton Mere, Blackpool
38 Forest of Bowland
39 Stocks Reservoir
40 Pendle Hill

North of the Ribble, the Pennine Hills sweep closer to the west coast so that the lowland plain, including the area known as the Fylde, narrows northwards. In the far north of the region lie the reedbeds and shallow mere of Leighton Moss, close by Morecambe Bay. The agricultural Fylde attracts geese in winter, while waders frequent the coastline. Marton Mere, lying behind Blackpool, attracts its share of rarities.

The Pennines themselves hold breeding moorland species on the higher plateau, while Goosanders are spreading on hill streams. The whaleback ridge of Pendle Hill stands above lower hills and valleys where walled and hedged fields are grazed by sheep.

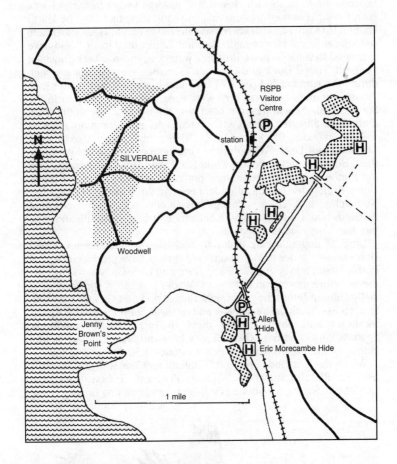

Habitat

Formerly an inlet of Morecambe Bay, Leighton Moss was claimed from the sea and drained, but flooded again, this time with fresh water, in 1917. Now an RSPB reserve of 321 acres (130 hectares), it lies between the villages of Yealand Redmayne on the east and Silverdale on the west, close to the eastern corner of Morecambe Bay. The reserve lies between limestone hills and comprises largely *Phragmites* swamp with invading willow scrub and shallow, open pools frequented by otters as well as a rich avifauna. Artificial scrapes and islands are overlooked from hides.

Meadow Rue is an uncommon plant growing at the edge of the marsh and the spikes of marestail protrude from shallower pools. The valley sides are clothed in woods of ash, oak, yew and birch which conceal red and roe deer. Purple hairstreak butterflies frequent the crowns of oak and ash trees, and high brown frittilliaries may be seen on the grassy slopes.

Species

Leighton Moss has long been famous for its breeding Bitterns and Bearded Tit, both species closely tied to large beds of *Phragmites* (a scarce habitat in northwestern England) and recently joined by Marsh Harrier. Up to 10 pairs of Bittern have nested in recent years either here or at the adjacent Haweswater. Bearded Tit first bred in 1973 and have increased to some 30 pairs. Breeding waterfowl include Teal, Shoveler, Pochard, Tufted Duck and Gadwall. Garganey are occasionally seen during the summer but proof of breeding is still awaited. Water Rail, though common here, are very elusive, as is their scarcer cousin the Spotted Crake which has also bred here. Shingle islands on the main mere have attracted breeding Oystercatchers and Common Terns as well as raucous Black-headed Gulls. Scrubby areas hold nesting Common and Lesser Whitethroats, Grasshopper and Sedge Warblers, Reed Buntings and Redpolls, while Reed Warblers, here approaching the northerly limit of their range, prefer the cleaner stands of reeds. Heron fly in to feed on the abundant eels. All three woodpeckers, a few Nuthatches and elusive Hawfinches inhabit local ashwoods and Buzzards float overhead. Woodcocks rode at dusk in spring and summer and Marsh Tits are plentiful.

Unusual migrants may occur in both spring and autumn. Marsh Harriers often arrive in May and recent springs have produced Osprey, Purple Heron and Spoonbill. Black Terns and Little Gulls hawk over the meres before moving on to the east. Wader passage in spring or especially autumn brings the occasional Ruff, Wood and Green Sandpiper, Spotted Redshank or Greenshank and, at dusk, Starlings, Pied Wagtails, Swallows and Sand Martins mass to roost in the reedbeds. Sparrowhawks and Barn Owls all prey here and Merlin, Peregrine and Hobby all dash in from time to time to snatch a Starling or Swallow.

Winter ducks include up to 1,000 Mallard and Teal with smaller numbers of Pintail, Shoveler, Wigeon, Pochard, Tufted Duck and Goldeneye. Skeins of gibbering Pink-footed and honking Greylag Geese

Marsh Harriers

pass overhead but seldom land unless the meres are frozen. Resident Mute Swans are joined at times by small parties of Whooper or Bewick's Swans. Hen Harrier cover the reedbeds on the lookout for unwary mammals or birds such as Snipe and uncommon Jack Snipe that crouch in the marsh.

Timing
The marsh is at its liveliest in spring and summer when Black-headed Gulls bring a sense of urgency to the proceedings and singing warblers and other marsh birds are visible from the paths between hides. Bittern are difficult to see except in frosty weather when the pools freeze rapidly, forcing the birds to feed in the open. However, they tend to be bolder in May when feeding young and may then be glimpsed briefly as they flap low over the reeds. Water Rail are also easier to see in frosty weather. Autumn and winter visits should be timed to allow a dusk watch over the passerine roosts to see hunting predators.

Access
Leighton Moss can be reached from the A6 north of Carnforth through Yealand Conyers and Yealand Redmayne to Myers Farm near Silverdale railway station. There is an information centre, with a bookshop, at the farm. Permits are available on payment at the shop and allow access via clearly marked paths and walkways to the hides but there is a public causeway running across the north end of the reserve which allows free access to a public hide.

31 CARNFORTH MARSH/ HEST BANK (RSPB)

OS Map 97
SD 46, 47

Habitat and Species
These two saltmarshes are formed either side of the estuary of the River Keer and as such provide one of the most important roost sites for waders, wildfowl and gulls on the south side of the Bay. They become particularly important during the winter and spring peak high tides, when numbers are large, having moved out of smaller roosts at lower levels. Greylag Goose, Shelduck, Wigeon, Teal and Pintail gather in large numbers along with a few Shoveler and Goldeneye. Ten thousand Oystercatcher can be found on a peak tide here along with over 5,000 Knot and Dunlin, Lapwing, Golden Plover, Bar-tailed Godwit, Curlew and Redshank can also reach large numbers here.

On Carnforth Marsh several pools, scrapes and embankments have been formed by the RSPB to make an excellent habitat, which is overlooked by two hides, the Allen Hide and Eric Morecambe Hide (see map on p. 89). Several hundred pairs of Black-headed Gulls nest here but the visiting birdwatcher can expect to see something a little different here at any time of year. In the last few years this has included rarities such as Little Egret, Black Stork, Red-footed Falcon, or Wilson's

Phalarope mixed in with more regular passage birds such as Garganey, Marsh Harrier from nearby Leighton Moss, Ruff, Greenshank, sandpipers, Mediterranean and Little Gulls and Black Terns.

To the south end are several large slag banks which are remnants of a long gone iron industry in Carnforth, providing shelter for passage migrants, particularly in hard winter weather for birds such as Snow Bunting, Twite and the odd Lapland Bunting..

At Hest Bank saltmarsh, to the south of Carnforth, large flocks of Ringed Plover, Knot, Dunlin, Redshank and Turnstone can be seen, along with Shelduck and larger gulls.

Access

For the Allen Pools follow the road for Warton, past Carnforth railway station, under two bridges, after 1 mile (1.6 km) turn left to Silverdale. Follow the road round Warton Fell to Crag Foot, where a track to the left (SD 477738) follows the dyke, under the railway to the car park for both hides. Hest Bank saltmarsh is very easily accessible as most of it can be viewed from the shore car park at the railway crossing or from the northernmost point of the Morecambe Promenade at Teal Bay (SD464660).

From Morecambe take the A5105 along the Promenade over the railway to Hest Bank. Turn left over the level crossing by the signal box and park on the grassy ridge overlooking the marsh. This area overlooks the RSPB reserve and a small parking fee may be required, but the car is an excellent hide.

32 DOCKACRES GRAVEL PITS

OS Map 97
SD 513723

Habitat and Species

These former gravel workings lie in the centre of the Keer Valley flightline and attract many interesting birds. In addition, grain feeding by the shooting syndicate during the winter months has greatly increased the diving duck numbers, especially Pochard. 'Dockacres' in pre-1987 literature actually referred to what is now known as Pine Lake (a time share/water sports complex). 'Dockacres back pool' has just recently (May 1996) been labelled as 'Borwick Lake' by the owners. In the absence of an official name, 'Dockacres' remains the pool to the east of the M6. It is doubtful whether the widely used 'Babydoc' will end up as the permanent name of the pool next to the Burton Road to the north.

In winter, the diving ducks can be found in the northeast corner of Pine Lake or on 'Babydoc' or Dockacres. Borwick Lake is frequently the best place to see Smew. There is sometimes a mass exodus to Leighton Moss, especially when the Sunday evening shooting on Dockacres coincides with water sports on Pine Lake. However, the diving duck are becoming increasingly tolerant of water-skiing and can remain on Pine Lake in some numbers, even on busy weekends. Ferruginous Duck, Lesser Scaup, Ring-necked Duck (both male and female), Greater

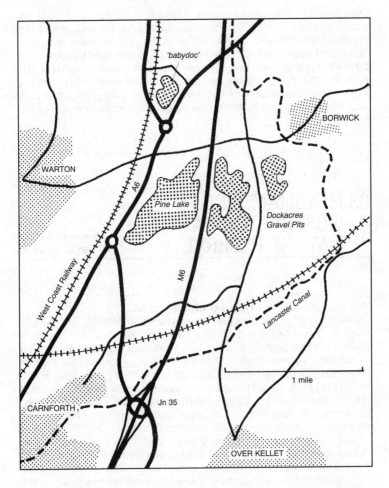

Scaup and Red-crested Pochard have all been recorded here at various times. Long-tailed Duck, Great Northern and Red-throated Divers are occasional visitors but the complex has a very poor track-record for the rarer grebes.

On passage almost anything can turn up, although the habitat for 'freshwater' waders is rather limited. Terns are regular and have included single White-winged Black Tern, a Whiskered Tern in 1996 and one count of over 100 Black Terns. Little and Mediterranean Gulls are fairly regular. The rocky islet on Dockacres tends to be the focal point for passage birds and temporary residents have included Glaucous Gull and Osprey. The grassy areas around Dockacres are very good for migrant pipits and wagtails (especially White Wagtail in mid–late April). The small areas of Common Reed and Reed Mace have hosted Bittern and Bearded Tit (notably at the northern end of Pine Lake).

Access

From Junction 35 of the M6 follow the motorway spur to Pine Lake Resort. Please note that Pine Lake Resort is a private venue and permission must be sought for access. At this roundabout travel north on the A6 and take the A6070 to Burton. Take the first left and park by the gate to view 'Babydoc', then continue to the A6 (one way) and, after the interchange, take the left turn at the crossroads signposted to Borwick; cross the M6, take the right turn at the next crossroads and park by the double gates on the right-hand side. After viewing Dockacres, Borwick Lake can be looked over by taking the public footpath about 50 metres from the parking spot and walking across to the fence.

33 HEYSHAM BIRD OBSERVATORY AND NATURE RESERVE

OS Maps 97 and 102
SD 35, 36, 45, 46

Habitat and Species

This Observatory covers the area around Heysham Harbour and the two Nuclear Power Stations, including two sites for observing northerly seabird passage (spring) or storm-blown seabirds making their way out of the bay (winter/autumn). It is a reasonably good site for Leach's Petrel, usually on the second (and subsequent) day of a WSW–WNW blow in September–mid October, occasionally to late October. The best place to watch Leach's Petrels is from the north harbour wall. However, the warm water outfalls from the power stations produce a dilute 'soup' which is very attractive to gulls and terns. Therefore, it might be more productive to watch for seabirds from the outfalls hide where the more distant views of Leach's Petrels will be compensated for by a variety of species including Black and Arctic Terns, Little and Mediterranean Gull.

In spring, significant numbers of seabirds enter the bay in all weather conditions on northerly passage, especially on early morning incoming tides. The most interesting involves Arctic Terns, which appear most regularly in easterly (offshore) winds. For example, 504 flew north in 45 minutes on 2 May 1996. Some species, such as the skuas, often spiral up and progress overland when they reach the inner bay. Other species, for example Kittiwake flocks, make half-hearted attempts to go overland but usually end up sitting on the sea, then floating/flying out on the dropping tide.

In midwinter, severe onshore gales produce large Kittiwake movements, sometimes in conjunction with large numbers of Little Gulls, depending on whether they are wintering in the Irish Sea within the 'catchment area' of the gale. This appears to vary considerably from winter to winter. Little Auks, Grey Phalaropes and skuas are occasionally recorded in midwinter.

The northeast corner of the power station land comprises the Nature Reserve and this contains an array of wet and dry land habitats in this relatively small area. It is also the site of the ringing and visible migration observations. This geographically unpromising location has pro-

Sabine's Gull

duced a surprising number of rare birds, mainly of eastern origin. Perhaps the lighthouse effect of the power station complex plays a major role in 'grounding' large numbers of night migrants, especially during southeast winds with poor offshore visibility. No fewer than 12 Yellow-browed Warblers have been recorded, and other rarities have included Dusky Warbler, Thrush Nightingale, Common Rosefinch, Pallas's Warbler, Melodious Warbler, Marsh Warbler and Wryneck. Visible migration recording also takes place here, which involves a 'hear; look for; count' sequence with respect to birds flying overhead, mainly during the early morning. Many silent high-flying birds are obviously missed! Oddities have included Serin, Woodlark and Bee-eater.

Red Nab and the helipad are two good wader roosts although Red Nab will be covered rather too quickly on spring tides. The helipad is sometimes 'carpeted' in Knot. Unfortunately, the well publicised Purple Sandpiper flock has now diminished to one or two individuals, which are very difficult to find.

Access

Follow the A683 from Junction 34 of the M6. This road has recently been extended as a by-pass leading straight to Heysham Harbour. At the Moneyclose Inn traffic lights (the first ones since Lancaster), turn right for the north harbour wall then left at the 'T' junction by the helipad, then immediately right and progress down the seawall road. This becomes narrower after the British Gas offices and also changes into a 'private' road which you use at your own risk. For the Nature Reserve/Observatory turn left at the Moneyclose Inn traffic lights and take the first right after about 300 metres. For Red Nab, carry on past the Nature Reserve entrance and park sensibly in the Ocean Edge Caravan Site car park. Then walk down any one of several routes to the shore, turn to your right and follow the seawall to the outfalls (and hide). Please remember Ocean Edge is a private site and access is by courtesy of the management.

The reserve is open at all times with vehicle access to the car park from at least 0900–1700 hrs. There will usually be someone at the Observatory building in the morning during migration times. For organ-

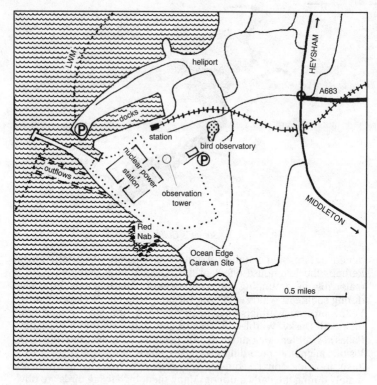

ised visits to observe ringing, visible migration etc., please telephone 01524 855624.

Timing

The spring seabird passage is usually most productive early in the morning, preferably on an incoming tide. Mid April to mid May is the best period. At other times of the year, periods of strong onshore winds are needed. The outfalls are most productive about 2–3 hours before high tide, especially if there is an offshore wind. They are frequently birdless at high tide during calm weather. The best time for migratory passerines is the early morning unless special weather conditions, notably a front approaching from the south with accompanying east/southeast winds, materialise. The Common Rosefinch was found during these conditions late in the day, after a 'birdless' early morning .

Habitat and Species

As with the other river estuaries on Morecambe Bay, the Lune has several important roost sites for wildfowl and waders. The prime roost sites are Pilling Marsh, Cockerham Sands, around Glasson Dock at Conder Green and Middleton Sands on the north shore.

The fields in the area of Cockerham Moss hold good numbers of Pink-footed Geese from February to April, often peaking at around 5,000 birds. These birds roost on Pilling Sands and may bring stragglers of other species with them including White-fronted, Barnacle and Brent Geese. Good numbers of Golden Plover and Lapwing are to be found in these fields in winter, often being molested by preying Sparrowhawk and Peregrine. Breeding species include Partridge, Whitethroat, occasional Lesser Whitethroat and Corn Bunting, the latter a bird which is rare north of the Lune.

Middleton Sands to Sunderland Point on the north shore of the estuary is fairly difficult for access and, as a result, is not watched as closely as other areas of the estuary. However, the monthly wader counts reveal good numbers of Ringed Plover, Knot, Dunlin, Sanderling and Redshank. Around Sunderland Point there are Grey Plover, Bar-tailed Godwit and Greenshank. This headland sees a movement of passage passerines with winter thrushes in cold conditions and pipits in spring and autumn. Richard's Pipit was recorded here in 1980 and Water Pipit in 1982.

The south shore of the estuary has much easier access as the old railway embankment from Glasson Dock to Lancaster carries a well maintained footpath with parking facilities provided at Conder Green. Apart from the regular wildfowl and waders, Conder Green, with its creeks and mudflats, has been visited by a few notable birds such as White-rumped and Buff-breasted Sandpipers.

Travelling south of Glasson Dock into the Fylde towards Pilling Sands you pass Cockerham Point with its prominent sandstone Abbey, before coming to the vast expanse of sands of Cockerham and Pilling. A Pacific Golden Plover was found here in July 1990. Here amongst the scarcer shorebirds seen on this length of coast have been Little Egret, Spoonbill, Little Ringed Plover, Little Stint, Curlew and Wood Sandpiper, Ruff, and odd Little Gull and Arctic Skua and occasional Lapland and Snow Buntings in winter. Just inland from this area Quail have been heard in summer and in 1987 a Crane was seen.

Access

For Middleton Sands take the A589 in Heysham to the traffic lights at High Heysham, continuing straight on down the minor road to Middleton. In the village take the first right to Middleton Tower Holiday Campsite following the road to its end at Patts Corner, where good views of the sands can be had. For Sunderland Point, pass through Middleton for Overton where you turn right for Sunderland. Park in the village and walk to Sunderland Point. Beware of high tides as the road crosses the saltmarsh at several points and is flooded twice a day.

To reach Conder Green take the A588 from Lancaster. At Conder

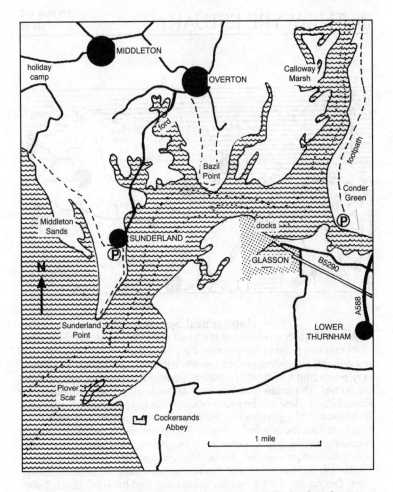

Green village turn right at the Stork Inn and park in the foreshore car park by the railway embankment. For Cockerham Point turn right off the A588 a mile (1.6 km) further south, at Thurnham and follow the road to the Abbey. Good views of the sands can also be had from the car park placed on the new flood prevention embankment near Pilling Hall off the A588 5 miles (8 km) south of Cockerham (SD 416495).

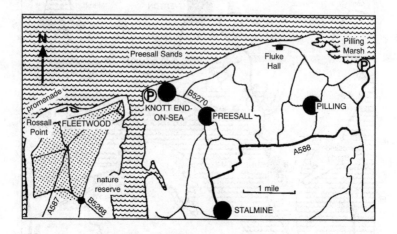

Habitat and Species

Fleetwood which is situated at the head of the Wyre Estuary, forms the southernmost point of Morecambe Bay. Its prominent position makes it not only an interesting place to watch wildfowl and waders but also a very rewarding site during migration periods for seabirds and passage passerines. The prime watchpoint is at the head of the promenade at Rossall Point. Here can be found offshore flocks of Common Scoter and Red-breasted Merganser while the flocks of common waders often contain both species of godwit, Purple Sandpiper and Sanderling. During migration periods, auks, Kittiwake, terns, Arctic and Great Skua can be seen. In autumn gales, Manx Shearwater, Leach's Petrel, Grey Phalarope, Sabine's Gull and Pomarine Skua have all been recorded here. During the winter months occasional Red-throated Diver, Twite and Snow Bunting can be found.

On the Wyre Estuary, the pools around the ICI works and Power Station attract grebes, Tufted Duck, Pochard, Wigeon, Teal, Goldeneye and a summer peak of moulting Mute Swans, Little Stint, Curlew and Wood Sandpiper, Little and Mediterranean Gull have been recorded on passage. Unfortunately, these pools are gradually being infilled for a land reclamation project, thus reducing the attraction for these birds.

Knott End on the opposite shore holds common waders with good numbers of Redshank and Turnstone. Occasional Eider and Scaup may venture up the estuary here and Glaucous Gull have been seen here as in other sites around Fleetwood in winter. The Wyre Estuary has long been noted for migrating flocks of Black-tailed Godwit.

Access

Rossall Point to the Lifeboat Station on the Wyre has easy access as viewing can be done from any point along the promenade.

The pools near the Power Station and at the ICI Chemical Works can be reached by following the A585, by-passing Thornton to a roundabout at the Cala Gran Caravan Park. Turn right and then left down a minor road to the Waste Re-cycling Centre. View the ICI pools from the railway bridge, where the Fleetwood Nature Reserve is sited on the opposite side of the road. The Power Station pools are half a mile (0.8 km) further down the road.

37 MARTON MERE, BLACKPOOL

OS Map 102
SD 33
SD 343353

This mere on the outskirts of Blackpool is an area of open water, marsh and reedbed which is a local nature reserve. It holds breeding Little and Great Crested Grebes, Sedge and Reed Warblers. It is best known for its migrant waders, which regularly include Little Ringed Plover, Jack Snipe, Green and Wood Sandpipers. Other migrants include Little Gull, Glaucous Gull, sea terns, Black Tern and Short-eared Owl. In winter it holds good wildfowl numbers, particularly Wigeon, Teal, Shoveler, Pochard, Tufted Duck, Goldeneye and Ruddy Duck. Bewick's Swan, Garganey, Scaup and Common Scoter have also been recorded here. Scarcer visitors have included Red-necked Grebe, Marsh Harrier, Osprey, Turtle Dove, Wryneck and Black Redstart.

An American Bittern stayed during the winter of 1990/91.

Access
From Preston take the M55 to Junction 4 and then the A583 to Great Marton. Turn right for Stanley Park and after half a mile (0.8 km) turn right again down Lawson Road. Halfway down the road, walk across the football pitch to Marton Mere.

38 FOREST OF BOWLAND

OS Maps 102 and 103
SD 55, 64 and 65

Habitat
The Forest of Bowland is an upland area of great scenic beauty with its narrow valleys and steep-sided fells punctuated by small pastures, drystone walls and small area of mature woodland. On the western side is Wyresdale surrounded by Tarnbrook Fell to the north and Hawthornthwaite Fell to the south. Through the valley flows the upper part of the River Wyre from its source, and it is joined by several streams and becks to form a lake at Abbeystead before continuing its journey westwards to the sea. Passing through the upland Trough of Bowland the heather moorland reverts to a scene of upland grassland and fell

farmsteads. At Dunsop Bridge the River Dunsop joins the River Hodder to flow southwards through the lower part of Bowland Forest to meet the River Ribble at Little Mitton. This is 'an area of outstanding natural beauty' with its fine stands of beech woodland and heather covered hills. To the northeast, amongst the open grass upland, is Stocks Reservoir and the large conifer stands of Gisburn Forest beyond.

Species

A very large gull colony centred in the Tarnbrook area holds some 5,000 Herring and Lesser Black-backed Gulls. A large part of the high open fells are well stocked with Red Grouse. On the high tops one can expect to encounter the odd Merlin and Hen Harrier with Golden Plover, Curlew, Dunlin, Short-eared Owl and on the rocky crags, Raven, Ring Ouzel and Twite. Lower down, the fellside streams have their resident Dippers, wagtails and in some areas Stonechat added to in summer by breeding pairs of Wheatear and Whinchat. In the valley bottoms amongst the wooded riversides there are Oystercatcher, Snipe, Woodcock, Red-breasted Merganser and some Goosander. Some river embankments have Sand Martin and Kingfisher and on the woodland

Golden Plover

fringes there are still the odd pair of Blackcock with Buzzard and Sparrowhawk hunting overhead in places. The beech woodland has Redstart, Pied Flycatcher, Wood Warbler, Little and Tawny Owls and a few pairs of Long-eared Owls with the occasional Green Woodpecker and Nuthatch. Amongst the more unusual species recorded in the Bowland area recently are Rough-legged Buzzard, Golden Eagle, Osprey and Hobby, with Wood Sandpiper at Abbeystead Reservoir. Winter brings good passage numbers of winter thrushes and Brambling with a few Snow Bunting on the highest tops and flighting Greylag and Pink-footed Geese.

Access

Make Dunsop Bridge the centre point. Take Junction 33 off the M6 and follow the A6 to Galgate, then taking the minor road for Dolphinholme and Abbeystead, which continues through the Trough of Bowland for Dunsop Bridge. Access to the summits of Tarnbrook Fell and Brennand can be gained by turning left beyond Abbeystead for Grizedale Bridge (SD 566554). Turn right along the valley to Tarnbrook where a footpath takes you to the top of Tarnbrook Fell and Wolfhole Crag. From the east, Dunsop Bridge can be reached from Clitheroe taking the B6478 via Newton Fell and Newton or the more scenic route from Clitheroe via the B6243 to Edisford Hall. Turn right for Bashall Eaves and Whitewell for Dunsop Bridge.

39 STOCKS RESERVOIR (NORTH WEST WATER)

OS Map 103
SD 75

Habitat and Species

Stocks Reservoir is some 700 ft (220 m) up amongst the grouse moors near Slaidburn and the North Yorkshire border. It covers some 344 acres (140 hectares) and is visable from the road and picnic site provided by NWWA. The central island is a refuge and breeding site for Canada and Greylag Geese, Teal, Tufted Duck and waders including Oystercatcher, Ringed Plover, Snipe and Redshank. Around 500 pairs of Black-headed Gull also breed here. In winter the reservoir holds a large gull roost and wildfowl numbers increase with Whooper Swan, Wigeon, Pochard, Goldeneye, an occasional Smew and Goosander to add interest. Also at this time have been recorded Hen Harrier, Golden Plover, Dunlin, winter thrushes and Great Grey Shrike. Ring-necked Duck have been recorded twice here in winter. The reservoir is part of a notable trans-Pennine migration route and as such produces some interesting passage migrants in spring and autumn. These have included Shelduck, Scaup, Common Scoter, Osprey, Little Ringed Plover, Little Stint, Curlew Sandpiper, Ruff, Black-tailed Godwit, Greenshank, sandpipers, Arctic Skua, Little Gull and Common and Black Terns, and an Isabelline Shrike in 1996.

On the northern edge of the reservoir lies the large expanse of Gisburn Forest, a Forestry Commission plantation which holds good woodland species such as Sparrowhawk, Long-eared Owl, Tree Pipit, Redstart, Wood Warbler, Siskin, Redpoll and a few Crossbill.

Access

From the A65 Kendal to Skipton road take the B6478 at Long Preston for Slaidburn. Some 8 miles (13 km) on, having passed through the villages of Wigglesworth and Tosside, turn right at the crossroads on Stephen Moor (SD 748543) for Stocks Reservoir and Clapham. A further 2.5 miles (4 km) will bring you to the north bank of the reservoir and the car park. Good views of most of the reservoir can be obtained here or along the road. From the west, travel through the Trough of Bowland to Dunsop Bridge and Slaidburn where the B6478 will take you to the crossroads at Stephen Moor.

Timing

The area is important for both breeding and passage wildfowl and waders. Spring and autumn can produce the unexpected, while in winter the large gull roost and the increase in wildfowl numbers are the main attractions.

40 PENDLE HILL

OS Map 103
SE 795410

Habitat

The summit of Pendle Hill is occupied by grass moor with some sparse heather. The rocky slopes are covered with bracken in places, and below these are pasture fields bounded by stone walls or hedges. Fast-flowing streams are home to riparian birds.

Species

Pendle is best known as a spring passage haunt of Dotterel, which crouch on the barren, windswept top of this rounded hill. The first birds arrive in mid April, but most are present in early May prior to a mass departure in mid month. In 1988, for example, 32 birds were counted. Greenland Wheatear often pass through around this time.

Earlier in the spring Golden Plover and Curlew flock in lower-lying pastures before dispersing to breeding territories, and Snipe and a few Redshank return to rushy fields which later attract Yellow Wagtail. The hill itself still holds small numbers of resident Red Grouse and a few Golden Plover, but these latter birds resent disturbance from ramblers. Twite return in April, and remain through the summer, forming small parties in August. Ring Ouzel in March and Whinchat in April are as likely to be passing through as holding territory, but Wheatear breed on the rocky slopes.

Dotterel

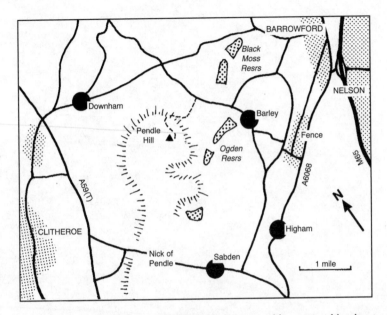

Redstart favour the lower, bracken-clad slopes with scattered bushes or trees. Where old hedgerow trees and semi-derelict barns stand together, listen for the curlew-hoot of Little Owl. Grey Wagtail are numerous along hill streams, where Dipper also breed. Goosander have bred locally too.

This tall, isolated hill attracts predators, for example Merlin and Short-eared Owl, and all Pennine hills may occasionally produce exciting birds in winter. Snow Bunting are irregular visitors, but in winter of 1989/90 a flock of 25 spent some weeks here, feeding on moorland grass seeds. Overgrown thorn hedges attract berry-eating thrushes and, in invasion years, Waxwing.

Timing

The area generally is popular walking country, but the chief bird season is from March to May. Dotterel enthusiasts concentrate their efforts in the first two weeks of May. The summit itself is often relatively crowded on fine weekends.

Access

The most direct route to the summit follows a stepped path up from minor roads north of Barley, but there are numerous footpaths, particularly around the lower slopes. Dotterel favour the flat summit around the triangulation point at the Barley end.

Calendar

All year: Red Grouse on moors; Little Owl on farmland; Dipper and Grey Wagtail on streams.

March–May: Ring Ouzel, Golden Plover and other moorland species on passage; Redshank, Snipe and Curlew in pastures; Dotterel on tops in early May. Twite, Redstart and other migrants arrive during April.

SOUTH LANCASHIRE, MERSEYSIDE AND GREATER MANCHESTER

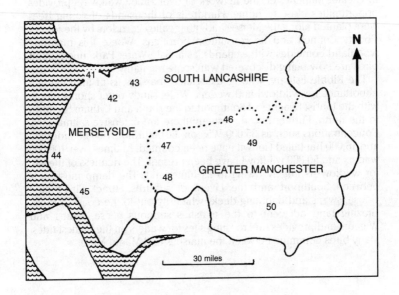

SOUTH LANCASHIRE

MERSEYSIDE

GREATER MANCHESTER

N

30 miles

41 South Ribble Marshes
42 Martin Mere and the South
   Lancashire Mosslands
43 Mere Sands Wood
44 Sefton Coast
45 Seaforth Nature Reserve
   and Crosby Marina

46 Bolton Area and the West
   Pennine Moors
47 Wigan Flashes
48 Pennington Flash
49 Elton Reservoir, Bury
50 Mersey Valley

The shallow coastline of South Lancashire is marked by wide, sandy beaches which, together with the estuaries of Ribble and Alt, attract thousands of waders. The beaches are fringed to landward by extensive dune systems, lost to development in places, although many of the surviving dunes are now protected. The low-lying mosslands between the Ribble and Liverpool have been drained to create rich farmland. The Wildfowl and Wetlands Trust reserve at Martin Mere and the Ribble Marshes National Nature Reserve together attract vast numbers of wildfowl which fly out to feed on farmland elsewhere.

A legacy of the Industrial Revolution, much of which was concentrated in the south Lancashire region, is a variety of rich ornithological sites which arose accidentally as a result of industrial development. The Seaforth Dock Pools in Liverpool and the coal-mining subsidence flashes at Leigh and Wigan are good examples. Fast-flowing streams off the Pennines were harnessed to power textile mills. As the population grew, larger drinking water reservoirs were constructed to supply the cities. The cluster of reservoirs around Bolton attract a wide range of birds, but all such reservoirs are worth a look on occasion, or could be adopted as a 'local patch'.

Few heather moors remain, but Twite still nest on grass moors towards the Yorkshire border. For many urban birdwatchers, especially in Greater Manchester, the network of river valley walkways provides opportunities close to home. Hundreds of thousands of young trees were planted along the Mersey and other valley corridors by the former County Council and its constituent boroughs. Where this maturing woodland coincides with wetlands, as at Sale Water Park, uncommon birds are now being discovered with some regularity.

The Ribble Estuary, with its associated marshes, is of international importance for wildfowl and waders. Wide, sandy outer shores merge with the tourist beaches of Southport to the south and Lytham St Annes to the north. Further into the estuary there are extensive saltmarshes. Concentrations such as 35,000 Wigeon, 60,000 Knot, 7,000 Sanderling and 16,000 Bar-tailed Godwit have been counted. At times over 100,000 waders and 50,000 wildfowl have been present. The richness of the site for wildfowl is largely owing to its hinterland. The damp mosslands between Southport and the Liverpool suburbs attract Pink-footed Goose, swans and dabbling ducks which fly out to the coast to roost. Grazing land adjacent to the marshes supports geese, swans and Wigeon, and provides safe roosting sites for waders on the highest tides. Many birds commute between the marshes and Martin Mere.

Habitat

The Ribble Marshes National Nature Reserve was established following the threat of agricultural destruction of its wildlife potential in 1979. Banks and Crossens Marshes now form the bulk of 5430 acres (2182 hectares) of reserve, with 300 acres (120 hectares) added at Hesketh Out Marsh. Some wildfowling is permitted, chiefly for Wigeon and Pink-footed Goose, but wildfowl numbers have increased since the establishment of the reserve.

The marshes consist of mudbanks and saltmarsh, the latter grazed by cattle during the summer. The wet fields at Marshside and Crossens are frequented by wildfowl and waders, especially at high tide. Southwards from the Marshside sand workings, the expansive beach is largely free of vegetation and backed by small dunes behind the road. The coast is exposed to autumnal gales, which may drive seabirds over the marshes or onto the sheltered marine lake at Southport.

Species

Wildfowl frequenting the marshes peak between late November and March. Bewick's Swans number several hundred. Small numbers of Whooper Swans are usually also present and may mingle with the smaller Bewick's, allowing direct comparison of two species which can pose identification problems when seen alone. The main focus for Whoopers has now shifted to Martin Mere. Pink-footed Goose flocks sometimes total 10,000 or more birds. Other goose species are often represented by stragglers, picked up on the journey from Iceland or Greenland. Sooty Greenland White-fronted, pale Greylag or brown, orange-legged Bean Geese are not so easily spotted as Barnacle Goose or the occasional Snow Goose. This last, rare species has accompanied the Pink-footed in several winters. Parties of Eurasian White-fronted Goose have occasionally settled. White-breasted Pintail drakes are conspicuous among the Wigeon flocks, although more careful scrutiny is required to detect the grey females. Shelducks are numerous, both on the marshes and on the beaches beyond. Mallard, Teal and a few Gadwall sit around the pools on the marsh, flying inland towards dusk

Sanderling

to feed. Brent Goose are infrequent on this coast. Take careful note of the race to which any birds seen belong. Dark and pale-bellied races both occur.

At high tide, rafts of dabbling ducks float on the sea at the edge of the marsh. Small parties of Scaup and a few Merganser or Eider occasionally drift in with the tide. The highest tides may flood the saltmarsh, driving a few Water Rails from cover.

The grazing marsh at Crossens and Marshside is a favourite haunt of Golden Plover, with several thousand present in winter. Over 1,000 Black-tailed Godwit roost at high tide, and parties of Curlew may be seen. Shorter-legged Bar-tailed Godwit and Grey Plover prefer the beaches. As the tide rises, packs of Knot swirl over the Southport beaches before settling to roost. Sanderling, Turnstone and Ringed Plover may also be seen, with the inevitable Dunlin and piping Oystercatcher. Tiny numbers of Little Stint and the occasional Spotted Redshank or Greenshank may be seen in winter. Ruff are more usual, with perhaps several dozen feeding with Redshank in the damp fields. Spring passage brings a variety of marshland waders to the Marshside pools in late April and May—few in number but smart in plumage. Ruff have been seen gathering at this season. There may still be thousands of Knot on the beaches, and northward passage may bring several hundred arctic Ringed Plover to Marshside.

White Wagtails are a feature of spring passage all along the coast in April and early May, but Yellow Wagtails are fewer than formerly. Wheatear are frequently present during April, many of them also bound for Iceland. Whinchat pass through in early May. A Marsh Harrier may appear, floating low over the marsh, at almost any time from spring to autumn. Garganey may be seen on the pools in spring or early summer. The marshes are nationally important for breeding species. Several hundred pairs of Common Tern, a few Arctic Tern, and several thousand pairs of Black-headed Gull breed, as do up to 500 pairs of Redshank. Lapwing, Ringed Plover and Oystercatcher also breed, and Dunlin have done so. Several hundred pairs of Lesser Black-backed and Herring Gulls nest, with a few Great Black-backed. Grey Partridge are numerous in neighbouring fields where the jangling song of Corn Buntings may still be heard. Shelduck breed in good numbers, and a few pairs of Shovelers are worth looking out for. Other ducks, such as Teal, Pintail and Tufted Duck, linger into the summer and sometimes attempt to breed.

By August the estuarine waders are starting to build up again. Several thousand Black-tailed Godwit may be present by the end of the month. This is also the most likely time to encounter Curlew Sandpiper, Little Stint and such species as Green or Wood Sandpiper on muddy pools. Ruffs again reach double or even treble figures. September gales may blow seabirds over the Marine Drive, but this is not a recognised seawatching site—at low tide the absence of the sea at Southport is legendary! However both Grey and Red-necked Phalaropes have appeared on sheltered pools after autumnal storms. Towards the end of the month the first Pink-footed Geese arrive on northwesterly winds from Iceland. October sees the return of the winter predators. Several Hen Harriers hunt the marshes throughout the winter, as do Merlins and increasing number of Peregrine. Short-eared Owl numbers vary, but there may be ten or more of these birds scattered along the coastline.

During the winter, Reed Bunting, Linnet and Greenfinch feed along the tideline around the sand workings at Marshside. Twite are often present, recognised by their abrupt flight call and the diagnostic twang after which they are named. A Black Redstart has been seen here on several occasions. Stonechats too are often present, as are Rock Pipits. Lapland Buntings feed out on the marsh, but are unlikely to be seen except in flight, when a knowledge of their calls is essential. Brambling numbers vary from year to year.

The Southport Marine Lake is a regular haunt of Cormorant, Goldeneye, and a few Merganser, and provides a haven for storm-blown sea-duck, and the odd Shag or diver. Snow Buntings sometimes feed around its shoreline, or along the beach nearby.

Timing

At low tide the saltmarshes look almost deserted, but they liven up rapidly as the tide pushes birds in. High tides between late August and mid April are best. During the winter there are always interesting birds to be seen on the grazing marshes. There is some shooting between 1 September and 20 February, but this seldom detracts from birdwatching. The highest tides in winter (32 ft (10.5 m) or more) may flood the marsh and flush out Water Rail or Jack Snipe.

Access

Marshside, the area most popular with birdwatchers, lies adjacent to Crossens Marsh. Both can be viewed from the Marine Drive which runs north from the Southport pleasure beach past the Marine Lake up to the A565 Banks roundabout. Stopping along the Marine Drive is prohibited, but it is possible to pull off at various points, and there are car parks adjacent to the marine lake and by the sand-washing plant at Marshside. Trees opposite Crossens sewage works often hold Bramblings in winter. Crossens Out Marsh may also be viewed by turning first left on reaching the Banks roundabout, crossing the river then walking left along the footpath which follows the top of the seawall. This embankment also provides a vantage point over Banks and

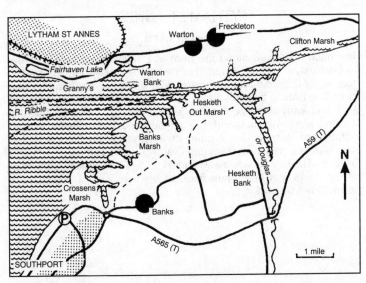

111

Hesketh Out Marshes. A further embankment path runs from Hundred End around Ribble Bank Farm, turning in beside the River Douglas to Hesketh Bank. During onshore gales, seawatching from the end of Southport Pier may be worthwhile.

CLIFTON MARSH

OS ref: SD 465285

This stretch of saltmarsh may hold large herds of wild swans when they are absent from Marshside or Martin Mere. The usual saltmarsh predators (Hen Harrier, Merlin, Peregrine, Short-eared Owl) may be seen. Access is difficult, but viewing is possible across the river from the embankment on the south shore. Access at various points in Higher Penwortham or Bottom of Hutton.

WARTON MARSH

OS ref: SD 400270

From Warton Marsh village take Bank Lane which runs past the end of the airfield. This lane narrows into a rough track where parking is difficult. Muddy footpaths lead east and west along the raised inner edge of the marsh, fringed in places by thorn scrub. In winter, flocks of Tree Sparrow, Linnet and other seed-eaters frequent this scrub, flying onto the strand line to feed on saltmarsh seeds. Twite and Brambling are sometimes present. On the highest spring tides the marsh may flood, driving Water Rail from cover. To the east this path is also accessible off Naze Lane East to the south of Freckleton village.

LYTHAM ST ANNES

OS ref: SD 375270

The main A584 runs along the front at Lytham. Walk east from the lifeboat station past the windmill to view the saltmarsh. Linnets congregate along the strand line in winter with other finches, buntings and larks. The Lytham beaches attract many waders, notably Sanderling in May and early autumn. Black-tailed Godwit may exceed 1,000 in autumn, along with thousands of Knot, hundreds of Dunlin and smaller numbers of other species. A mile (1.6 km) west of the lifeboat station take Marine Drive which leads past Granny's Bay to Fairhaven Lake (SD 340273). The bay attracts many waders at high tide. Small numbers of diving ducks and Cormorant frequent the lake, with a possibility of storm-blown seafowl.

Habitat

The mosslands of southern Lancashire comprise an extensive area of former peatlands, now converted to rich, arable farmland. The area generally is low-lying and flat, with narrow, reedy drainage ditches and small scattered woodlands. Many fields hold shallow puddles in winter. The Wildfowl and Wetlands Trust reserve at Martin Mere covers 363 acres (150 hectares) of damp pasture land, shallow pools and scrapes which attract wildfowl and waders. It is a RAMSAR site, EEC Special Protection Area, and SSSI for ornithological and botanical interest. There is a large collection of penned wildfowl from around the world.

Species

Martin Mere in winter is probably the best site in the region for watching wild geese. Up to 34,000 Pink-footed Geese have been counted on the mosses in early winter, and there are regularly several thousand visible from the hides at the Trust centre—more than 22,000 were seen in October 1994. Careful searching through the flocks will often reveal odd birds of other species, perhaps a family group of White-fronted or a solitary Bean, Brent or Snow Goose. Wild Greylag and Barnacle Geese also occur in small numbers, but identification is made confusing by the presence of feral birds. A small flock of feral Barnacles is present throughout the year (numbering up to 39 in 1994), and up to 400 or more Greylags feed on the reserve outside the nesting season, with smaller numbers during April to July. A few pairs may nest. These geese, and a small flock of feral Pink-footed which consort with them all year, fly out from Scarisbrick Hall. Canada Geese are only likely to be numerous during August when up to 200 freshly moulted birds may visit the mere. In some winters, tiny, small-billed Canada Geese of one of the small races with a high-pitched, cackling voice have accompanied the Pink-feet—perhaps genuine vagrants from North America. Lesser White-fronted Goose has also been recorded. Injured or old Pink-feet and wild swans occasionally stay over the summer. While scanning through the Pink-feet, check for plastic rings with numbers which can be read

Pink-footed Geese

through a telescope, and report any sightings to the staff.

Provision of grain attracts concentrations of wild swans into the grounds. Up to 700 Whoopers and 500–600 Bewick's Swans are present at peak times, with up to 20 Mute Swans on the mere in winter. Teal and Mallard are present in their thousands, and Wigeon have exceeded 25,000. Pintail, though highly mobile and erratic in their appearances, may top 3,000 in early winter. Gadwall have increased considerably since the Trust established their collection here, perhaps aided in part by collection-reared birds which, having flown free up until the early 1980s, now behave as wild birds. Up to 50 or so may be seen scattered amongst the Mallard and Teal. A similar number of Shoveler, particularly in autumn or early winter, show a clearer preference for the company of their own species. Up to 250 or more Shelduck feed around muddy pools in late winter. All the regular freshwater ducks appear from time to time. Recently dredged areas of the mere have held up to 500 Pochard, several dozen Tufted Duck, and a few Goldeneye, with occasional Scaup, Goosander or Ruddy Duck. Ferruginous Duck and Common Scoter have also occurred. North American stragglers, sighted in several recent winters, are one or two Green-winged Teal and American Wigeon among their Eurasian counterparts.

Ducks nesting in a wild state include Shelduck, Gadwall, many Mallard (400 pairs in 1988), Shoveler and Pochard. Wigeon, Teal and possibly Pintail may spend the summer here in small numbers. Garganey are occasional visitors in spring or autumn. The abundance of nesting waders gives some idea of the productivity of the mosslands in general before they were drained. Some dozens of pairs of Lapwing and a few pairs of Snipe and Redshank nest. Oystercatcher, Little Ringed Plover and (at least once) Ruff have been known to do so. Non-breeding Black-tailed Godwit may be present in numbers through the summer, with larger flocks at passage times in some years.

Autumn brings a fair variety of waders to the pools. Curlew and Dunlin, Ringed and Little Ringed Plovers regularly reach double figures, while Snipe may be numbered in hundreds. Many other species occur less predictably and in small numbers. Several Pectoral Sandpipers have been recorded while Collared Pratincole, Lesser Yellowlegs, Red-necked Phalarope and other rarities have occurred. Thousands of Lapwing and decreasing Golden Plover flock during autumn and winter in the damp, rushy pastures, where they are joined by many Ruff. A hundred or more of these often red-legged, hunch-backed waders may be present. Gulls visiting the mere in winter have included such rarities as Franklin's, Ring-billed, Mediterranean, Glaucous, Iceland and Yellow-legged. Spring wader passage, during April and May, is again dominated by Black-tailed Godwit, but Spotted Redshank, Greenshank and others may visit.

Short-eared Owl, Kestrel and Hen Harrier are quite likely to be seen during a winter afternoon's watch from the hides. Merlin and Peregrine too will take Snipe, and the larger falcon may tackle a duck. A Barn Owl is sometimes seen hunting mice or small passerines along the rough grass of field edges. These scarce, white owls breed on the reserve.

Within the pens of the wildfowl collection, Moorhen and Collared Dove help themselves to the inmates' food, as do Corn Buntings in winter. Although this species is declining in the region, this remains a fairly reliable site to see the birds. A flock overhead sounds rather like a bowl of 'rice crispies'—appropriate for a grain-eating species! Starlings may roost in their thousands, attracting raptors as the light fades, and Tree Sparrows regularly flock here in midwinter. While summer is often regarded as the quiet season at Martin Mere, there is still much to be seen. Spring passage of hirundines brings flocks of Sand Martin, while parties of White and Yellow Wagtails scurry along the mere edge. The occasional Black Tern or Little Gull may hawk over the water. One or two Marsh Harriers generally appear at this season and there is a possibility of sightings throughout the summer. Some 45 pairs of Sedge Warbler nest, while fewer pairs of Reed Bunting and Meadow Pipit breed. Skylarks are also common. Up to 20 or so Grey Herons fish the pools at any season. Spoonbill and Little Egret have been recorded as rare visitors.

Although nowadays geese are generally present on the reserve in winter, some watchers still tour the lanes across the more southern mosslands to seek flocks which often feed in carrot fields. Fields beside the lanes at Plex Moss, Halsall Moss and Altcar Moss at times hold thousands of geese, with Wigeon, Pintail and other ducks in damper areas. Grey Partridge and Pheasant are numerous throughout the area, with a few Red-legged Partridge too. There is also a chance of seeing raptors—the same species as at Martin Mere itself—attracted by the mixed finch, bunting and sparrow flocks which venture from thorn hedges into the stubbles. Mossland Birchwoods beyond the reserve hold a sprinkling of nesting Woodcock, Turtle Dove and Long-eared Owl—the last two both increasingly scarce and hard to locate. Barn Owl frequent old farm buildings. The breeding population of this species on the mosslands has held up in the face of a national decline. There is a healthy population of Little Owls. Wader passage in both seasons brings a range of marshland species to flooded fields. A feature of spring passage in some years is the appearance of trips of Dotterel in the flat fields, most regularly at Altcar Moss, although they may occur anywhere in ploughed fields. Plex Moss is often good for Whimbrel in spring. Marsh Harriers sometimes favour Altcar Moss in summer.

Access

Martin Mere (SD 423143) is conspicuously signposted for miles around, even from the M6. The reserve is open from 9.30 am till dusk or 5.30 pm, whichever comes sooner, throughout the year except for Christmas Eve and Christmas Day. There is an admission fee for non-members of the Wildfowl and Wetlands Trust, currently £3.50 for adults, £2 OAP, £1.50 children. Coach parties should book in advance (tel. 01704 895181)—concessionary rates may be claimed for parties of more than twenty.

The mosslands to the south are best explored by car, although increased road traffic means greater care has to be taken to pull off the carriageway where possible. Goose flocks are wary and highly mobile, so it is often necessary to tour the lanes for some time before a flock is located. Scan carefully from the cover of a vehicle if possible to avoid flushing the birds. Plex Moss Lane is often particularly good.

The area lies between the A5147 to the east and A565(T) to the west. All transverse lanes between the B5195 and the A570 are worth exploring, as is the area to the north of Bescar Lane Station (SD 396145).

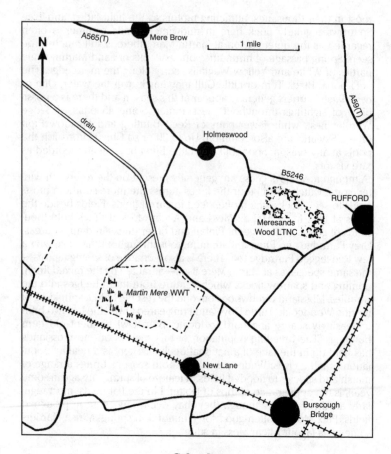

Calendar

All year: Feral wildfowl including Greylag Goose; Grey Partridge, Barn Owl, Little Owl, Collared Dove, Corn Bunting, Tree Sparrow.

December–February: Whooper and Bewick's Swans, Pink-footed and other geese; Shelduck, Wigeon, Teal, Gadwall, Mallard, Pochard and Tufted Duck; good chance of a rarer duck or goose; predators include regular Hen Harrier, Merlin, Short-eared Owl, perhaps Peregrine; large plover flocks with many Ruff and Snipe; finch and bunting flocks visit pens at Martin Mere, or stubbles elsewhere.

March–May: Winter wildfowl and raptors depart from March: Garganey and a sprinkling of waders on spring passage; Black-tailed Godwit may be numerous. White Wagtail pass through, and Sedge Warbler arrive. Snipe, Lapwing and other waders in display flights. Whimbrel and per-haps Dotterel on mosslands in May. Chance of Marsh Harrier.

June–July: Wader display tails off. Duck and feral goose broods hatch. Perhaps the quietest time of year, although waders start to trickle through in July. Possible Marsh Harrier.

August–November: Ducks in drab plumage in August, starting to resume smart plumage by end of the period. Wader passage now more diverse, with Greenshank, Spotted Redshank, Green and Wood Sandpipers regular. Pink-footed Goose start to return in mid September, as duck flocks gather. Usually five or six individual Marsh Harrier on passage, and a few Garganey. Predators more in evidence from October.

43 MERE SANDS WOOD

OS Map 108
SD44–15–

Habitat

Mere Sands Wood at Rufford is managed by the Lancashire Wildlife Trust. The reserve covers some 105 acres and contains a number of disused, flooded sandpits in a wooded, heathland setting. There are extensive areas of birch and oak woodland, and plantations of Scots Pine. Red squirrels occur around the car park. The site is a geological SSSI.

Species

The woods hold a variety of common woodland species, such as Redpoll, Nuthatch, and Coal and Willow Tits, with Blackcap, Chiffchaff, Willow and Garden Warbler in summer. Linnet and Yellowhammer frequent the more open areas. Little Ringed Plover have bred in the pits, where a wader scrape attracts Snipe, Green Sandpiper and other passage species such as Ringed Plover and Common Sandpiper. Ruddy Duck, Great Crested and Little Grebes breed. By August a wide variety of eclipse-plumaged ducks on the reserve may include Gadwall, Wigeon and Shoveler. Winter brings much larger numbers of wildfowl. Gadwall have topped 100, with over 1,000 each of Teal and Mallard at times. A few dozen Pochard and Tufted Duck are generally present.

Access

Mere Sands Wood lies off the B5246 between Rufford and Holmeswood, only a few minutes drive from Martin Mere. The reserve is signposted (at SJ 448162) along a track to the car park set in the wood. The LWT information centre lies close to one of the hides overlooking the flooded workings of the old quarry. There is a charge of £1 per car for non-members of LWT. The car park is locked at dusk or at 8 pm in summer. Circular walks lead around the pools and direct visitors to a series of public hides which provide good views of the water areas and wader scrape.

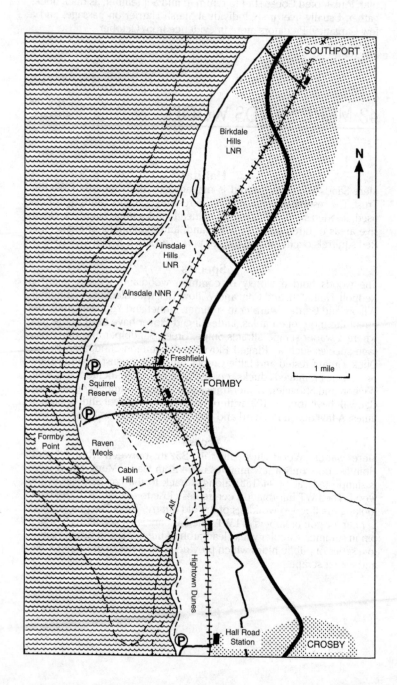

Between Southport and the northern suburbs of Liverpool lies an area of wide, sandy beaches backed by a dune system of outstanding botanical and entomological interest. The extensive sandflats linking those of the Ribble to those of North Wirral and the Dee are feeding and roosting grounds for large flocks of waders. Breeding birds include Shelduck, Whinchat, Stonechat and Grasshopper Warbler. The dunes shelter a wide range of migrants in both spring and autumn. The Sefton Coast is used intensively for recreation, with much of the area wardened by Sefton Council's Coast Management Scheme, which aims to harmonise recreation with the natural interest of the area. Other sections are managed by the National Trust and English Nature. It is difficult to split the area into separate birdwatching sites. Indeed the whole area is contiguous, with ornithologically outstanding coastline to both north and south. The following access points are suggested.

44A ALT ESTUARY AND HIGHTOWN DUNES

OS ref: SJ 29–03–

The River Alt emerges at Hightown, past a small saltmarsh and reedbed, meandering across mud and sandflats. Access to the north shore is restricted by the presence of the Altcar rifle range. The dunes between Hightown and Crosby include areas of stunted poplar, willow and sycamore scrub which hold migrants at the appropriate seasons.

Species

The Alt estuary is internationally important for Knot, Bar-tailed Godwit and Sanderling, and nationally important for Grey Plover. Other waders, Shelduck, terns and gulls also occur in good numbers. At high tide small parties of Turnstones, Ringed Plovers and Sanderlings may roost on the south side amongst the bricks and rubble of the shoreline. As the tide ebbs, these birds are joined by others which fly in from the main roost (at Formby) to feed on the newly exposed mud. While the estuary waders are present from late summer to spring, marshland species also appear on spring and autumn passage, preferring the muddier areas

Firecrest

near to the river. Greenshank, Common Sandpiper, Little Stint and Curlew Sandpiper may appear. Rarities have included Kentish Plover. In winter a few Merganser, Scaup and Goldeneye dive in the river channels. Little Gull are frequent and may number as many as 50 or more in spring. Mediterranean, Glaucous and Iceland Gulls have also occurred. In fact the range of species mirrors the pattern at Seaforth Docks (Site 45). For example Common Tern are numerous offshore in August, with smaller numbers of Sandwich, Little and Arctic Terns. Meadow Pipits nesting in the dunes are sometimes parasitised by Cuckoo. Other nesting species include Skylark (with one of the highest concentrations in the region), Redpoll, Willow Warbler, Whitethroat, Grasshopper Warbler and possibly Stonechat. In both spring and autumn passage warblers and chats appear in the stunted sycamore and poplar thickets. Regular coverage has turned up less common species such as Barred Warbler and Red-backed Shrike.

Access

Take the road from Hall Road Station (on the northern outskirts of Crosby) down to the seafront, turn right and park by the Coastguard Station (SD 298004). This car park forms a useful vantage point for seawatching during onshore winds, although a wide beach is exposed at low tide. Walk north from the car park, checking weedy areas for pipits or buntings. Bushes, especially the larger clumps towards Hightown, should be checked for migrants. From the dunes above the moorings of the sailing club, scan the estuary for wildfowl and waders. The wader roosts can be seen gathering in the distance as the tide rises. Access is also possible from Hightown. Cross the station road bridge and turn right at the roundabout up Lower Alt Road. A footpath at the end gives access to the saltmarsh and dunes (SD 296037).

44B FORMBY POINT

OS ref: SD 267068

An area of dunes backed by woodland of pines and poplars, Formby is a noted haunt of passerine migrants and of interest for other wildlife too. Red squirrels, introduced from the continent, may be seen throughout the area, but most easily at the National Trust's squirrel reserve at Victoria Road, Freshfield. At high tide the Point provides good seawatching. At low tide the Formby Channel area is an important feeding ground for waders. It is also a major high-tide roost. The Cabin Hill National Nature Reserve is sandwiched between Raven Meols LNR and the Altcar rifle range. On clear days it is possible to see along the North Wales coast to Anglesey.

Species

Seawatches can be exciting at any time of year. In winter Red-throated Diver and Great Crested Grebe fish offshore, with other divers or grebes on occasion. Common Scoter are often present, varying in numbers between a few individuals and several hundred. Other sea-ducks, such as Eider, Long-tailed Duck, Red-breasted Merganser or Velvet Scoter are occasionally present. Little Gulls visit the Formby Channel in spring and during onshore winds. Gannet and Fulmar appear during summer storms, when Kittiwake may be numerous. Manx Shearwaters also occur at this season, with a chance of an accompanying Mediterranean Shearwater or, in early autumn, a Sooty Shearwater. It is autumnal westerlies that bring the greatest variety of birds, with Leach's Petrel, Arctic and Great Skuas and Guillemot being typical. Razorbills appear regularly in small numbers. Long-tailed and Pomarine Skuas, Sabine's Gull and Grey Phalarope have all been reported during storms. Puffin and Black Guillemot are scarce winter visitors.

At high tide one of the region's major wader roosts gathers near the rifle range at Formby Channel. From September to March, Knot are counted in their tens of thousands, Bar-tailed Godwit and Dunlin in thousands, and Oystercatcher, Grey Plover, Redshank and Sanderling in hundreds. Smaller numbers of various other species are also expected. Sanderling and Ringed Plover are more numerous on spring and autumn passage in May and August/September. At low tide these birds are scattered over the flats, with some flying to feed along the North Wirral shore or in the Dee estuary. Common Tern fish in the Channel on spring passage in May, often joined by a few Little and Sandwich Terns. From July to September there are regularly several hundred Common Tern, with smaller numbers of Sandwich and Little and, rarely, Arctic or Roseate. West coast passage stations seldom attract the range of landbirds seen at their east coast counterparts. In spring, White and Yellow Wagtails, Willow and Sedge Warblers, Whitethroat, Wheatear and a few Whinchat are staple birds, with other warblers, chats and flycatchers in smaller numbers. A similar range of species migrates through in the autumn, when there is an increased chance of rarities. The first British Eleanora's Falcon to be recorded was watched at Cabin Hill in July 1977. Other highlights have included Melodious and Barred Warblers, Bearded Tit, Red-breasted Flycatcher, Rough-legged Buzzard, Osprey, Golden Oriole, Great Grey Shrike, Wryneck and Greenland Redpoll. Yellow-browed Warbler have occurred in October, when Goldcrest may be numerous. Firecrests have been found on several occasions.

Access

From Formby take the road past the main station or the parallel Raven Meols Road which converge and become Lifeboat Road. There is a free car park at the end (SJ 275065). The sea can be scanned from various points straight out from or to the north of the car park. Numerous footpaths enable exploration of bushes behind the dunes for migrants. Cabin Hill NNR lies a mile (1.6 km) to the south of the Point, beyond Raven Meols LNR.

The road past Freshfield Station in the northern outskirts of Formby leads down to a National Trust car park (parking charge) adjacent to the squirrel reserve (SJ 274083). There are good areas of bushes on either side, but especially to the south of this track.

44C AINSDALE AND BIRKDALE HILLS

OS ref: SD 300115 and 310138

North of the National Trust's holding at Formby Point, although largely separated by the Formby golf course, lie the 1216 acres (243 hectares) of Ainsdale National Nature Reserve. Dominated by high dunes, the habitat is similar to the adjacent Ainsdale and Birkdale LNRs but with the addition of areas of tall pines, with breeding natterjack toads (in the damp slacks) and sand lizards. Red squirrels are found in some numbers. On the LNRs, berries of sea buckthorn and hawthorn provide food for migrant birds in autumn. Insects are concentrated around the dune slacks where they are sought by hirundines and warblers. Just outside the Ainsdale LNR is a saline boating lake. This is generally too busy for good birdwatching in summer but may be more rewarding in winter.

Species

The range of nesting passerines is typical of the coastline, and includes a few Stonechat and Grasshopper Warbler. Ringed Plover and Oystercatcher have both been known to breed on the sand and outer dunes, and both are present through the winter when they are joined by Turnstone, Dunlin, Redshank, Bar-tailed Godwit and Curlew. Sanderling may gather in hundreds off Birkdale as the tide rises. Seawatching is worthwhile at high tide during onshore gales in summer or autumn, although shelter may be hard to find. Leach's Petrels are among species which may appear under such conditions.

During severe weather Stonechat feed along the tide line, and occasionally Shorelark and Snow Bunting are recorded. Outside the breeding season Merlin and Peregrine visit on occasion, as do Short-eared Owl and perhaps a Hen Harrier. In autumn Fieldfare and Redwing feast on berries and are often hunted by a Sparrowhawk. A few Jack Snipe feed in the damp slacks, especially in October. Ainsdale Lake in winter attracts small numbers of waterfowl, and is always worth checking after storms for sheltering sea-ducks or perhaps a phalarope. Glaucous Gull have been seen at Ainsdale in every month of the year, and Mediterranean Gull appear with some regularity. The pinewoods sometimes hold Crossbill and Siskin, which have nested. Long-eared Owls formerly occurred.

Access

Ainsdale and Birkdale Sandhills LNRs are administered by Sefton Borough Council. There is free parking near the boating lake at the end of the Ainsdale beach road (SD 301129)—a walk of 1 mile (1.6 km) from Ainsdale railway station. Birkdale Hills lie to the North and Ainsdale Hills to the south of this road. The National Nature Reserve starts about 1 mile (1.6 km) to the south. Footpaths are well marked. A permit is required to wander off these, but it is not necessary to leave the paths for normal watching.

Timing

During the summer months the coast is very popular with trippers. Its interest is then primarily in plants and other aspects of natural history. Early morning visits are advisable at passage times, especially in spring. Autumn migrants may linger longer in less busy areas. To see waders or seabirds, time visits around the high tide. Wader roosts begin to gather a couple of hours before the tide peaks. Seawatching at Formby Point can be productive in onshore gales. Watching is possible in greater comfort from the Hall Road car park, although the setting is not so good.

45 SEAFORTH NATURE RESERVE AND CROSBY MARINA

Habitat

Seaforth Nature Reserve comprises freshwater and saltwater pools bordered by overgrown piles of rubble with small numbers of recently planted shrubs. The area, lying within Liverpool Freeport and overlooked by the Radar Tower, appears unprepossessing, but it regularly supports impressive numbers of gulls, terns and waders, including the largest spring passage of Little Gulls in the country. The area is owned by the Mersey Docks and Harbour Company and managed as a reserve by Lancashire Wildlife Trust.

Crosby Marina, immediately adjacent to the north, is used extensively for water sports, but may hold birds when less disturbed. Quieter areas of the shoreline and surrounding grass attract waders during passage periods and gulls in winter.

Species

This reserve is of great interest for the gull enthusiast. Regular observation here is clarifying the pattern of occurrence of several species in northwestern England. Mediterranean Gulls are seen in all months, most frequently between March and August. Winter flocks of Little Gulls have been present offshore in Liverpool Bay and the southern Irish Sea for many years, and birds from this population often visit the reserve, particularly during westerly gales when up to 100 have taken refuge on the pools. Generally, however, few birds are seen at this season. Spring passage to the east starts in late March, and peaks in mid April with over 200 present at times. The 1989 count of 683 in this month has not been equalled. A small summering population of immature birds usually remains. Return passage may bring up to 50 birds in September and October, particularly with onshore winds.

Black-headed Gulls may exceed 10,000 but are much less numerous from April to the end of June. Common Gull number 3,000 or more at times in winter and spring. Lesser Black-backed Gull reach 1,000 in autumn, and Herring Gull may exceed 3,000. Great Black-backed are less numerous and appear in large numbers mainly in cold or windy weather. Kittiwake are seen on most days, but are much less numerous than formerly. Largest numbers of a few dozen birds occur during strong winds when birds shelter on the reserve. Sabine's Gulls appear during onshore gales in autumn, but not every autumn provides suitable conditions. Iceland Gulls appear annually in small numbers and have been recorded in most months, particularly during late winter and spring. Glaucous Gull are rather more frequent but follow a similar pattern to Iceland Gull. There are records of Bonaparte's and Ross's Gulls—two real rarities. A very few Ring-billed Gulls are detected annually among passage flocks of Common Gulls. One bird wintered at Crosby Marina in 1987–8. Small numbers of 'Yellow-legged' Gulls are often found amongst the Herring Gulls in almost any month.

Common Terns are the most frequent in their family, arriving in small numbers in April but reaching well over 1,000 in August. A few pairs nest. Arctic and Black Terns are scarce, the former occurring mainly in

Little Gull — first winter

spring and the latter in autumn—at least 60 were present during the national influx on 11 September 1992. Sandwich Terns are rather more regular, especially in August, but Little Terns have been scarce of late. Roseate Tern have appeared on a handful of occasions in autumn, while a Forster's Tern was a major find in March 1987. Two White-winged Black terns called in during the autumn of 1993.

Surface-feeding waterfowl are represented by moderate winter numbers of Mallard, Teal and Shelduck, with some Gadwall present most of the year. Diving species are more of a feature. Over 100 Cormorant are regular outside the nesting season and over 400 have been counted. In winter several dozen Pochard and fewer Tufted Duck feed on the pools, often joined at high tide by a small flock of Scaup. Goldeneye and Red-breasted Merganser are present in winter. Moderate flocks of Coot are to be seen from August to March and a few breed. Any stretch of water on this coast will attract waders and at least 30 species have been recorded, including Temminck's Stint, Grey Phalarope and White-rumped Sandpiper. Ringed Plover and Lapwing breed regularly here and Oystercatcher, Redshank and Little Ringed Plover have done so. The high-tide wader roost consists mainly of two species, Oystercatcher (up to 1,800) and Redshank (up to 1,000), with smaller numbers of Dunlin, Ringed Plover and Turnstone. Black-tailed and, in summer, Bar-tailed Godwits have shown signs of becoming regular features. Whimbrel and Common Sandpiper are regular passage birds. Curlew Sandpiper, Little Stint and Sanderling occur chiefly in autumn in small numbers. The grass at Crosby Marina may be productive for these three species. A few Jack Snipe join good numbers of Snipe in winter. Shore waders on Crosby beach include Knot, Bar-tailed Godwit and the occasional Grey Plover.

Breeding landbirds are scarce, but include Skylark and Meadow Pipit. As planted shrubs mature this list should increase. Greater interest will undoubtedly focus on migrant passerines which should stop off in increasing numbers. To date the chief evidence of passage has been for those species which are not dependent on such cover. White Wagtail may pass through in hundreds in spring and Wheatear have exceeded

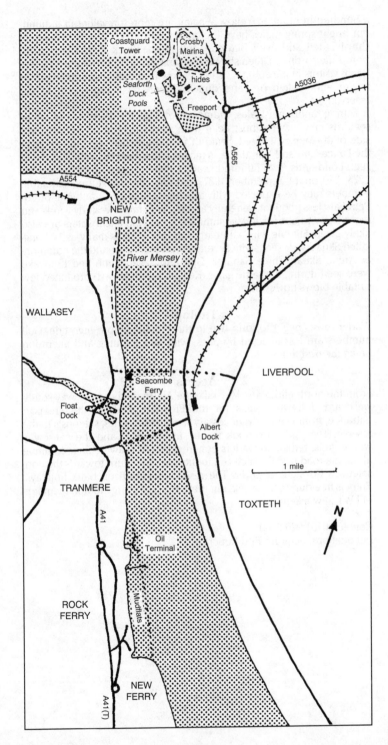

a hundred in number. Yellow Wagtail are more prevalent in autumn, but bright spring males have included odd birds of the Blue-headed, Grey-headed and even Black-headed races. Black Redstarts pop up from time to time. Greenish Warbler and Song Sparrow were exceptional visitors in the autumn of 1994. Snow Buntings occur erratically in winter, more often on sand dunes around the Marina than in the reserve.

During autumnal gales, numbers of Leach's Petrels and other seabirds may exceed those seen from New Brighton on the opposite side of the Mersey. Indeed, Seaforth's exposed position in the angle of the Lancashire and Wirral coasts makes it the ideal seawatching site in such conditions. Two hundred Leach's Petrel passed on 30 September 1978, 370 on 14 September 1987, and smaller, but still considerable numbers may be expected with any onshore blow in autumn. Storm Petrel are less frequent, generally arriving with more westerly winds and more likely to appear in late summer. Skuas and shearwaters are also likely given suitable winds. In early October 1988 as many as 17 Long-tailed Skuas were seen, with several Pomarine, Great and the commoner Arctic Skuas. Three Sabine's Gull and several hundred Kittiwake were seen during the same gales. Recent autumns have produced few suitable blows however.

Timing

Wader roosts begin to form two to three hours before high tide. Gull numbers are less affected by tides, with late morning and afternoon being the best times.

Access

From the north end of the M57 take the A5036 dual carriageway south-westward, following signs for the Freeport. Park at the Freeport entrance, from where it is necessary to walk, following signposts to the reserve. Two hides overlook the freshwater pool and the causeway where gulls, terns and waders congregate. For seawatching, continue along the road past the hides up to the river, then turn towards the conspicuous Coastguard tower. The reserve is closed on bank holidays. Entry is free during the week, but there is a 50p charge to non-members of LWT at weekends.

Contact: 0151 920 3769
Publications: Seaforth Bird Reports

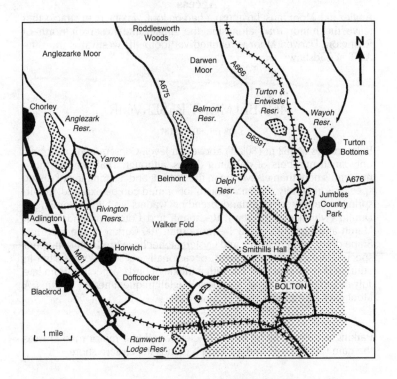

The area to the north of Bolton consists largely of pasture land, rising to grass moorland with some heather moor on the highest ground. There are areas of young conifer plantations on the moors, and more mature conifers around the margins of the many water supply reservoirs which lie within the steep-sided Pennine valleys. Tracts of old oak woodland add to the diversity. A large part of the area is covered by a countryside warden service, who can advise on quieter areas to visit. Public footpaths are well maintained and signposted. Some of the better sites are detailed below, but there is plenty of scope for exploration.

46A ANGLEZARKE AND DARWEN MOORS

OS ref: SD 63–17–, SD68–19–

Limited areas of heather support Red Grouse (keepered on Darwen Moor) and a few breeding Golden Plover. Twite nest in very small numbers, with a few pairs of Wheatear on rocky slopes. Young conifer plantations may hold nesting Whinchat, and there is a possibility of Short-eared Owl. Snipe are numerous in rushy areas. In winter the likelihood of raptors increases, with perhaps a Hen Harrier or Merlin. Ravens are now often present. Even a young Golden Eagle has visited. Snow Buntings are seen infrequently. Dotterels have been seen on the tops on spring passage, and might well make repeat visits.

Access

Anglezarke Moor must be approached on foot, via one of the tracks that leave the minor road alongside the Anglezarke Reservoir north of Rivington. Darwen Moor is reached via footpaths westwards from the A666 at Cadshaw.

46B BELMONT RESERVOIR

OS ref: SD 675167

Belmont lies at 262 m (800 ft) above sea level. Consequently it attracts only small numbers of dabbling ducks, although Teal may be more numerous here than elsewhere in the district, and a sprinkling of diving species is generally present. Quite a lot of mud can be exposed, and in spring a variety of moorland breeding waders visit the shoreline— Dunlin (which may display), Redshank and Common Sandpiper. In March and April there may be more than 100 Curlew in the pastures. Snipe drum conspicuously and Oystercatcher have bred. Other migrant species, such as Ringed Plover, occasionally visit. Wader passage in autumn may be more varied, with a trickle of birds, especially from late July to September. Dipper and Grey Wagtail frequent nearby streams. A Montagu's Harrier was seen in June 1988.

Access

Parking is difficult along the A675 clearway, but a minor road crosses the dam (SD 675164) and a footpath climbs the eastern shore.

46C RODDLESWORTH WOODS

OS ref: SD 664214

An extensive area of upland, broadleaved woodland, the Roddlesworth Woods hold small numbers of Pied Flycatcher, Redstart and occasional Wood Warbler. Tree Pipit, Woodcock and resident Green and Great Spotted Woodpecker are other interesting woodland species. Redpoll may be numerous in winter.

Access

The woods lie alongside the A675 some 4 miles (6.4 km) north of Belmont, just south of Abbey Village. One mile (1.6 km) north from Belmont Reservoir, turn right onto a minor road for Tockholes. There is a car park and nature trail at Ryal Fold.

46D JUMBLES COUNTRY PARK RESERVOIR

OS ref: SD 734145

Jumbles Reservoir, flooded in 1970, is surrounded by farmland and mixed, recently planted woodlands. Being in a country park, the reservoir is used for sailing and fishing, but there are quieter areas. A range of common waterfowl occurs, including Great Crested Grebe, Teal, Tufted Duck and Pochard. Goosander are often present, with Goldeneye on occasion. Kingfisher hunt from perches overhanging the water and in streams. A variety of scrubland species nests in the planted woodlands, for example Bullfinch, Goldfinch and Redpoll. Fieldfare and Redwing may be abundant in October and November. A logbook of bird sightings is kept in the information centre, and the list of species recorded at the reservoir is growing steadily. Many of these are only fleeting visitors, but have included Spotted Sandpiper, Pomarine Skua, Little and Iceland Gulls, Black Tern and Hobby.

Access

The Country Park is signposted off the A676 Bolton to Ramsbottom Road (take the left turn at SD 737133). Alternatively there is a second car park at Ousel's Nest off the B6391 on the west bank, giving a more circuitous walk. Footpaths encircle the reservoir, and connect with Wayoh and Entwistle Reservoirs.

46E WAYOH RESERVOIR, EDGWORTH

OS ref: SD 733166

Lying a short distance to the north of Jumbles, at 147m (550 ft) above sea level, Wayoh is fringed for much of its circumference by mixed woodland. The northern inlet is very shallow with muddy, well vegetated margins. Some 100 species have been recorded, including Bittern and Grey Phalarope. Common Sandpiper nest along the shoreline, and Little Ringed Plover have settled in briefly when the water level is low. Few waterfowl breed because of the fluctuating water levels, but Great Crested Grebe may gather to fish in late summer. In winter there is a strong likelihood of a party of Whooper Swan or a few Goosander. Scrubland habitats hold a variety of breeding finches and warblers, with Goldcrest and occasional Crossbill in the conifers. Sparrowhawks often hunt the smaller birds.

Access

From Edgworth crossroads (SD 741169) take the minor road to the northwest. After half a mile (0.8 km) take the very narrow road at SD 736175 (easily missed—look out for the little church on the left to Entwistle station). Park beyond the causeway which crosses the top end of the reservoir. A path leads around the entire reservoir and connects with Turton and Entwistle Reservoir. It passes through woodland and scrub habitats, with a good chance of Siskin in winter, and excellent views across the two wildfowl refuges.

46F TURTON AND ENTWISTLE RESERVOIR

OS ref: SD 720175

This is a stone-sided reservoir surrounded by mature conifer plantations which often hold Siskin and occasionally Crossbill. It attracts small numbers of diving waterfowl, notably Goosanders on occasion, and perhaps a party of 'wild' swans.

Access

A car park below the dam is accessible off the B6391 (turn right at SD 724168). A public footpath skirts the north shore.

46G WALKER FOLD CLOUGH

OS ref: SD 676124

Broadleaved woodland to the south and conifers to the north give way to rough pasture and the heather moorland of Winter Hill with its Red Grouse, Twite and other moorland species.

Access

By the minor road between the B6226 and the A675. Footpaths lead northwestward onto the moor.

46H SMITHILLS HALL

OS ref: SD 700120

A good variety of woodland birds, including Nuthatch, may be seen from the nature trail through the woodlands.

Access

By minor road off the A58 between Doffcocker and Astley Bridge.

46I RIVINGTON, ANGLEZARKE AND YARROW RESERVOIRS

SD 61

A chain of large reservoirs running north from Horwich, Rivington and Anglezarke are, like other reservoirs in the area, bounded by rocky shores with areas of mud restricted to the tops of inlets. Rivington in particular is heavily disturbed by visitors, especially in summer, and it is as a haunt of winter wildfowl that the reservoirs are best known. There are extensive woodlands, however, and while those around Lever Park may swarm with picnickers, there are quieter areas to be found.

Dabbling ducks never reach the abundance in which they are encountered on lowland waters, although several hundred Mallard may be present at times. Most standard species do occur however. Diving ducks are better represented by Pochard, Tufted Duck and Goldeneye, with increasing Goosander. Smew and Merganser appear infrequently, with perhaps a Common Scoter or two at passage times. Scarce grebes and storm-blown divers find conditions to their liking and may stay for weeks following their rare arrival. Whooper Swan are often present. There is a sizeable winter gull roost on the Lower Rivington Reservoir which attracts 11,000 or more gulls, including many from the tips near Horwich. There may be in excess of 200 Great Black-backed Gull, and odd Glaucous and Iceland Gulls occasionally join the roost. A few Kittiwake may appear on passage in early spring, or after winter storms. Terns and Little Gull appear occasionally at passage times. Common Sandpiper nest around the margins, with Grey Wagtail and Dipper being found by inlet streams. A Spotted Sandpiper was a recent highlight.

Undisturbed oak woods hold a good range of common woodland birds, with Redstart, Wood Warbler, Tree Pipit and Pied Flycatcher in the better areas. Green Woodpecker favour the edge between woodland and moorland, and the odd pair of Lesser Spotted Woodpecker may nest in alders near the waterside. Woodcock rode in the twilight.

Goldeneye

Access

The wider, southern end of Rivington is favoured by waterfowl and roosting gulls. It can be viewed from the A675 Bolton–Chorley road just west of Horwich (SD 626127), or by turning right off that road immediately after a small roundabout, following signs for the West Pennine Moors Information Centre. On this side, viewing is best from the vicinity of the castle (SD 628130). Minor roads and footpaths provide viewing of Anglezarke from both banks. The causeway roads between reservoirs are also good vantage points.

There are interesting woodland areas at the north end of Anglezarke and between there and White Coppice. Dean Wood, accessible by permit only but skirted by a public footpath on its north side, is managed jointly by North West Water and the Lancashire Trust for Nature Conservation. From Anglezarke Quarry, take the minor road signposted to Belmont and the wood lies on the right after almost a mile (1.6 km), just beyond Wilcock's Farm (SD 632155).

46J RUMWORTH LODGE RESERVOIR

OS ref: SD 678078

Rumworth has shallower margins than the other reservoirs—consequently it is more attractive to surface-feeding waterfowl and to waders. It was formerly much favoured in winter by Whooper Swan, which may still occur but in smaller numbers. Pochard, Tufted Duck and Coot may be present in large numbers, and Wigeon may graze with Canada Goose on neighbouring pastures. Wild geese, such as White-fronts, alight rarely. Cormorant often visit outside the breeding season. Small flocks of Shoveler sometimes gather in autumn. Uncommon visitors have included Great Northern Diver and Black-necked Grebe.

A flock of Lapwing often wanders around the shoreline from autumn to spring. Often they are joined by a few passage waders. Dunlin and Redshank are typical, but other species occur each year, and rarities have included Pectoral Sandpiper and Temminck's Stint. Snipe are common in the surrounding marsh, where they are joined by a few, elusive Jack Snipe. Oystercatchers may nest.

Grey Heron may generally be seen fishing in areas unoccupied by human anglers. Little Egret and Ruddy Shelduck visited briefly in 1995.

Access

Rumworth may be viewed from Beaumont Road (A58) to the east, where a short, dead-end public footpath gives views over the southern end (SD 680077). Continue westward and turn right at the lights into Junction Road for further viewing over the wall. On the south side take the cobbled Lock Lane between Chew Moor and Hunger Hill, walk up the private road to Tempest Court and follow a footpath marked by stiles to the right. This passes close to the southern edge of the reservoir at SD 676076.

46K DOFFCOCKER

OS ref: SD 684103

Bordered on one side by a housing estate, Doffcocker Lodge is nevertheless extensively fringed by tall ruderal and marsh vegetation. It holds breeding Great Crested Grebe and possibly Ruddy Duck, with Reed Bunting and Sedge and other warblers in surrounding scrub. In winter it is visited by large numbers of waterfowl in better variety, with Snipe and Jack Snipe in the marsh. Other waders appear infrequently at passage times.

Access

A causeway runs south from the A58 dual carriageway at SD 682104. Parking is easier, however, on the minor road through the housing estate on the south side. This road starts from opposite the B6402 junction on the A58 (SD 681101).

Calendar

All year: Red Grouse, Raven and Short-eared Owl on the moors; Kingfisher, Dipper and Grey Wagtail along watercourses; woodpeckers and other common woodland species.

December–February: Raptors on the moors, where Snow Bunting are a slim possibility; Whooper Swan, Goosander and other wildfowl on the reservoirs.

March–May: Summer visitors include Wheatear and Twite from late March with Whinchat, Pied Flycatcher, Wood Warbler and Redstart a month later. Small passage of waders by reservoirs includes moorland breeders moving onto breeding areas.

June–July: Common Sandpiper and perhaps Little Ringed Plover by reservoirs. Generally a rather quiet time.

August–November: Wildfowl return; wader passage at Rumworth and elsewhere; large thrush flocks in Wayoh–Jumbles area.

47 WIGAN FLASHES

OS Map 108
SD 50

The Wigan flashes resemble Pennington Flash (Site 45) in that they are the result of coal-mining. Indeed their proximity to Pennington ensures a degree of interchange by birds between the two sites. A number of wetland habitats near the Leeds and Liverpool Canal further link the major flashes. A rubbish tip attracts gulls and corvids. Extensive scrub of sallow and other species supports a range of breeding finches and warblers, the latter also favoured by reedbed and tall marsh vegetation. A small, feral population of Mandarins is established in the vicinity of Haigh Country Park (SD59-08-).

Species

The Wigan flashes attract a range of birds similar to those at Pennington (site 48), although since they lack the protective management offered at the latter site, numbers of birds tend to be smaller. Up to 100 or more Cormorants have visited in recent winters. An exceptional record in April 1992 was of an assemblage of 16 migrant Red-throated Divers. Breeding waterfowl include Little and Great Crested Grebes, and Tufted and Ruddy Ducks. Odd birds of other species, such as Teal, Shoveler or Pochard may linger into spring. Greylag Geese have bred. Little Ringed Plover breed in the area, and Snipe and Redshank may do so. Common Sandpiper are present with such regularity on spring passage that they too are suspected of breeding intent. Common Terns have bred in several years, as also have Black-headed Gull. Ruddy Shelduck and a Great White Egret visited in the summer of 1995. Scrubland species are better represented, with a good variety of finches, Reed Bunting and Yellowhammer, and warblers include Reed, Sedge, Lesser Whitethroat and Grasshopper breeding locally. A River Warbler was a rare visitor in 1995, holding territory for several days. Yellow Wagtail and Meadow Pipit also nest. Cuckoos parasitise the pipits and Reed Warblers.

Resident Kingfisher are a further attraction, and Long-eared Owl have been seen in winter. Waders pass through in small numbers, as also do terns in spring and autumn. Outside the breeding season, large numbers of wildfowl are generally present. Water Rail frequent marshy areas throughout the winter, and have been known to stay in summer and breed. Bitterns are seen in most winters, but generally remain hidden in reeds. The rubbish tip to the south of Pearson's Flash attracts large numbers of gulls including occasional Glaucous or Iceland.

Access

From Wigan centre take the A49 then B5238 Warrington road. Park below the conspicuous tower of St James with St Thomas church, Poolstock (SD 578045). Cross the main road and walk south along the canal towpath. The canal is traversed by bridges and lock gates, with viewing of the various flashes to either side. Paths may be muddy.

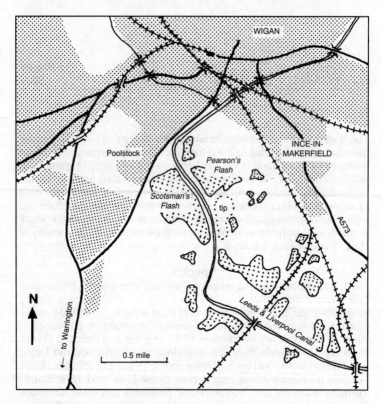

48 PENNINGTON FLASH

Habitat

Pennington Flash lies one mile (1.6 km) to the southwest of Leigh (SD 638990). Since 1981 its 170 acres (68 hectares) of water have been incorporated into a Country Park of more than 1000 acres (400 hectares). The flash owes its origin to subsidence following coal-mining at the adjacent Bickershaw colliery which dominates the view to the north. Resulting shallow marshes attract wildfowl, waders and other wetland species, whose numbers have increased considerably since wardening reduced shooting over the flashes to a minimum. Former spoil tips from the mine have been landscaped and planted with trees which are beginning to attract woodland species. The Country Park is heavily used by anglers and a sailing club, as well as the general public, but areas of shallow water and reedbeds are reserved for wildlife and overlooked by hides.

Species

Waterfowl dominate the winter scene. Up to 30 Little Grebe and at times dozens of Cormorant feed on fish, the latter often perching on stumps below Sorrowcow Farm. Great Crested Grebe are present in small numbers. Three species of diver and Red-necked, Black-necked and Slavonian Grebes have been known to visit, especially in severe weather. Bittern may lurk unseen in reedbeds and flooded areas, where Water Rail are more conspicuous on frosty days. Two or three pairs of Kingfisher are resident and may be seen on most days of the year.

Several hundred Mallard form the bulk of the dabbling ducks, with up to 200 or more Teal, small numbers of Pintail, Wigeon and Gadwall, with Shoveler in mild winters. Two hundred or so Pochard are normally present, with 600 or more in some winters. They are accompanied by lesser numbers of Tufted Duck, and often a few round-headed Scaup. Goldeneye increase to a maximum in late winter or early spring. Ruddy Duck are becoming more frequent. Scarcer diving ducks, such as Long-tailed Duck, Smew, Merganser and Goosander visit infrequently. Coot flocks vary in size from one winter to the next: in 1984 nearly 1,000 were present. Pennington is not a noted goose haunt, although a few White-fronted Geese have been known to settle in winter and a few feral Greylag Geese are seen. Parties of Canada Goose visit erratically, and skeins of Pink-footed Goose pass overhead from time to time.

Large plover flocks frequent fields by the A580 to the south, where there may be hundreds of Golden Plover and several thousand Lapwing. Some of these visit the park, perhaps bringing an accompanying Redshank or other wader. A hundred or more Snipe are often present in damp areas, with a sprinkling of Jack Snipe around Pengy's Pond, where they generally crouch unseen.

There is a sizeable gull roost, often containing 4–5,000 Black-headed, and 1–2,000 Herring Gulls in late December, with smaller numbers of other common species. Determined scanning of these flocks may reveal a Glaucous or Iceland Gull.

Such species as Great Spotted Woodpecker, Marsh and Coal Tit, and Nuthatch remain uncommon winter visitors owing to the absence of suitable habitat, although this situation is changing as planted wood-lands mature. Any black-capped tit seen is almost certain to be one of the resident Willow Tit. Long-tailed Tit and Chaffinch are two other species just returning to the area: air pollution obliterated the mosses from which they build their nests, but industrial decline has reversed this trend. Siskin and Goldfinch are increasing as winter residents as planted alder begin to fruit.

Short-eared Owl roost within the park in some winters. As many as five have been noted hunting for voles. Long-eared Owls may also be present, roosting in scrub. Merlin dash through on occasion. An even smaller predator, the Great Grey Shrike, has been recorded in several winters.

Early spring sees the departure of winter visitors and the return of breeding species. Great Crested Grebe build up to a peak of 40–50 birds, many of these displaying in front of the hides. In March, flocks of winter thrushes head northeast and parties of Bewick's Swan stop off briefly. Meadow Pipit return from mid March, often with fresh-plumaged Pied Wagtail and Reed Bunting. A Black-faced Bunting in March 1994 was an exceptional sighting. Summer visitors drift in from the end of March, with more pronounced passage from mid April. Hirundines swirl over the water, and parties of wagtails scurry over short turf at the water's edge. Both Yellow and White Wagtails reach a peak towards the end of April. Blue-headed Wagtail or a pink-breasted Water Pipit may add to the spectacle, with a few Common Sandpiper.

The shingle should always be checked for waders. At this season these include species prospecting for possible nest sites, such as Oystercatcher, Ringed and Little Ringed Plover, and such long distance migrants as arctic Ringed Plover, Sanderling and Turnstone. A few Dunlin are often present, and there is the possibility of odd individuals of several other species. Rarities have included Kentish Plover, Avocet, Temminck's Stint and Red-necked Phalarope.

A small passage of terns may be evident, most likely Common or per-haps Arctic Tern, although Black Tern may well appear following east-erly winds. White-winged Black Tern have appeared twice. Other scarce migrants have included Osprey on several occasions, Little Egret, Alpine Swift, Nightingale and Great Reed Warbler—the rewards of persistent watching.

By now breeding waterfowl have settled into their territories. Nesting ducks may include Gadwall, Pochard and Ruddy, as well as the more usual Mallard and Tufted. Good numbers of Little and Great Crested Grebes breed. Garganey and Black-necked Grebe have lingered in spring. Twenty to 30 Grey Herons feed by the flash in spring and sum-mer. Common Scoter are infrequent passage migrants at this time. Little Ringed Plover breed within the park, and Ringed Plover and Redshank have done so. Common Terns have nested lately. Nesting passerines include Meadow Pipit, Grasshopper, Sedge and Reed Warbler, Lesser and Common Whitethroats. Reed Bunting and Linnet are common, with small numbers of Tree Sparrow, Goldfinch, Yellowhammer and Redpoll. Days with bad weather in June or July may see 1,000 or more Swift feeding over the flash, accompanied by fewer House Martin.

By August, Goldfinch flock to feed on thistle seed, and Mistle Thrush to strip berries from rowans. In late summer, Kestrel and their fledged young hover over rougher areas, returning Water Rail may be heard squealing from cover, and Lapwing flocks begin to increase.

Autumn wader passage is light since the shingle is then often occupied by anglers, although Greenshank are more likely to appear than in spring. Terns are less numerous at this season. A feature of autumn passage is the large gathering of hirundines. In some years up to 5,000 or 10,000 Sand Martins may roost in the reedbeds. There may also be several thousand Swallow at the height of passage in September. There is a moderate diurnal passage of wagtails and pipits, and the occasional Whinchat, Redstart or perhaps Tree Pipit may settle in the plantations. In late autumn, Fieldfare, Redwing and Blackbird gather in the hedges to the south of the flash, with fewer grey, continental Song Thrush. Parties of migrant Chaffinch and Brambling may alight to join local finches in weedy arable fields. By this season the resident Partridge and Tawny Owl begin to call at dusk, advertising their territories.

Timing
Summer visits in fine weather are likely to be the least rewarding owing to the popularity of the Country Park with day-trippers, although a Leach's Petrel was found one hot day in July 1995. During this season, early morning visits are advisable. At passage times, showery weather may cause migrants to drop in. Dusk visits are advisable in autumn to view hirundine roosts, which may attract predators. Storm-driven seabirds are a possibility following gales. Frosty weather may drive Water Rail from cover.

Access
The entrance to the country park lies on the A572 St Helens Road (SJ 646986). Park near the information centre, and explore the nature reserve area to the north from obvious footpaths. Paths along the south side of the flash are recommended in the autumn, and at the west end in winter.

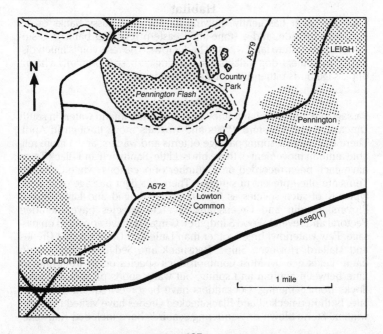

Calendar
All year: Partridge, Kingfisher, Willow Tit.

December–February: Good variety of waterfowl including Gadwall, Pochard, Tufted Duck, Goldeneye and Ruddy Duck. Gull roost may include 'white-winged' birds. Short-eared Owl in some years.

March–May: Passage of pipits, wagtails and Reed Bunting in March/April; small wader passage continuing into June; breeding warblers arrive.

June–July: Swifts congregate in wet weather; breeding waterfowl have young.

August–November: Rather quiet during August, but Swallow roost may be spectacular in September. Winter visitors arrive from October.

Reference
Wilson, J. D. (1985) *Birds and Birdwatching at Pennington Flash*, Pennington Flash Joint Committee.

49 ELTON RESERVOIR, BURY

OS Map 109
SD788094

Habitat
Elton Reservoir has gently shelving muddy and grassy banks on its northwestern side, and a stone-lined eastern retaining bank. It is surrounded by pasture land with tall hedgerows. The reservoir is much disturbed by anglers, dog walkers and a sailing club, so is primarily a haunt of passage birds rather than long-term residents.

Species
Passage at Elton is similar to movements at other inland waters in south Lancashire and Cheshire. Pipits and wagtails move through in April. There is a variable spring passage of terns and waders, and a more reliable autumn movement of these birds. Little, Sandwich and Black Terns have each been recorded on a number of occasions, while Common Terns are often present in summer. There is a light passage of waders, typically of such species as Oystercatcher, Ringed and Little Ringed Plovers, Dunlin and Greenshank. Scarcer species have included Pectoral and several Wood Sandpiper. Garganey have appeared on passage. Few waterfowl breed, other than Little and Great Crested Grebes and Mallard. However, Snipe, Redshank and Sedge Warbler nest in damp fields nearby. Most common duck species occur from time to time between autumn and spring, but water sports prevent any large flocks from gathering. Goosanders have become frequent visitors of late. Both Red-necked and Black-necked Grebes have visited in recent winters. Storm-blown or wandering seabirds have included Kittiwake,

Fulmar and Velvet Scoter, with several records of Red-breasted
Merganser.

Timing

Elton is an ideal local patch, requiring persistent coverage, rather than
a place for a one-off visit. Early morning visits are likely to be more
rewarding than later in the day when the shoreline is increasingly disturbed.

Access

Various access points are available, the most straightforward being
down Kitchener Street, to the east off the A58, signposted to the reservoir and Florence Nightingale Hospital. A track leads past the hospital
to a car park at the north end of the reservoir. Footpaths lead around
almost the entire shoreline, only skirting the sailing club's compound.

50 MERSEY VALLEY

The floodplain of the River Mersey between Stockport and the
Manchester Ship Canal contains a variety of habitats—mature woodland
and agricultural land, golf courses and playing fields, working and
reclaimed tips and sewage works, 'natural' and canalised river. Many
sites are managed for wildlife and recreation by the Mersey Valley
Warden Service, and around 200 species have been recorded in the last
decade, including such rarities as Caspian Tern, Crane and Black-throated Thrush. Some of the best sites for birdwatching are described below.

Timing

Convenience of access from the city and suburbs means that the
Mersey Valley (and others in the network of Greater Manchester river
valley access schemes) forms an excellent 'local patch' that will repay
regular coverage. Sale Water Park is worth a visit at any time of year,
although hot summer weather produces more people and fewer birds.
Chorlton Water Park is arguably at its best for waterfowl in winter.

50A CHORLTON WATER PARK

OS ref: SJ 820919

The attractively landscaped former borrow pit, from which material was
taken for building the adjacent motorway, forms the centrepiece of the
park. Two islands and several compounds containing marginal vegetation attract a range of species. In winter the lake is closed to boats and
regularly attracts large numbers of wildfowl. The Water Park also
includes many acres of rough grassland and young tree plantations
popular with passerines.

Species

In winter there may be 1,000 or more Pochard and 200 or so Tufted Ducks on the lake, with a few Goldeneye and Great Crested and Little Grebes. Scarcer diving duck appear in with the Pochard from time to time. Scaup appear each winter in very small numbers, and Red-crested Pochard, Ring-necked and Ferruginous Ducks have occurred. Do not be misled by odd hybrids! These ducks flight at dusk to the Salford Docks to feed. By day they return either to Chorlton, to Rostherne Mere or to the lake in Heaton Park, north Manchester. There is thus regular mixing of birds between these three waters.

Parties of terns appear on both spring and autumn passage. A Spotted Crake was a rare visitor in July 1995.

Pochard

Access

Chorlton Water Park can be visited by turning off Barlow Moor Road (A5145) opposite Southern Cemetery (SJ 825925) into Maitland Avenue and proceeding to the car park at the south end. Alternatively the site may be reached from Sale Water Park by walking up Rifle Road to Jackson's Bridge (SJ 810926), then turning right and following obvious paths beside the river for about a mile (1.6 km).

50B SALE WATER PARK AND BROAD EES DOLE NATURE RESERVE

OS ref: SJ 800930

Another large gravel pit dominates Sale Water Park. Its popularity for water sports and its depth limit its value for wildlife. Around the park are several mature hedgerows and substantial areas of rough grassland. Lying between the lake and the River Mersey is Broad Ees Dole Nature Reserve, which has been developed by the Mersey Valley Warden Service since 1985. A hide overlooks a lagoon area popular with waders, a wet marsh and willow and alder scrub. The site is closed to the public, but excellent views can be obtained from the perimeter. In winter Cormorant fly in from Rostherne to fish, and may perch on the electricity pylons after feeding. Great Crested Grebe are generally present. Up to 70 Teal join the Mallard on the reserve where over 100 Snipe probe for food. Jack Snipe often reach double figures, and with luck can be watched feeding, using their strange, bobbing, 'sewing machine' action. Water Pipits are now irregular winter visitors. Little Ringed Plover and Common Sandpiper appear on spring passage, with a chance of other waders, although the variety is better in the autumn. Terns pass through at both seasons and a Kittiwake may appear from time to time. Whitethroat, Redpoll and other passerines breed in the scrubby areas. Herons roost by day on the Broad Ees Dole scrape.

Access
Sale Water Park lies between Junctions 7 and 8 of the M63. From Junction 8 follow Rifle Road to the northeast, turning very shortly into the drive to the park.

50C CHORLTON EES NATURE RESERVE

OS ref: SJ 811928

Occupying the site of a former sewage works, Chorlton Ees is a fine example of reclamation for wildlife. Young woodland, tall reedy grassland and several ponds provide a range of habitats, in turn attracting a wide variety of species. A network of footpaths makes for easy exploration. The reserve holds a range of commoner woodland species. Less common migrants such as Wood Warbler, Pied Flycatcher, Redstart and Whinchat pass through. Short-eared Owl and Great Grey Shrike have been recorded in winter.

Access
Cross the Mersey from Sale Water Park via Jackson's Bridge (SJ 810926) and turn left. The Ees lie directly across the river from the Water Park. From the north side, turn south off the A5145 in Chorlton-cum-Hardy, onto Barlow Moor Road, into Beech Road then almost immediately into Reynard Road. This becomes Claude Road and, shortly after, Brookburn Road. There are car parks on Brookburn Road and along the cobbled road to the west.

50D CARRINGTON MOSS

OS ref: SJ 743916

Carrington Moss is an extensive area of arable land lying south of the Mersey. It is criss-crossed by a network of footpaths, many alongside mature hedgerows, and there are several areas of mature woodland, mostly reserves managed by the Cheshire Wildlife Trust. Views can be obtained of the large wetland and scrub area within the Shell UK complex, an important site for wildfowl.

Species
The arable fields attract flocks of seed-eating birds in winter, such as Chaffinch, Goldfinch and Corn Bunting, Partridge, Stock Dove and Skylark. These in turn attract raptors, usually Sparrowhawk but less often Merlin or Peregrine. This is now one of the more reliable sites in

the region for the declining Corn Bunting. Flocks of Canada Geese occasionally visit the stubbles. Willow Tit and Redpolls nest in the birchwoods, and there is a range of common farmland breeding species. Corn Buntings have declined in recent summers, but a pair or two still breed. Whitethroats and Willow Warblers nest commonly in scrub, and Grasshopper Warblers can sometimes be seen or heard reeling. A few Wheatears and Whinchats are noted at passage seasons, when flocks of Meadow Pipits appear. Pipit flocks should always be checked for less common companions.

The Shell Pond regularly attracts Canada Geese and small to moderate numbers of waterfowl such as Teal, Wigeon and Gadwall. Ruddy Ducks have bred and Tufted Ducks are present all year. A party of White-fronted Geese visited in November 1993, while in January of that year a Gannet appeared. In summer and early autumn there may be large gatherings of hirundines over the wetland, notably of Sand Martins from the nesting colonies in the banks of the Mersey. These hirundines attract the occasional Hobby, a species which is becoming more numerous in the region. A vagrant Bee-eater called in briefly one recent spring day.

Both Ringed and Little Ringed Plovers are resident in summer. Waders are more varied at passage periods when a sprinkling of other species may occur. A Dotterel in spring of 1992 was an exceptional visitor, but there have been a few records of such species as Wood Sandpiper, Black-tailed Godwit, Grey Plover and Oystercatcher.

Any sheet of water attracts gulls. Notable recent records here have been of Mediterranean and Yellow-legged Gull.

Access

From the A56 through Sale, take Carrington Lane (A6144) northwestwards from Ashton upon Mersey. At the crossroads with Flixton Road (B5158) turn left into Isherwood Road (SJ 745930). This deteriorates into the cinder track of Ackers Lane. Park here and follow footpaths to the right around the edge of the petrochemical compound.

50E FLETCHER MOSS GARDENS, STENNER WOODS AND MILLGATE FIELDS

OS ref: SJ 847903

These adjacent sites offer a variety of habitats within a surprisingly small area close to the city. Fletcher Moss Gardens provide excellent formal parkland, while Stenner Woods is an area of mature wet woodland dominated by willows and oaks. Millgate Fields includes a large hay meadow and pasture land popular with larks and Lapwings. In 1971 only two species of lichens were found growing on the trees here. Now there are at least 25—a measure of both air pollution abatement and general wildlife habitat improvement.

Access

Via Millgate Lane off the A5145 Wilmslow Road in Didsbury.

CHESHIRE AND WIRRAL

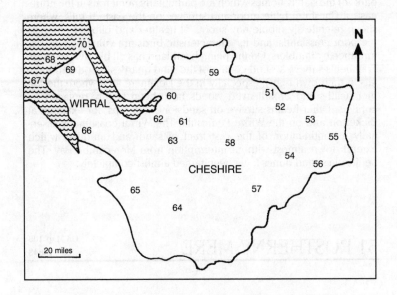

The Cheshire Plain is dotted with dairy farms and oak-lined hedgerows. Many flooded marl-pits survive, but many more have been and continue to be lost. Little Owls and Lesser Whitethroats are two of the most typical species of the agricultural landscape, the latter being the commonest warbler across much of the southwest of the county. The principal ornithological sites on the plain are the meres, many of them of glacial origin, and the flashes—shallow lakes created by the pumping of brine from underground salt-fields. Salt processing has also provided a number of sludge beds, some of which are now attractive to waders.

Dredging of the Manchester Ship Canal and the Weaver Navigation has given rise to large, wet sludge beds of great ornithological value. A few ancient woodlands are accessible to birdwatchers, the oak woods at Peckforton are particularly rewarding. Mature trees are common in the parks of the stately homes which are particularly numerous in the north-east of Cheshire. Little moorland survives on the eastern hills, where sheep relentlessly nibble any shoots of heather and bilberry amongst the poor grasslands, and its characteristic birds are vulnerable to disturbance by ramblers. On the plain, heathland has all but disappeared. Fragments survive around certain of the sand quarries (good bird habitats in their own right), especially in the Delamere area where the former heaths and broadleaved woods have been largely replaced by conifers. Other heaths survive on sandstone outcrops, for example at Bickerton and on the Wirral Peninsula. The Wirral coastline is essentially a continuation of the vast tract of sand- and mudflats which extend down almost without interruption from Morecambe Bay. The peninsula's sand dunes have been tamed almost completely.

51 ROSTHERNE MERE

OS Map 109
SJ 743843

Habitat

Rostherne Mere lies in a deep, natural hollow. It extends to 48 hectares with a maximum depth of 30 metres. The banks shelve steeply for the most part and, while much of the mere is fringed by narrow reedbeds, there is little submerged vegetation and few waterfowl breed. Muddy cattle drinks and sandy spits provide limited habitat for passing waders. Mixed woodlands run down to the mere edge for more than half of its circumference. Elsewhere it is bordered by pasture land. The mere, woods and pastures together comprise the Rostherne Mere National Nature Reserve. The mere is known mainly as a winter haunt of wildfowl which can be watched in relative comfort from the A.W. Boyd Memorial Observatory.

Species

From October to March hundreds of ducks line the edges of the mere, roosting amongst the reedbeds or on overhanging branches. Mallard predominate in autumn, but may be outnumbered by several hundred Teal in winter. Wigeon, Coot and Canada Geese graze the pastures. Two to 300 of these feral geese may be present, and the flock should always be checked for oddities. The proliferation of wildfowl collections has led to an increase in sightings of escaped birds and it is now not unusual to find one or two Barnacle Geese with the Canadas. Snow, Lesser White-fronted and Bar-headed Geese have turned up from time to time, and hybrid birds of questionable parentage also occur. A few Shovelers generally remain through the winter although this species is more numerous in autumn. In recent years flocks of 100 or more Gadwall have been present in late autumn, but Pintail have become scarce winter visitors.

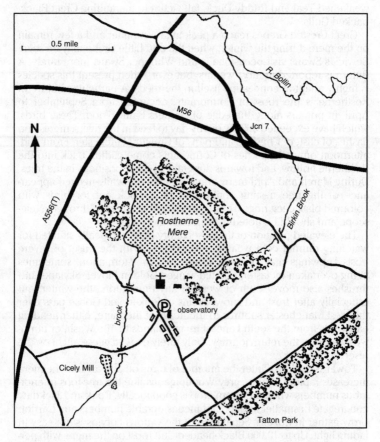

Pochard form the bulk of the diving duck population. In recent winters a large flock of more than 1,000 birds has based itself on the Mersey valley, spending time at Rostherne. Several dozen Tufted Duck generally mingle with the Pochard and a few of the larger, heavier-billed Scaup arrive on occasion. With careful searching a Ferruginous Duck or a hybrid diving duck might be found. Assorted hybrids are seen in most winters. In midwinter 20 or more Goldeneye spread out across the back of the mere to feed, and for some years now Rostherne has been as good a place as any in Cheshire to see Smew—one or two red-headed females often rest under Gale Bog in the northwestern corner of the mere. The introduced Ruddy Duck is common here as elsewhere in the region, although culling of the species is proposed. Scarcer waterfowl, such as Goosander and the rarer grebes, turn up from time to time, and there have been records of Green-winged Teal and American Wigeon.

Severe weather concentrates wildfowl on the mere. Owing to its depth Rostherne hardly ever freezes over completely and remains open long after other meres and flashes have frozen. When prolonged frosts cause the Baltic Sea to freeze over, and when alternative duck roosts in Greater Manchester are ice-bound, numbers of Pochard and Tufted Duck may run into thousands. Under such conditions the ducks are crowded into a small pool of open water and the smaller birds, such as weakened Teal and Ruddy Duck, fall victim to marauding Great Black-backed Gulls.

Great Crested Grebes reach a peak in late summer and a few remain on the mere during the winter, when the odd Little Grebe may be seen. Bewick's Swans visit occasionally and Whooper Swans more rarely. A Bittern is reported in most winters, but even when present this species is highly adept at concealing itself in the reeds. A particular feature of Rostherne is the roost of Cormorants, occupied from September to April, in poplars along the edge of Harpers Bank Wood. These birds, which have exceeded 300, fly out by day to feed in the rivers, meres and flashes of eastern Cheshire and parts of Greater Manchester. From mid-afternoon onwards, parties of Cormorants come gliding back into the Rostherne hollow, and towards dusk take up their positions in the trees. During March and April many adults assume the white-necked appearance of the tree nesting continental race. Look out for birds with coloured plastic leg rings. These can sometimes be read through a telescope and should be noted in the observatory logbook.

The elevated position of the observatory makes it ideally situated for watching diurnal cold weather movements. With the onset of severe frosts Lapwings may be seen flying west in V-formation, sometimes being overtaken by faster, pointed-winged Golden Plover. Skylarks and thrushes also move south or west. At any time during the winter, but especially after frost and snow, skeins of Pink-footed Goose pass over the west Manchester suburbs to the north of the mere, either heading eastwards from the south Lancashire mosslands to The Wash, or north-westwards on the return journey. Only rarely do wild geese alight on the reserve.

Towards dusk in winter the number of birds on and around the mere increases rapidly. Plump, grey Woodpigeons line the tree-tops in enormous numbers when the acorn crop is good locally. Rook and Jackdaw congregate in smaller, though not inconsiderable numbers and Carrion Crow gather in dozens. Separation of the various corvids is not easy in fading light. Up to 10,000 Black-headed Gull roost on the mere, with perhaps a few hundred of the larger gull species, but the latter have become less numerous since the refuse tip closed at Lindow Moss, near

Cormorants

Wilmslow. Glaucous and Iceland Gulls have become correspondingly scarce. Common Gull may reach 1,000 or more between January and March. Kittiwake are infrequent visitors after storms at sea.

From late summer to early winter thousands of Starling wheel over the mere at dusk before roosting in the reedbeds. In recent years these have often been harassed in spectacular fashion by a Peregrine or two, and Sparrowhawk are even more likely to appear, sometimes becoming entrapped in the swirling flocks. Hobbies have been seen with increasing frequency in recent summers.

Woodland birds move through the alder trees at the mere's edge, giving views of Siskin, Goldfinch, woodpeckers and possibly Marsh Tit. Nuthatch, Long-tailed and Coal Tit, and Jay will take food from a bird table just below the observatory. The winter flocks of wildfowl disperse during March and the reserve then becomes relatively quiet for the summer months.

Stock Doves displaying in front of the observatory are one of the first signs of spring, and Lesser Spotted Woodpeckers call and drum from mereside alders, Curlews visit the pastures by day and at dusk in some years Woodcocks rode around the woodlands. Passage in April and May brings a few Common Sandpipers and other waders to the shoreline. Far more conspicuous are the swirling flocks of hirundines and Swifts which feed over the mere. Parties of terns, Common, Arctic or Black, may visit at this time.

Breeding species include Kestrel, Sparrowhawk and Little Owl, with such woodland species as Blackcap, Nuthatch and Spotted Flycatcher. Buzzards are often present. Grey Wagtail may be present along the inlet stream and a Kingfisher may perch on posts by the old boathouse. A well-studied population of Reed Warbler breeds in the reedbeds, some nests being parasitised by Cuckoos. A few pairs of Sedge Warbler breed. Nesting waterfowl include Great Crested Grebe, and sometimes Tufted and Ruddy Ducks. The odd non-breeding Cormorant, Wigeon or Shoveler may spend the summer on the mere, and scores of feral Greylag Geese arrive to moult with the Canada Geese.

Late summer and early autumn may see a build-up of Great Crested Grebe, resting in a flock out on the open water. Parties of drake Pochard may arrive in July from breeding waters, and Tufted Duck may be more numerous than at any other season (except for severe winter weather). Shoveler numbers reach a peak in September or October. A few terns and waders may pass through, and autumn gales may blow a shearwater or other seabird inland.

Timing

For general viewing of wildfowl a visit at any time of day will do. During the winter months, however, afternoon and dusk visits are recommended for roosting birds. Persistent frosts concentrate wildfowl, driven off other waters. Westerly or northwesterly gales at any time of year may blow in seabirds.

Access

Leave the M56 at Junction 7, turning south onto the A556(T). After a mile (1.6 km) take the second turning on the left, continue along this winding road for three quarters of a mile (1.2 km), past the church, and park on the left opposite a T-junction, outside the warden's house, 'Rowans' (SJ 743837). Otherwise follow signs for the main, north entrance to Tatton Park (SJ 748827), and take the minor road north-wards directly opposite the park gate. Access to the mere is prohibited. Permits for the observatory are readily available, however, costing £5 per person, £7.50 for a family and £1 for OAPs. They are valid from 1 January to 31 December, and are available from D.A. Clarke, 1 Hart Avenue, Sale, Cheshire on submission of a stamped, addressed envelope. Cheques or postal orders should be made payable to the Manchester Ornithological Society. Directions from Rostherne village to the Observatory are given on the back of the permit. Limited viewing of the mere is possible from the churchyard, but day permits are now available for £1 per person. Escorted tours are available for groups by arrangement with the Warden, English Nature, 'Rowans', Rostherne, Knutsford, Cheshire, WA16 6RY.

Calendar

All year: Great Crested Grebe, Cormorant (non-breeding), Canada Goose, Tufted Duck, Sparrowhawk, Kestrel, Stock Dove, Little Owl, all three woodpeckers, Nuthatch, Jay.

December–February: Cormorant, Wigeon, Teal, Pochard, Tufted Duck, Goldeneye, Ruddy Duck, perhaps Gadwall and Smew, other wildfowl. Gulls and crows roosting. Siskin below the observatory.

March–May: Gull roost vacated and wildfowl disperse. Curlew and Common Sandpiper, possibly other waders; Swift, hirundines and occasional terns over the mere.

June–July: Non-breeding waterfowl may include Wigeon, Shoveler and Cormorant. Few wildfowl breed but Greylag Geese join the Canada Geese in June for the moult, and Pochard and Tufted Duck increase in July. Reed Warbler numerous in reedbeds.

August–November: Great Crested Grebe, Shoveler and Tufted Duck numerous. Occasional terns or waders.

Reference

Harrison, R. & Rogers, D. A. (1977) *The Birds of Rostherne Mere*, NCC.

52 TATTON PARK AND KNUTSFORD MOOR

OS Map 109, 118
SJ 77, 78

Habitat

Tatton Park consists of open grassland with scattered clumps of trees and some larger mixed woods of oak, chestnut, beech and pine. Grazing by sheep, cattle and both red and fallow deer prevents the development of a scrub layer in all but a few, fenced woods. The smaller of the two meres, Melchett Mere, has boggy areas of rushes along its banks. It acts as a refuge for wildfowl when the main mere is disturbed by boats and windsurfers. Tatton Mere itself, dammed by the monks of Mobberley Priory in medieval times, has little marginal vegetation except at the southern end where carr woodland has developed on either side. An extensive reedbed separates the mere from Knutsford Moor pool, which lies outside the park. The mere is often heavily disturbed by water sports. At the northeast corner of the park is a mill pool, backed by a large bed of sedges. The fast-flowing brook downstream from the mill attracts riparian species. To the north of the mill is the deer enclosure, a secluded area of grassland with scattered, old trees standing on ancient field boundaries.

Species

The meres are one of the main attractions of the park, but the plentiful mature timber makes Tatton outstanding for characteristic parkland birds. All three woodpeckers breed regularly, the ground-feeding Green Woodpecker favouring the combination of permanent pasture and old trees. Nuthatch and Treecreeper are abundant, and Jackdaw, Stock Dove and Little Owl nest in holes in trees. Dog Wood, along the eastern side of Tatton Mere, has held both black-capped tit species. The Marsh Tit, which favours the drier mature woodland with its oaks and chestnuts, has become scarce of late. The 'big headed' Willow Tit prefers the damper carr where it can excavate nest-holes in soft stumps of alder and birch. Goldcrests nest in the scattered pines. Blackcaps sing from the canopy over rhododendrons, and a few Garden Warblers may answer back from scrubbier areas. Wood Warblers are present in some springs and have bred. An area of rough grassland and bramble scrub, just outside the park, borders Dog Wood to the south. Whitethroats dance above the scrub, uttering their scratchy song before plummeting back into cover. Several pairs of Garden Warbler breed and Willow Warbler sing from the birches. There is just a chance of hearing the reeling of a Grasshopper Warbler on a spring evening. On the fringe of the reedbed a pair or two of Sedge Warblers continue to nest. Several pairs of Reed Warbler nest in the *Phragmites*, and probably a pair or two of Water Rail, whose weird wailing and trilling 'song' may be heard as the light fades. Curlews nest in the remoter areas of parkland, arriving in March as a vociferous flock, then splitting up as pairs establish territories. Lapwings tumble in wild display flights over rushy patches. Woodcock rode along the northern edge of the park.

Breeding waterfowl include Ruddy and Tufted Ducks, which also nest on the mill-pool where Grey Wagtails breed and Kingfishers are often seen fishing. Little and Great Crested Grebes also nest on the meres. This may be the only place where Great Cresteds have nested in a blackcurrant bush, for the shrub grows wild here and a pair once built their nest amongst emergent stems at the water's edge. Canada Geese nest along the rushy fringes of the meres and even beneath trees up to 100 metres or more from the water. In several years escaped Barnacle Geese have paired with Canada Geese here. Other birds of captive origin which have been seen with some regularity are Red-crested Pochard, Mandarin and Wood Duck.

Buzzards are seen regularly, up to 12 in 1996, and have attempted to nest. A Red Kite spent several months recently in the area of the deer enclosure, Ospreys occasionally pass through in spring or autumn, and there is a recent autumn record of Rough-legged Buzzard.

Winter wildfowl include Teal, Pochard and Goldeneye, with a chance of Smew. Tufted Duck are always present. Cormorants fly in from Rostherne, and later haul themselves out on the banks of Melchett Mere to digest their scaly meals. As spring approaches, the Goldeneye display regularly and their numbers increase as passage to the northeast commences. Scarcer waterfowl are seen in most winters, perhaps a diver or rare grebe.

Snipe and Jack Snipe winter in the treacherous marshes around Melchett Mere where elusive Water Rail are often present. Rails are more easily seen around the Moor reedbed, even from the railings beside the playing field in the centre of Knutsford where a motley selection of overfed ducks waits for junk food. Bearded Tits have occurred here. In autumn the reedbed holds roosts of Pied Wagtail and Swallow, and in winter Redwing and Blackbird roost in birch scrub and rhododendrons nearby. Also in winter Siskin and Redpoll feed in mereside alder and birch trees. Greenfinch and Chaffinch gather to stubble fields around the park, and Brambling often appear either there or under beeches.

March brings the first passerine migrants to the mereside when parties of Meadow Pipit, Pied Wagtail and Reed Bunting comb the short turf, and the odd Wheatear flits along the shoreline. During showery weather in April the flocks are joined by White and Yellow Wagtails and perhaps a Water or Rock Pipit. Common Sandpipers rise from the water's edge and fly away low across the mere. The first Sand Martins are seen in late March, to be joined by Swallow and then House Martin during April, and Swift by the end of that month. Terns are recorded annually on either passage, with perhaps more chance of a young Little Gull in the autumn. Migrant parties of hirundines again appear over the meres in September and October, when their numbers may change markedly from hour to hour as flocks arrive in dribs and drabs from the north, feed for a while as they reassemble, then depart *en masse* to the south.

Timing

The park is open from 10 am until dusk daily except for Christmas Day. Sunny weekends, bank holidays and special events days should be avoided. Morning visits are recommended as disturbance increases during the day and waterfowl may then leave the park and fly to Rostherne. Evening visits in spring can be rewarding. Showery weather at passage times produces most migrants, particularly when the wind is from a southerly quarter in spring.

Access

Three entrances allow access to Tatton, and the park is well signposted on all approach roads to Knutsford, but most birdwatchers enter through Dog Lodge. Take the B5085 from the A537 out of Knutsford, pass a brick church, then pull into a loop behind a grass verge on the left and park (SD 754786). Continue walking in the same direction and turn left into Teal Avenue. Take the first left into Mallard Close, cross the railway bridge, and the stile into the park will then be obvious. Knutsford Moor and scrub areas are visible to the left. Otherwise park in the car park below the lower shopping street in Knutsford itself, from where the Moor with its hungry ducks can be seen. Cross the Moor, keeping the railings on the left, then follow a rough track to the left

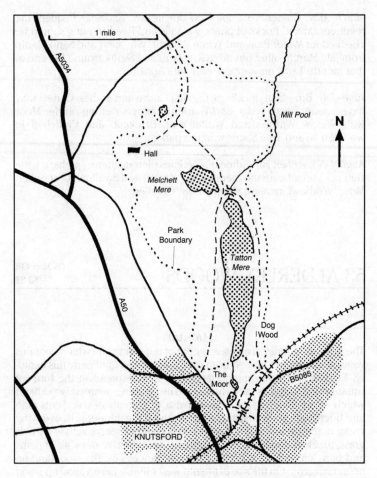

through the scrub. This track eventually leads through to Dog Wood. On a short visit it is customary to walk up the east side of the mere inspecting the wildfowl and any migrants, then continue to Melchett Mere which can be scanned from the southeast corner. It is then possible to complete the circuit of the mere, perhaps following an avenue of mature beeches down the west side of the park to the Knutsford gate. On evening visits however this gate may be locked, so it is advisable to retrace one's steps.

Calendar

All year: Little Grebe, Great Crested Grebe, Canada Goose, Tufted Duck, Ruddy Duck; Woodcock; Stock Dove, Little Owl, all three woodpeckers, woodland species.

December–February: Cormorant, Teal, Pochard and Goldeneye on the meres, Water Rail, Snipe and Jack Snipe in marshy ground, Brambling under beeches, Redpoll in birches and Siskin in alders. Thrushes roosting at the Moor.

March–May: Goldeneye display conspicuously; Shoveler frequent the reedbeds. Mixed flocks of pipits, wagtails and Reed Bunting should be checked for Water Pipit and White Wagtail. Wheatear and Sand Martin from late March, other hirundines in April and Swifts around the end of that month. Terns may appear from late April.

June–July: Broods of ducklings, Canada Goose and grebes. Curlew may have young. Reed, Sedge and Garden Warblers nesting on the Moor with Willow Warbler and Whitethroat. Blackcap and Chiffchaff in woodlands, and Tree Sparrow in the parkland.

August–November: Hirundines sometimes plentiful; terns, perhaps Little Gull occasional over the meres. Pied Wagtail and Swallow roost on the Moor. Wildfowl increase sharply from October.

53 ALDERLEY WOODS

OS Map 118
SJ 87

Habitat

The Edge at Alderley is an escarpment of red sandstone which contains veins of copper ore, mined from prehistoric times until early this century. Evidence of these mining activities is widespread in the form of square-sided cuttings and tunnels. The mature, planted woodland which covers much of the edge consists principally of oak, Scots pine and birch, with some chestnut and beech on the thinner soils overlying rocky outcrops, and larch. Ground flora is rather sparse with wavy hair grass, bracken and brambles dominant. An extensive network of paths and bare, eroded areas around mine entrances give the woodland an open character. On the site of the old west mine, where a spoil tip stood into the 1960s, an area of open ground is developing into birch scrub. Stands of gorse and sallow here are attractive to small finches and warblers.

Species

During the winter months, the woods contain large tit flocks, generally accompanied by a few Goldcrest, Nuthatch, Treecreeper and the occasional Lesser Spotted Woodpecker. The black-capped Marsh and Willow tits are scarce here. Coal and Great Tits in particular feed on beechmast, and both species may outnumber the Blue Tit in winter. When there is a good mast crop they are joined under the beeches by Chaffinch and Brambling. Parties of Redpoll feed in the birches, a food source also used by small groups of Bullfinch. Siskins also feed in the birches, moving into larches towards spring. Redwings move into the woods to feed on holly berries so long as these are available. Green Woodpeckers are seen each winter, often remaining into April. As spring approaches their ringing 'yaffle' echoes through the woods with increasing frequency, but the birds usually disappear without nesting. Great Spotted Woodpecker nest commonly in the less accessible reaches of the woods, a scatter of chippings at the base of a birch tree sometimes betraying the presence of a nest. In June the strident calls of the young birds also give the nest away. These calls have a remarkable resemblance to the clearer 'pee-pee-pee . . .' note of the Lesser Spotted Woodpecker which also nests here in small numbers. In spring, Wood Warblers are the chief attraction at Alderley, and easily located by their song—a shivering trill sometimes replaced or preceded by a series of clear 'peu' notes on a descending scale. The first Wood Warblers arrive in late April and soon after that the breathtaking display flight may be seen, in which the bird flies rapidly through the branches, changing direction with such speed and frequency that its flight is very difficult to follow. Redstart and Pied Flycatcher also breed in some years. Like the Wood Warbler, these are species which have a restricted upland distribution in the region. Tree Pipits may also nest, finding the numerous clearings to their liking. Treecreeper and Nuthatch are both plentiful breeders, the latter even plastering up fissures in the exposed rock faces to nest. From the middle of May Spotted Flycatchers stammer their weak song while Chiffchaffs, which arrived in early April, are still singing vigorously. Coal Tits nest in mouse-holes beneath the pines where the numerous Goldcrests hang their flimsy structures. Reports of Firecrest in recent summers are unsubstantiated though not improbable.

The heath and scrubland area at the West Mine site supports a quite distinct breeding community with Whitethroat, Garden Warbler, Linnet and Redpoll. Lesser Whitethroat and Grasshopper Warbler have occurred, but Yellowhammer, once plentiful, have undergone a rapid decline both here and elsewhere in eastern Cheshire in the last few years. Adjacent pastures support a few pairs of Lapwing—now primarily a bird of arable land hereabouts in the breeding season. A Kestrel often hunts the area. Though not noted as a Woodcock site, one or two birds do rode over the woods in spring, passing over the main car park. In May the hoarse hunger calls of young Tawny Owl may be heard.

Timing

The woods are mostly owned by the National Trust and attract many visitors so that at times, particularly at weekend and on sunny evenings in spring and summer, they may become too crowded for the liking of many birdwatchers. Early morning visits may then be advisable. In spring birdsong is at its best at this time of day, although evening visits generally give sufficient time to locate most species. In winter timing is less important. Few birds are then in territory, so that if the woods are heavily disturbed, the flocks move to quieter parts.

Access

The woods straddle the B5087 Alderley Edge–Macclesfield road some 2 kilometres out from Alderley. Several lay-bys border the road and there is a large car park, which may be locked at dusk, just to the east of the Wizard restaurant (SJ 860773). Numerous paths criss-cross the woods to such an extent that it should be no trouble for visitors to remain on paths to avoid contributing to the erosion which is an increasing problem. Most of the woodland species can be located in that part of the woods lying to the north of the road. To reach the West Mine area, enter the southern part of the woods by a track opposite an unmade car park some 200 metres to the west of the Wizard. Follow this main track past the conifer plantations until the gorse is reached.

Calendar

All year: Good range of common woodland birds.

December–February: Large mixed tit flocks roam the woods, accompanied by other woodland species. Green Woodpecker in winter residence. Redwing strip berries off hollies; Bullfinch and Redpoll, along with Siskin, take birch seed; and Brambling may join Chaffinch under beeches.

March–May: Summer visitors arrive during April and by early May most warblers will be present. Lesser Spotted Woodpecker may be conspicuous in March or April. Woodcock rode and by May young Tawny Owl call to be fed.

June–July: Residents and summer visitors busy with nesting duties, although unmated Wood Warbler continue to sing regularly. Redstart, Spotted and perhaps Pied Flycatchers, possibly Tree Pipit present in woods with Chiffchaff and Blackcap. Redpoll and Linnet, Whitethroat and Garden Warbler nest on the heathland.

August–November: Wood Warblers slip away unnoticed as other migrants depart.

54 RUDHEATH SAND QUARRIES
OS Map 118
SJ 77

Habitat

Rudheath was once an extensive heathland area to north of Holmes Chapel. Most of the land has been turned over to agriculture, but small areas of heathland, birch woodland and pine plantations remain. Several flooded sand quarries add to the diversity of the area.

54A NEWPLATT WOOD SAND QUARRY

SJ 75–70–

This is a large, shallowly flooded sand quarry used for angling. A flock of Canada Geese is resident, and small numbers of several wildfowl species are generally present, especially between autumn and spring. These include Teal, Shoveler, Pochard and Tufted Duck. Less common species such as Goosander and Garganey have visited. Areas of sandy mud are often exposed around the gently shelving shoreline. This mud attracts waders such as Oystercatcher and Snipe, and occasionally other species such as Greenshank and Dunlin. The plentiful fish have attracted migrant Osprey.

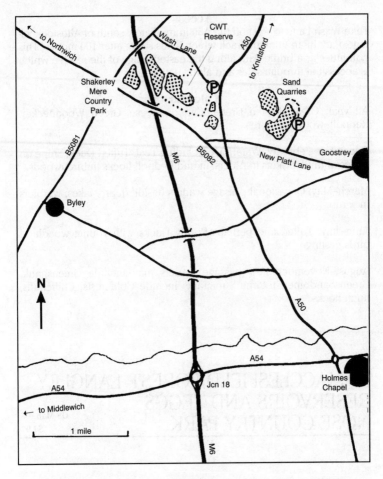

Access

The quarry lies to north of New Platt Lane and east of the A50 Holmes Chapel to Knutsford Road just south of Allostock village. A minor road runs up the eastern side of the site. From here a well-worn path skirts the eastern edge of the lake, giving interrupted views across the water.

54B RUDHEATH WOODS NATURE RESERVE

SJ 74–70–

An area of heathland and wet woodland managed by the Cheshire Wildlife Trust, this site regularly attracts moderate numbers of Redpolls, Siskins and mixed flocks of tits. Green Woodpeckers feed on the heathland while both Great and Lesser Spotted Woodpeckers visit the damp woodland where Willow Tits are resident. Hobbies have been seen in summer. Goldcrests are common in the scrub in autumn and winter. Chiffchaffs also frequent the scrub in early spring and autumn, less often in winter.

Access

Take Wash Lane to west off the A50 immediately south of Allostock village. Park in an unmade track which leads south after 100 metres. This continues as a bridle path along the eastern edge of the reserve which is accessible through stiles and along paths.

Calendar

All year: Great Crested Grebe, Canada Geese, Green Woodpecker, Redpoll, woodland birds.

December–February: Waterfowl including Teal, Tufted Duck; Snipe on exposed mud; Siskins in Alders; tit and Redpoll flocks in birchwoods.

March–May: Occasional passage waders beside quarry lakes; warblers in scrub.

June–July: Tufted and perhaps Ruddy Ducks with young; woodland birds nesting.

August–November: Few passage waders may include Greenshank, Green Sandpiper; returning migrants include Goldcrests, Chiffchaffs, finch flocks.

55 MACCLESFIELD FOREST, LANGLEY RESERVOIRS AND TEGGS NOSE COUNTRY PARK

OS Map 108
SJ 97

Habitat

Lying on the slopes of the Pennines and covering the catchment of a chain of reservoirs, the conifer plantations of Macclesfield Forest are home to a limited but specialised community of birds. Pine, spruce and larch are the principal trees, with some sycamore and a few other broadleaved trees, notably beech, along the roadsides. The plantations should improve for birds as the first generation of trees matures, and felling and replanting become more prevalent. The forest is surrounded by upland pasture and rough, sheep-grazed moorland. Red deer frequent the plantations, emerging into the open by night. The reservoirs are steep-sided with rocky shores and, as the water level fluctuates markedly in summer, little marginal vegetation has developed. Submerged plants, exposed during dry weather, include the uncommon shoreweed (*Littorella uniflora*), needle spikerush (*Eleocharis acicularis*) and the lesser marshwort (*Apium inundatum*), a tiny umbellifer. The lower reservoirs, Teggs Nose, Bottoms and Ridgegate, are heavily fished. Trentabank, the topmost reservoir, is out of bounds to anglers but seldom holds many waterfowl.

Teggs Nose Country Park includes an area of mixed broadleaved woodland with oak, ash, beech and other trees, and plentiful dead wood. Cattle graze among the trees but there is nonetheless a considerable scrub layer of brambles and other undergrowth. At the bottom of the steep hillside the woodland changes to alder carr, and at higher altitudes it peters out and is replaced by stands of bracken and some heather.

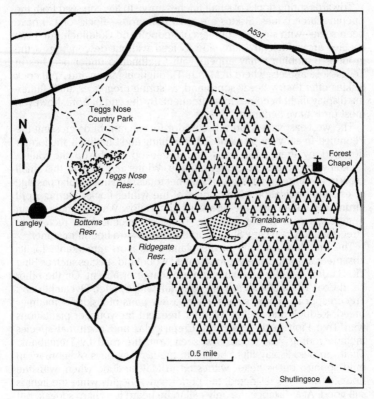

Species

Despite an overall impression of quietness, the forest does have some specialities, and unusual birds turn up with surprising frequency. During the winter months flocks of Goldcrest, Coal and Long-tailed Tits roam the plantations, their thin calls breaking the misty silence. With perseverance Crossbills are quite likely to be seen, often in flight across the valley, although they sometimes alight in roadside trees. Goshawks are seen with some regularity, perhaps dashing in at twilight in an attempt to snatch a Carrion Crow from the communal roost in larches at Trentabank. The forest has furnished winter records of a variety of other raptors, notably Hen Harrier and Rough-legged Buzzard. Ravens are often seen, or their deep croaks heard. A few common waterfowl winter on the reservoirs. Up to a dozen Goldeneye are usually present, and in late winter there is no better place than Ridgegate for watching their display. The drakes alternately stretch out their necks then throw back the head so that the bill points skyward, giving a strange creaking call at the same time. Often the displaying birds swim within a few yards of the roadside wall. A Smew spent several weeks here in 1990. In recent winters, a roost of Goosander has become established at Trentabank, the ducks arriving in late afternoon from rivers, fish ponds and lakes over a wide, surrounding area. Thirty or more are sometimes present, although the roost may settle at Lamaload Reservoir, a short distance to the north, if that water is not disturbed.

Towards spring flocks of small finches arrive to feed on seed from the opening larch cones. Siskins are most numerous—flocks of 150 have been seen—with smaller numbers of Redpoll and Goldfinch. All these species are sufficiently acrobatic to feed without descending to the ground. Bramblings may appear with Chaffinches under beeches at Teggs Nose and elsewhere in March. Throughout March and April cock Siskins utter their wheezy songs and, as spring progresses, their fluttering display flight becomes more frequent. By the end of April, however, most birds have departed.

The west-east valley forms a corridor for migrant birds crossing the Pennines. In early spring parties of Brambling and Chaffinch, the former detected by their nasal calls, fly at tree-top height up the valley. Jackdaws move east at greater altitude. Winter numbers of this small crow in Cheshire greatly exceed summer totals, and this regular passage gives some indication of the origin of the winter flocks. During April hirundines gather over the reservoirs and Yellow Wagtails, now few in numbers, return to the pastures. There are recent April records of Firecrest and Great Grey Shrike, probably eastward-bound migrants.

The breeding avifauna of the plantations is as remarkable for its absentees as for its variety. Broadleaved woodland species such as Blue Tit, Garden Warbler and Nuthatch are scarce or absent. On the other hand Coal Tit and Goldcrest are plentiful, with Spotted Flycatcher and Treecreeper in mature stands where a few pairs of Siskins sometimes breed. Redpoll and Willow Warbler frequent the younger plantations with Tree Pipit in the clearings. Crepuscular and nocturnal species include roding Woodcock, best seen from the road by Trentabank. Their curious display flight begins in the last few days of February in mild springs, but is better witnessed in May or June when, with the hours of darkness restricted, the performance begins while the light is still good. At a distance the only call to be heard is a sharp squeak, but as the birds pass overhead with deep, slow wingbeats, listen for a series of three or four deep grunts. Tawny Owls are common and make use of old crow nests, there being a lack of the cavities in trees that provide the usual nest-site. Long-eared Owls have bred and may still do so, hunting the moors above the forest. By day their place is taken by Kestrels which hover above the ridges on the lookout for field voles. Cleared areas appear suitable for Nightjars, but this bird is now very scarce in Cheshire.

A few waterfowl breed on the reservoirs. Both Great Crested and Little Grebes may nest on Bottoms Reservoir, and Tufted ducklings have been reared on Ridgegate. Canada Geese sit conspicuously on nests beneath trees near the water. Common Sandpipers, which feed along the shore-line, evade the anglers by nesting inside the plantations. As the young hatch the adults perch on roadside walls, bobbing and calling anxiously. Of particular interest is the heronry in larches beside Trentabank. Renovation of old nests may start in February, with new nests still being built in April. The Grey Herons fly out to fish in brooks, pools and rivers in the surrounding hills. Returning birds are greeted with much bill-clat-

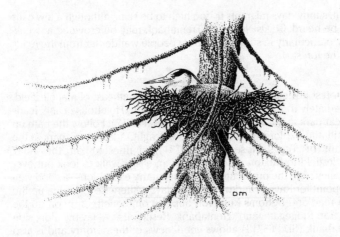

Grey Heron

tering by their mates. During May and June the growing young birds gabble and squawk noisily.

The woodlands at Teggs Nose come into their own during the summer. Wood Warblers trill beneath the oaks and are more easily located than the pair or two in the forest proper. Redstarts flit in and out of tree holes or warble from the cover of a thorn bush. Pied Flycatchers have become a regular breeding species in recent summers. All three woodpeckers are seen, although the Lesser Spotted is decidedly scarce. Nuthatch and Tree Pipit also nest, as do lowland species such as Garden Warbler. Autumn passage brings the occasional rarity to the forest—Honey Buzzard and Wryneck have been noted—but the area is best known for heavy movements of commoner species. On any cloudy or misty day from mid August to November, migrant pipits and wagtails, and later thrushes and finches pass low over the ridges above the forest, where the skilled observer can separate the various species by their calls. White Wagtails often feed beside the reservoirs in late August and September. Autumn passage of these pearly grey birds down the Pennines is inadequately documented. Migrant Bramblings are often recorded here even when they appear to be absent elsewhere in the county. Easterly winds in October or November bring the largest movements, with thousands of Redwing or Fieldfare, hundreds of Blackbirds and dozens of Song Thrushes on the best days. Starlings and Jackdaws are other important species. Tired migrant thrushes and finches will often settle in the scrub and woodland at Teggs Nose, where they make easy pickings for the resident Sparrowhawks.

Timing

Evening visits are advisable for watching roosting and crepuscular species. Clear mornings are best for raptors. On cloudy days mist may obscure the valley, although on cold winter days when fog blankets the lowlands the sun may well be shining on the hills. Diurnal passage over ridges above the forest is heaviest on autumn days with mist, hazy cloud or when it is totally overcast, although very large movements have occurred with a clear sky and light wind from an easterly quarter. Passage stops abruptly in heavy or persistent rain or in high winds. On bright, sunny days migrants fly too high to be seen, although a few calls may be heard. Teggs Nose and Trentabank may be crowded at week-ends, particularly in summer, but few people wander far from the roads into the forest.

Access

The forest lies east of Langley village to the southeast of Macclesfield. Immediately through Langley village a left turn, Holehouse Lane, leads to a car park at the foot of Teggs Nose (SD 946717). Follow the path up the hill and explore scrubby areas to the right. A larger car park at the summit of Teggs Nose (SD 949731), signposted off the A537 Macclesfield to Buxton road, provides an easier walk to look out over the valley from the promontory near the quarry exhibition—a good van-tage point for Ravens and on passage days. Otherwise continue up the main road and Bottoms Reservoir appears on the left. Carry on up the road for Ridgegate and Trentabank Reservoirs. A lay-by alongside Trentabank (SD 963713) allows good views of the heronry and is also one of the best viewpoints for the forest as a whole. For watching autumn migration continue up the road past Trentabank to the hilltop, then walk right along the footpath on the ridge and wait. If there is a pas-sage, birds will pass low over this ridge. The Forest Chapel road is gen-erally most productive for Crossbill, although these may be seen from any of the tracks through the forest.

Calendar

All year: Tufted Duck; Sparrowhawk, Kestrel, Tawny Owl; Goldcrest, Long-tailed and Coal Tits, Raven, Crossbill.

December–February: Goldeneye on the reservoirs, with perhaps a few Pochard, Teal or Wigeon; Goshawk and other raptors occasionally; Carrion Crow roost in large numbers; Goosander roost either here or at Lamaload Reservoir.

March–May: Goldeneye displaying by March when Canada Geese take up territory and Heron renovate nests; Woodcock start to rode and Crossbill may be nesting. Passing migrants in March include Jackdaw, Chaffinch and Brambling. Finch flocks in early spring include Siskin, Redpoll and Goldfinch. In April hirundines and Yellow Wagtail pass through. Summer visitors arrive including Common Sandpiper, Pied Flycatcher and Tree Pipit.

June–July: Young Heron fledge during this period; Great Crested Grebe, Tufted Duck and Common Sandpiper may also have young. Redstart, Wood Warbler and Pied Flycatcher at Teggs Nose. Possibility of Siskin in the conifers.

August–November: Summer visitors depart. Goldeneye may return from August, more likely in October. Diurnal passage includes Meadow and Tree Pipits and White Wagtail in August and September, Meadows con-tinuing to pass through in October. Pied Wagtail more numerous in October and a few Grey Wagtail likely; Siskin from mid-September; Chaffinch and Brambling in October. Large-scale thrush movements in October/November including Redwing, Fieldfare, Blackbird and Song Thrush. Goosanders may build up at Trentabank.

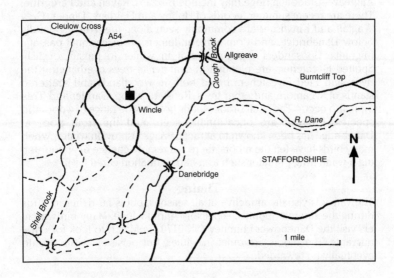

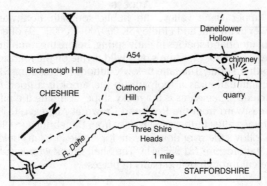

Habitat

The River Dane is a clean trout stream forming the boundary between Cheshire and Staffordshire. Its waters are rich in invertebrates (look for banded agrion damselflies in the lower reaches) which provide food for a good number of riparian birds. Danebower is a gritstone hill topped with peat moorland. Rocky slopes and mixed woodlands, including those at Shell Brook, support a diverse range of breeding species. There are red deer in the woods.

Species

Golden Plover still breed on the Danebower moors in small numbers, but have been increasingly disturbed by ramblers. Red Grouse are easily seen, however, and there is a chance of Twite or a passing Merlin. Curlews nest on moorland and rough pastures. The Ring Ouzels which used to feed in the pastures around the quarry chimney have become scarce, transient visitors of late. Wheatears still nest commonly along rocky slopes, where Cuckoos seek pipit nests, and there are several pairs of Little Owls in the area. Birds soaring above the Allgreave–Gradbach ridge may include Buzzard, Raven and Peregrine. There are recent summer records of Hobby and Fieldfare. Dipper, Grey Wagtail and Kingfisher are commonly seen along the river, especially below Danebridge, and Common Sandpipers are occasional passage migrants. Goosanders sometimes visit in winter in pursuit of fish. Spotted Flycatchers are plentiful in summer in trees overhanging the river, and Pied Flycatchers breed both in woodlands and scattered stands of Sycamore and other trees. Redstart, Wood Warbler and Tree Pipit also occur. The Shell Brook woods hold a wide range of woodland species. Buzzard are occasionally seen, and the trout pool at Danebridge has been known to attract passage Osprey. In winter, when many birds have left the moors, there is a remote chance of encountering a wandering predator such as a harrier or Short-eared Owl.

Timing

The valley is visually attractive at all seasons, but is far richer in birds during the summer months, especially April to June. Many birdwatchers visit the Danebower chimney (SK 0170) in March to look for early migrants. The moors are quiet in winter, but persistent visits should eventually be rewarded.

Access

For the upper Dane valley, the public footpath northwards from Danebower to the Cat and Fiddle (SK 009700–SK 000719) offers a good chance of moorland species in early spring, before the rambling season intensifies. (Look for Cheshire's only wild thyme on the roadside verges at the northern end.) The lane below Cutthorn Hill (starting SJ 999686) and its continuation as a footpath up the brook is a good place for moorland-edge species, as is the rocky slope alongside the minor road running eastward from the Rose and Crown at Allgreave (SJ 973669). Access to the valley further west is easy from Danebridge (SJ 964651): a footpath follows the river downstream for a mile (1.6 km) before crossing into Staffordshire (SJ 955641). The Shell Brook woods (SJ 9463–SJ 9466) are cut through by footpaths in places.

Calendar

All year: Red Grouse, Little Owl, Dipper, Grey Wagtail, Kingfisher, Sparrowhawk, woodland birds.

Spring–summer: Golden Plover, Curlew, Meadow Pipit and Skylark return to the moors in March; Ring Ouzel and Wheatear appear on scree slopes, where Cuckoo often perch in May; Wood Warbler, Redstart, Pied and Spotted Flycatcher sing in woods from late April.

Habitat

A series of shallow pools formed in recent decades as a result of salt mining, the flashes lie in a triangle between Sandbach, Middlewich and Crewe. The larger flashes at Elton Hall and Watch Lane have extensive muddy margins attractive to wading birds. The Elton Hall flashes are a diurnal roost for wildfowl, and an adjacent disused sludge bed is popular with wildfowl and waders. Watch Lane and several of the smaller flashes have marginal stands of reedmace (*Typha*) or reed-grass and the true reed (*Phragmites*) is spreading at Watch Lane. The most important *Typha* bed is at Fodens Flash, a small pool backed by carr of alder and willow—the only woodland of consequence in the area. Across the road from Fodens Flash a partly derelict market garden is producing a useful cover of willow and hawthorn scrub. This site, and industrial wasteland in the area, furnish a good supply of weed seed for winter finches and other birds. Sunken rushy areas in pastures and tall thorn hedges form further valuable habitats. A pool between Watch Lane Flash and the Trent and Mersey Canal is fed in part by a saline spring. The inland saltmarshes which develop in such sites are a botanical speciality of Cheshire. This particular site holds lesser sea spurrey, reflexed saltmarsh grass, sea aster and other species typical of coastal marshes. Their seeds may originally have been carried inland by birds, or perhaps on barges plying up and down the Weaver valley. However, wild celery, a recent arrival at Watch Lane, is more likely to have travelled on the muddy boots of some birdwatcher from the Weaver Bend at Frodsham where the plant thrives.

Rapid siltation of the Elton Hall flashes, intensification of agriculture in the surrounding fields, and drainage of Railway Farm Flash (despite its SSSI status) have reduced the attractiveness of the site in recent years.

Species

With over 200 species recorded to date, the Flashes are one of the best known birdwatching sites in Cheshire. Passage waders are fewer than formerly, but winter wildfowl remain varied.

Spring passage begins in March with Little Ringed Plover one of the first immigrants. Wheatear passage traditionally starts around 21 March, and birds linger so long around rabbit burrows as to give rise to suspicions of breeding. In late March and April, southwesterly winds and showers may bring large movements of Meadow Pipits. Feeding flocks spread out across the short turf bordering Watch Lane and other flashes in company with Reed Bunting, Pied, White and later Yellow Wagtails and, rarely, Water Pipit. Common Sandpipers, *en route* to their Pennine nesting streams, also mingle with these flocks, snapping at yellow dung-flies on cow-pats. If the wind blows from the east in mid April, there is just a chance of a migrant Osprey deflected westward from the usual line of passage.

Wader passage picks up gradually during April and May. Most of the typical autumn species occur in small numbers. Arctic Ringed Plover in

May or early June may be accompanied by Sanderling. Dunlin, regularly present in small numbers, may utter their purring song. Terns are seen occasionally.

Fodens Flash comes into its own during the summer months with Reed Bunting, Sedge and Reed Warblers nesting in the marsh; Great Crested Grebes, perhaps Ruddy Duck and Little Grebes on the flash; and Willow Tit, Treecreeper, Spotted Flycatcher, sometimes Lesser Spotted Woodpecker and possibly Water Rail in the carr. The adjacent market gardens are alive with Whitethroats in the nettle-beds and Willow Warblers in the scrub. Bullfinches are common here, their presence betrayed by a thin whistle or a white rump glimpsed as a bird flies into a thorn bush.

The area of the flashes as a whole supports important breeding populations of several wetland species. Little Grebe are present on several of the smaller pools. Throughout the spring Great Crested Grebe can be seen displaying, at times very close to the car park, from the end of Watch Lane. A pair of grebes will face each other so that they are almost touching, and shake their heads vigorously from side to side. In more advanced versions of this display the birds may rear up out of the water and shake limp water weeds or algae in their bill. One other aquatic species nesting on all pools is the Coot. Throughout the breeding season territorial Coot may be seen rearing up out of the water and thrashing away with legs and beak at any intruding rival, while non-breeders of the same species swim meekly in a sociable flock. Shelduck nest annually. Birds return from the moult from December onwards and by spring they too are displaying aggressively. By the time the ducks are sitting on eggs, the drakes will be busy driving ducks of all species, and even Grey Heron, off their adopted flash. Few waders now breed, although Little Ringed Plover still nest in the area. Ringed Plover have also attempted to nest. Redshank may be seen displaying from December onwards, but rarely settle at Sandbach.

Lesser Whitethroats nest in overgrown hedges at Watch Lane, Elton Hall and elsewhere, but are more often heard than seen. Little Owls breed in hedgerow trees throughout the area. Their yelping calls are often heard by day, especially in showery weather. Corn Bunting and Yellow Wagtail, present around arable fields, have recently become

Ruddy Duck

rather scarce. The local population of Yellow Wagtails is of particular interest since aberrant birds resembling Sykes' or Blue-headed Wagtails occur from time to time, and have been seen feeding young on several occasions.

'Autumn' wader passage may begin by the end of June with the first Green Sandpiper, perhaps a Greenshank or 'black' Spotted Redshank, presumably failed or non-breeders. Common Sandpiper passage peaks in July when the odd Turnstone or Sanderling may also occur, and Green Sandpiper increase, their liquid calls carrying on the twilight air. As Elton Hall Flash has become more overgrown, Green Sandpipers have become a major feature of autumn passage. Ruff, Greenshank and Spotted Redshank, and possibly a Wood Sandpiper may appear in August. Little Stint or Curlew Sandpiper may latch on to parties of Dunlin, and a Godwit or Grey Plover may turn up, even quite late in the autumn. The flashes have provided several records of rare waders.

Other autumn migrants tend to be neglected by birdwatchers, but are not without interest. Whinchats still occur, perching on fenceposts around Watch Lane, although numbers are decreasing, and Redstarts flicker along the hedgerows. The line of Crack Willows at Elton Hall provides rich pickings for passing warblers. A small but regular passage of Water and Rock Pipits is most obvious during the first few days of October when birds comb the edge of Watch Lane Flash, picking freshwater shrimps from amongst the debris. In some years Garganey are present among the Teal, but they often escape detection through their habit of sleeping for much of the day. When seen with their heads up however, the stripy face pattern, with broad supercilium, and the heavier bill are diagnostic.

In winter the Elton Hall flashes are an excellent locality to see all the common dabbling duck species. Of particular interest is the flock of Pintail which has visited the site annually since the 1960s. Numbers vary between 25 and 60 from year to year. The Teal is the most numerous duck with several hundred present at times, the constant 'prip . . . prip' of the drakes merging with the deeper calls of Pintail and the loud 'whee-oo' of Wigeon. A flock of up to 400 or more of this latter species join with Coots to graze the pastures around the flash. In severe weather less usual fowl appear, perhaps a family party of Bewick's or Whooper Swans or a small flock of White-fronted Geese. So long as the weather remains mild large numbers of Lapwing (up to 3,000 or more) feed on surrounding pastures and roost on the sludge bed at Elton Hall. Snipe conceal themselves in the marshes where they are hunted by hovering Kestrel, or by Sparrowhawk which adopt a peculiar slow flight to enable them to spot the stripe backed waders crouching in the rushes. Dunlin may be present right through the winter, and a few Redshank, Ruff, Curlew and Golden Plover wander down from their haunts around Northwich and Middlewich. The sloping field to the north of Pumphouse Flash regularly supports several dozen Moorhen. A flock of Skylark winters on the stubble fields between Elton Hall and Railway Flash—this species is remarkably local hereabouts at this season. Fieldfare and Redwing strip berries from the hedges and may fall prey to a Peregrine, sallying out from a perch on a nearby electricity pylon. A Great Grey Shrike is as likely to turn up here as anywhere in Cheshire, although the chances of encountering one are still very slim.

At Elton Hall as elsewhere, the behaviour of the large flocks of birds gives warning of the presence of predators. A hovering Kestrel may

cause only local consternation amongst the smaller waders and Starling. A passing Merlin or soaring Sparrowhawk will cause the Lapwing flocks to scramble, and the impending arrival of a Peregrine or migrant harrier (rare here) causes panic among the ducks as well.

Watch Lane holds a few diving ducks in winter, but it freezes over rapidly and ducks and Great Crested Grebes are then displaced to the coast. A few Jack Snipe winter in the *Typha* beds along with the odd Water Rail, and a Green Sandpiper may feed in the northeastern corner of the flash. The pool below the canal sometimes attracts a Kingfisher. A holly hedge to the north of this pool is popular with roosting Greenfinch and Linnet. Stonechat are regular winter residents in the area when their population is at a high level, and can be seen perching on thistle stems and fenceposts.

In winter Fodens Flash is a good place to see Water Rail. These shy birds perform particularly well in frosty weather when they feed by open puddles or ditches in the willow carr. Willow Tit are resident—as good a place as any to get to know this species for Marsh Tit are almost unknown here. A long-established roost of Magpie in scrub behind the flash has held over 470 birds. Long-eared Owl have been recorded in at least three winters, roosting in scrub.

Timing

In spring, showery weather from a southerly quarter or else misty days are more likely to bring down migrants, as is wet or stormy weather in the autumn. In winter duck numbers tend to increase during the day as feeding birds are flushed off field ponds and minor flashes back to the roosts. Prolonged frosts concentrate waterfowl at Elton Hall where the river Wheelock provides some open water.

Access

Turn south off the A533 Middlewich–Sandbach road by The Fox public house just north of Sandbach station. Continue round the perimeter of the lorry works until a narrow humpback bridge over the canal is reached (SJ 733611). For Fodens Flash turn right immediately at this bridge and park at the roadside by the flash shortly after the first corner. A bridlepath runs westward through the carr just beyond the flash. For Watch Lane Flash return to the canal bridge and take the other fork. Turn left by the telephone box into Red Lane and continue round until Watch Lane appears as a minor road joining from the right. Car parking at the end of Watch Lane (SJ 727606) allows good views of the flash. To reach Elton Hall take roads around the eastern side of the flash, viewing at intervals over the hedges. Turn right at the main road past the chemical works, then left after one kilometre at the first crossroads. This road runs between Elton Hall Flash (to the east at SJ 725595) and Pumphouse Flash. Visitors should not wander off the roads at Elton Hall or Watch Lane.

Calendar

All year: Great Crested and Little Grebes, Mute Swan, Shelduck; Lapwing, Dunlin (not breeding); Little Owl along hedgerows; Willow Tit and Bullfinch common at Fodens Flash.

December–February: Wigeon, Teal, Pintail at Elton Hall; Water Rail at Fodens; Lapwing and Snipe widespread, with a few Ruff, and perhaps

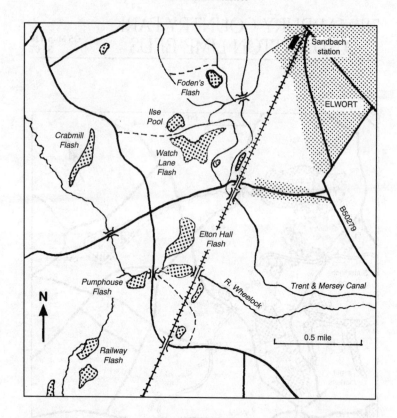

Jack Snipe or Green Sandpiper; Sparrowhawk and perhaps Peregrine hunt the area; a few Stonechat in mild winters. Magpies form huge roost at Fodens Flash.

March–May: Breeding waders appear in March and April, followed by passage birds in April and May: Little Ringed Plover, Ringed Plover, Oystercatcher, Common Sandpiper and other species. White and Yellow Wagtail may join flocks of Meadow Pipit and Reed Bunting; Wheatear generally present from late March. Wildfowl depart and summer visitors arrive.

June–July: Breeding species include Little and Great Crested Grebes and Ruddy Duck; Little Ringed Plover by flashes and on waste ground; Reed and Sedge Warblers, Whitethroat and Spotted Flycatcher all at Fodens Flash; Lesser Whitethroat and Reed Bunting widespread. Wader passage resumes in July.

August–November: Autumn duck flocks may include one or two Garganey sleeping amongst the Teal. Sprinkling of passage waders. In October, winter visitors arrive, including Water Rail. Duck flocks build up in late autumn.

58 MARBURY COUNTRY PARK AND WITTON LIME BEDS

OS Map 118
SJ 67

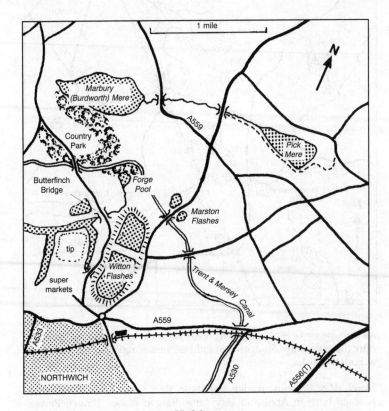

Habitat

A cluster of sites lying to the north of Northwich offer a considerable diversity of habitats, encompassing woodland, fresh water, reedbeds and industrial sludge tanks. Access has been greatly improved in recent years as part of the Mersey Forest initiative. A number of threats to 'develop' the area, most recently for a 'national angling centre', would destroy much of the ornithological interest, but have so far been resisted.

Northwich lies at the heart of the Cheshire salt and chemical industry. Consequently a great deal of land has been left in a rough state, with plentiful scrub and coarse grassland. Flashes, subsidence pools formed as a consequence of underground brine-pumping, have been used as sludge beds for lime-rich waste. They may contain pools of shallow water following rain and are then attractive to waders and wildfowl. Budworth Mere and Pickmere may also have formed as a consequence of the dissolution of rock salt, but by natural means and much longer ago.

168

58A WITTON FLASHES AND BUTTERFINCH BRIDGE

OS ref: SJ 665750 and SJ 661753

Habitat

The huge Witton Flashes have been filled with alkali waste and now resemble sludge beds. Shallow rainwater pools form in wet weather and attract passing waders. A tall embankment separates the grassy Ashton's Flash from the relatively bare Neumann's Flash to the north. The flashes support a range of lime-loving flowers which are otherwise hardly known in Cheshire: fragrant orchid, hoary mustard, ploughman's spikenard and yellow-wort are all abundant. The area in general is well endowed with hawthorn and other scrub. Immediately to the north-west of the Witton Flashes a narrow tributary flows underneath the road at Butterfinch Bridge to join the Witton Brook. To the west of the road it widens out onto mudflats, bordered on one side by *Phragmites* reeds. To the other side a stand of sea club-rush, sea aster, lesser sea spurrey, and several other species form one of the best inland saltmarshes in the county. Above this marsh is the embankment of Marbury No. 1 sludge bed. This tank was used to accommodate dredgings from the Weaver Navigation. More recently it has been restored as a wetland as part of the Mersey Forest in Vale Royal. The flowery banks of the tank support a wide range of butterflies.

Species

Grey Herons roost on the Witton flats on winter days, but their presence is eclipsed by the huge number of Lapwing. Up to 11,000 have been counted, with 3–5,000 in most years. They are accompanied by Golden Plover, varying in numbers from dozens to a few hundred. The plover flocks may be joined by a few Curlew, Dunlin or Redshank. So long as the weather remains mild, dozens of Snipe may feed on Neumann's Flash, but with the onset of frosts they disperse, and the plovers move out to the west. Shelduck are generally present through the winter months.

Depending on rainfall, Neumann's Flash may remain wet throughout summer and into the autumn. Over 100 Dunlin and more than 50 Ringed Plover have been present on occasion, with a dozen or more Ruff, a few Redshank and a good variety of other species, such as

Curlew

Curlew Sandpiper, Little Stint or Black-tailed Godwit. Sanderling, Knot and Turnstone occur in most years. A roost of Curlews in late summer may number several hundred birds. Over the years, the list of rarities has included Dotterel, Stilt and Broad-billed Sandpiper, Avocet, Temminck's Stint and Long-billed Dowitcher. Both Ringed and Little Ringed Plovers breed. Caspian Terns have visited on no fewer than four occasions over the years.

Shelduck have bred in the vicinity. In winter, small parties of ducks of various species may dabble by flood pools at Witton. Water Rails lurk in the Butterfinch Bridge reedbed.

Scrubland species nesting locally include Whitethroat, Lesser Whitethroat and Garden Warbler, with a few pairs of Grasshopper Warbler in bramble thickets and Reed Warbler beside Witton Brook. Long-tailed and Willow Tits are also common. A few pairs of Meadow Pipits nest among rough grass at the sides of the sludge tanks—the species is absent in summer from much of the Cheshire plain. Wheatears occur along the embankments on passage.

In winter a Blackcap or Chiffchaff may be found in the scrub, and towards dusk Pied Wagtails may gather on the mud at Witton before flying off west at sunset towards Winnington. Two scarcer visitors have been Great Grey Shrike, seen in several winters, and Long-eared Owl roosting in thorn scrub. Woodcocks often roost beneath the scrub, favouring the insulation of evergreen species such as Holly.

Marbury No. 1 Bed regularly attracts small numbers of Teal, Snipe and other ducks and waders. Wood Sandpipers have been seen in several recent autumns. Teal increase into the hundreds in winter, when Green Sandpipers are often present.

Timing

Plover flocks are at their largest around full moon in autumn and early winter. Severe weather soon drives them westwards. Wader passage is best in wet weather in May–June and August–October. Visits at any time of day may be rewarding. Dusk visits are advisable to hear Grasshopper Warbler in summer and to see the wagtail flocks in winter.

Access

From a roundabout on the A559 to the east of Northwich town centre take Leicester Street westward towards the waste disposal site and supermarkets. The flashes are visible behind an embankment to the north. Take the first turning to the right, called Old Warrington Road at its southern end, but renamed Marbury Lane beyond the tip entrance. Continue across the metal bridge and look for a gateway on the right, from which a stile leads to a path up the embankment. View from this point through a telescope, or walk north along the embankment until reaching an opening through the fence which leads to two screens overlooking Neumann's Flash. Do not venture onto either of the flashes. Butterfinch Bridge and Marbury No. 1 Bed lie 0.5 km to the north along this same road. Limited parking is sometimes possible in a wide, seldom used gateway to the east of the road. All gateways are in use by tenant farmers and rangers and should not be blocked, nor should the roadside passing places.

A footpath has been constructed alongside Witton Brook and reedbed. This continues through scrub towards Anderton Nature Park. A path leads up the eastern side of Marbury No.1 Tank to the Haydn

Hide from which wildfowl and waders may be viewed. A silent approach is recommended.

Calendar

All year: Grey Heron roost at Neumann's Flash. Scrubland species include Long-tailed and Willow Tits.

December–February: Flocks of Lapwing, Golden Plover and Snipe roost by day. A few Redshank or Ruff may winter. Pied Wagtail gather in large numbers at dusk prior to roosting. Water Rail at Butterfinch Bridge. Possibility of Long-eared Owl, Blackcap or Chiffchaff.

March–May: Gull and plover flocks disperse. Light wader passage; Redshank, Ringed and Little Ringed Plovers display. Scrubland comes to life as warblers arrive and take up territory. June–July: Breeding waders and Shelduck may have young. Warblers continue to sing well into June: Grasshopper, Reed and Garden Warblers, Whitethroat and Lesser Whitethroat among others. Lapwing flocks start to reform by the end of June and the first passage waders appear in July.

August–November: Wader passage at its most varied; plover flocks increase in size. Juvenile warblers roam the scrub, sometimes with mixed flocks of tits. In September they take berries from elder and other bushes, and perhaps utter subdued practice songs before departing. Lesser Black-backed Gulls may gather in a diurnal roost at Neumann's.

58B BUDWORTH (MARBURY) MERE AND PICK MERE

OS ref: SJ 655768 and 683772

(See map on p. 168)

Habitat

The Country Park lies within the grounds of the now demolished Marbury Hall. It consists for the most part of dog-walking grassland, the scrub which provided much ornithological interest having been largely cleared away. However, mature planted woodland of mixed broadleaved trees with some conifers encircles the park.

The mere, referred to as Budworth Mere to distinguish it from Marbury Mere near Whitchurch, is fringed by a narrow belt of *Phragmites* reeds for much of its perimeter. In places these reeds thicken out to form substantial beds, notably at the western end where a small woodland reserve has been set aside as a memorial to T.A. Coward, the great Cheshire naturalist. Other parts of the shoreline are subject to grazing and trampling by cattle. A sandy spit by the mouth of the Kid Brook on the north bank attracts bathing gulls and sometimes waders. The mere is subject to heavy disturbance by a sailing club based at the eastern end, and by members of the public visiting the park.

Species

The mere seldom supports large numbers of wildfowl, but most of the common species occur regularly in winter, and frequent counting has produced totals of more than 100 Wigeon and 200 each of Pochard and Tufted Duck on occasion. A few Goldeneye are usually present, and Cormorants fly in from Rostherne. The mere attracts more than its fair share of divers and the rarer grebes, with one or two in most winters. Canada Geese are becoming more frequent and skeins of Pink-footed Geese pass over occasionally in midwinter. A Bittern is sometimes seen in winter or spring.

In spring the reedbeds attract a good variety of waterfowl. Gadwall and Shoveler have displayed in recent years, the latter species having bred successfully, and Tufted Ducks nest annually, as do Little and Great Crested Grebes, while Ruddy Ducks may be present through the summer. Reed Warblers are present from late April, by which time the wintering Water Rails have departed. Kingfisher and Grey Wagtail nest in the vicinity. When Kingfisher numbers are high following mild winters, birds are often seen dashing low over the water within a few metres of the mereside footpath, their approach being heralded by a ringing 'chee' call. A heronry has been founded in recent years and held 80 nests in 1994.

Spring passage over and by the mere involves essentially the same species as at Tatton Mere (site 52), but Sand Martins tend to arrive here even earlier in March and Common Sandpipers are generally better represented. Oystercatchers may occur at this time. Other passage waders are more likely to be seen in autumn, when Dunlin, a Green Sandpiper or a Redshank may feed at the mouth of Kid Brook. Terns occur at Budworth more regularly and in better numbers than at any other inland site in the county. Black Terns are more likely to appear in the autumn, but Common and Arctic Terns usually appear on both migrations. The occasional Little Gull is also seen and Common Scoter may drop in.

All three species of woodpeckers nest locally. The woodlands fringing the park hold a good variety of birds including plentiful Long-tailed Tit and Nuthatch, with Blackcap, Spotted Flycatcher and Chiffchaff in summer. Marsh Tits still occur, but rarely now. The first Chiffchaff often sings at the mereside well before the end of March.

Pick Mere, some 2 kilometres to the east of Budworth Mere, attracts a similar range of species in winter and on passage, but lacks the woodland species. Its margins support Sedge and Reed Warblers and Reed Bunting, and damp fields alongside the mere are popular with migrant pipits and wagtails.

Timing

The sailing club is active on most days with even remotely favourable weather, but the presence of the boats generally only concentrates waterfowl in the western end. Here they may be disturbed by visitors to the Country Park, so in fine weather early morning visits are advisable. Tern passage is most likely in wet, windy weather from mid April to June and again from July to September. Black Tern arrive especially on easterly winds. Pick Mere is often worth a visit at passage times, especially during showery weather in spring. Winter visits may turn up unusual waterfowl.

Access

Marbury Country Park is signposted off the minor road between Anderton and Comberbach (SJ 648763). Otherwise it may be reached by continuing northward up the private road from Butterfinch Bridge to the "pay and display" car park. There is open access to the southwestern shores of the mere through the park. To reach Pick Mere either follow minor roads from the park, turning right in Comberbach and continuing through Great Budworth to Pickmere village, or take the B5391 eastwards from the A559 Lostock–Warrington road. From Pickmere village follow signs for 'Pickmere Lake'. Park at the fairground end and walk the very muddy footpath along the south bank of the mere, examining fields for migrants.

Calendar

All year: Woodland birds include Nuthatch, Treecreeper, Long-tailed and perhaps Marsh Tits, and all three woodpeckers. Great Crested and Little Grebes frequent the meres all year unless driven off by frosts. Grey Heron and Kingfisher seen daily.

December–February: Wildfowl include Pochard and Goldeneye, Wigeon and Teal. Pink-footed Goose overhead occasionally and rare grebes or divers seen most winters. Cormorant fish in the meres. Water Rails and Snipe along boggy parts of shoreline.

March–May: Sand Martin and Chiffchaff arrive by the end of March with other hirundines and Swift following in April. Common Sandpiper and occasionally other waders pass through in April and May. Waterfowl take up residence by reedbeds. Terns and sometimes a Little Gull may feed over meres.

June–July: Residents and summer visitors busy feeding young, including Reed Warbler, Blackcap and Spotted Flycatcher. Common Tern, or perhaps other tern species, visit occasionally.

August–November: Terns pass through in appropriate conditions until September, a few waders, such as Dunlin, Redshank or Green Sandpiper until October. Winter wildfowl then returning.

Contact: Witton Area Conservation Group, Mr Paul Hill, 1 Clive Cottage, London Road, Allostock, Knutsford, Cheshire, WA16 9LT.

59 WOOLSTON EYES

OS map 109
SJ 68

Habitat

The huge sludge tanks at the Woolston Deposit Grounds SSSI are managed in part as a nature reserve by the Eyes Conservation Group in agreement with the Manchester Ship Canal Company. Part of the site is still in use to accommodate dredgings from the Ship Canal. The site has been extensively altered in recent years, No. 3 Bed having been drained when the banks of the tank were judged to be in a dangerous state. The River Mersey has been diverted around the northern side of No. 3 Bed. No. 2 Bed is currently being used for pumping, but the former strategy of frequent small bouts of pumping has been replaced by occasional large-scale pumping which results in catastrophic changes in water level. Few areas of open mud are exposed, and the open water pools are densely fringed by *Typha* and *Phragmites*. No. 3 bed contains areas of marshy grassland with nettles, willow scrub and other rank vegetation. The river and canal are severely polluted, but both may hold wildfowl in severe weather and grebes have recently been observed catching fish on the river as the water quality slowly improves.

Species

More than 200 species have been recorded at the Eyes, including all five grebes, the three woodpeckers, and four species of owl. The principal interest nowadays lies in the huge populations of breeding warblers and in the waterfowl which favour the shallow pools.

Lying next to the Mersey, the flooded tanks inevitably attract large numbers of dabbling ducks moving inland from the estuary. The Mersey valley Pochard flock also spends time here in winter. Up to 1,000 or more Teal are present at this season, with dozens of Mallard, Shoveler, Tufted Duck and Pintail. Other standard duck species occur less frequently or in smaller numbers, and scarce or rare species such as Ferruginous and Long-tailed Duck, Green-winged Teal, Common Scoter and Smew have been noted. In late autumn and winter Pink-footed Geese occasionally fly over and have been known to alight briefly. The extensive shallow marshes form excellent nesting habitat for wildfowl. Teal, Shoveler, Mallard, Pochard, Tufted Duck and Ruddy Duck are all present through the summer. Gadwall nest in increasing numbers. Pintail, Wigeon and Garganey have lingered in some years. Broods of Tufted and Ruddy Ducks may appear in July and August respectively. Broods of the various dabbling ducks remain hidden in the marsh and are less easily seen. A few pairs of Little Grebe arrive in spring and stay to nest.

The Eyes support important nesting populations of several other marshland birds. More than 200 singing Sedge Warbler and over 100 Reed Bunting are present in summer, with smaller numbers of Reed Warbler. A pair of Marsh Warblers bred in one recent summer, an occurrence which is unlikely to be repeated. Water Rails may be heard squealing at any time of the year and sometimes nest. Bearded Tit and Marsh Harrier have both appeared on passage, with the latter now annual. Emergent tussocks are favoured as nest sites by several hundred pairs of Black-headed Gull, whose presence may attract a migrant Little or Mediterranean Gull in spring. Hundreds of Swifts often feed overhead.

Rank grass and brambles on the embankments are favoured by Grasshopper Warblers and Whitethroats, with Willow Warblers in taller scrub. Blackcap and Willow Tit nest along the more wooded stretches of riverbank, where Kingfisher are often seen, with Sand Martins in the banks of the Ship Canal. The scrub and *Typha* on No. 3 Bed hold large roosts of Starling from spring to autumn, comprising thousands of birds at times. In some autumns Pied Wagtails roost. In most years there is a

Swallow roost which may contain thousands of birds. A Hobby is often in attendance and has provided some spectacular performances. From October to early winter hundreds of Redwings and other thrushes may shelter by night. Mist-netting by day has revealed significant passage of Reed Buntings and various other passerines through the Eyes. Warblers and Goldcrest pass through in moderate numbers. In winter, roosts dwindle as food supplies diminish, although Magpies seldom seem to go hungry and continue to roost in the scrub. One or two Chiffchaffs remain in willow scrub during most winters. Merlins are seen annually in very small numbers and on occasion a Short-eared Owl hunts field voles in grassy areas. A Peregrine may visit from time to time.

Few waders now visit, owing to changes in the pumping regime into the tanks, but Snipe are regularly present in the marshes. Their numbers are notoriously difficult to estimate.

Timing

Whatever the timing of a visit there is always something to be seen. Even nocturnal visits might produce an array of surprising noises. Water Rail and Spotted Crake have been heard by night. Morning visits are generally most productive for birdsong. Since waterfowl are easily flushed from the tanks by unwitting members of the public standing on the skyline, mornings may also produce better views of waterfowl.

Access

Access is strictly limited to permit holders. A public path skirts No. 3 Bed, but viewing other than from hides is likely to disturb the birds and should not be attempted. Permits are available, at a cost of £3 per year (£6 for a family), from Brian Ankers, 9 Lynton Gardens, Appleton, Warrington, Cheshire W4 4ED. A stamped addressed envelope should be enclosed and cheques made payable to the Eyes Conservation Group. A permit entitles the holder to visit the Eyes on any number of occasions during the year and to make use of the several hides. The Eyes is not an easy reserve to find but is best approached by visitors from outside the area by leaving the M6 at Junction 21 and taking the A57 signposted to Warrington. After some 200 yards (200 m) turn left down Weir Lane and park by Woolston Weir (SJ 654888) or in more secure settings close to houses. All permit holders receive a map of the reserve giving details of the best viewing points and those areas which are out of bounds.

Calendar

All year: Teal, Shoveler, Pochard, Tufted Duck; Water Rail, Snipe, Black-headed Gull; Kingfisher, Willow Tit.

December–February: Wildfowl including Pintail and diving ducks. Pink-footed Goose occasional overhead. Short-eared Owl, Peregrine and Merlin occasionally hunt over reserve. Magpie roost in scrub where few Chiffchaffs often winter.

March–May: Little Grebes return; Ruddy and other ducks take up territory while winter wildfowl may linger and show signs of nesting. Reed Bunting appear from March onwards, with warblers arriving in April and May.

June–July: Wildfowl broods appearing include Tufted Duck and Gadwall. Gull colony gives impression of great activity, and hundreds of Swifts may wheel overhead. Warbler song tails off in July. Starlings roost in thousands.

August–November: Ruddy Duck broods still appearing in August; Shovelers increase in September and October. Snipe return. Warblers depart during August and September, when birds from outside the area pass through. Swallow roosts in early autumn replaced by incoming thrushes in October. Goldcrest and Reed Bunting pass through in October. By November large numbers of Teal have usually returned.

60 MOORE NATURE RESERVE

OS Map 108
SJ 58

Habitat

Moore Nature Reserve includes alder woodland, rough grassland, and two sizeable pools fringed by reeds. Sand is still being extracted from part of the area, where a third pool is proposed. The gorse scrub which once housed many breeding birds has largely been cleared, but there are areas of sparsely vegetated, sandy ground where gorse is beginning to regrow. Between the reserve and the River Mersey there are areas of arable land and coarse grassland, some of this now being lost to Mersey Forest plantations. A large refuse dump has replaced a once ornithologically excellent reedbed. The mudflats of the River Mersey are a further interesting habitat, while the Manchester Ship Canal and a flooded sand quarry to south of the reserve attract a few waterfowl.

Species

The alder woodlands have closed, high canopies and attract a limited range of species including Willow Tits, Treecreepers and all three species of Woodpeckers. In winter large flocks of Siskins are generally present in the woodlands, Reed Buntings feed on grass seeds in rough, open areas, and elusive Long-eared Owls favour areas of dense scrub.

In summer Whitethroats are plentiful where scrub and rank grassland meet, while Grasshopper Warblers favour stands of bramble and willowherb. The reedbeds around the pools shelter Sedge and Reed Warblers in summer, while several pairs of Little Grebes nest, and Black-necked Grebes have visited. Gadwall are seen with some regularity, but waterfowl are more varied in autumn and winter when small parties of Teal, Wigeon and Shoveler visit. Pochard, Tufted and Ruddy Duck are more likely to be seen on the deeper, western pool. The sandpit south of the Ship Canal attracts Tufted Duck, Goldeneye and infrequent Scaup. Great Crested Grebes also nest here.

To west of the reserve, a bend of the River Mersey approaches to within 20 metres of the Ship Canal, by Randell's Sluice. The river, here estuarine, has areas of exposed mud at low tide. Large flocks of Lapwing are present through the winter, numbering up to 10,000 at times with up to

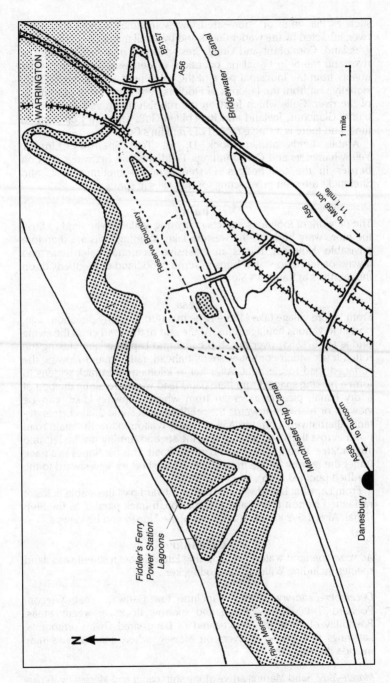

several hundred Golden Plovers. Other waders occur according to season and depending on tides elsewhere in the Mersey estuary. Up to 200 Dunlin have been seen; parties of Curlew visit; Redshank, Ruff, Black-tailed Godwit and occasionally less common species occur. Predators such as Peregrine or Short-eared Owl sometimes wander along the river, attracted by the wader flocks and by small mammals in the rough grassland. Cormorant and Great Crested Grebe now fish in both the river and the Ship Canal on occasion, evidence of improving water quality from the industrial parts of the catchment. Diving ducks occasionally visit from the lagoons of Fiddlers Ferry power station to north of the river. Gulls which feed on the rubbish dump visit the river to bathe. Glaucous, Iceland and Ring-billed Gulls are seen from time to time, and there is a single record of Franklin's Gull.

Arable fields attract Stock Doves, Tree Sparrows, Linnets, Yellowhammers and Corn Buntings. Fieldfares and Redwings feed on berries in the tall hedges. Oystercatchers sometimes nest, and Shelducks are seen prospecting for nest sites in spring.

Timing
The network of footpaths attracts many dog walkers, who tend to flush the more wary birds off the western lake. Morning visits are therefore advisable. However, this is an extensive area, and quiet areas can always be found to watch birds in scrub, woodland or reedbeds or on the mudflats at Randell's Sluice.

Access
From Moore village take Moore Lane in a northwesterly direction, signposted to various haulage firms. At the end of this road cross the swing bridge (SJ 578853) over the ship canal into Lapwing Lane, taking the rough track which continues straight ahead, rather than following the surfaced road to the right. After half a kilometre the track widens to form a parking space. From here paths lead westward along the bed of a dry canal, passing a screen from which 'Lapwing Lake' can be viewed, or eastward towards the reedbed pool some 2 kilometres distant. Alternatively from the A56 at Lower Walton follow the main road north across the ship canal, taking the second turning on the left into Taylor Street then first right into Eastford Road. This continues as a track under the railway bridge from where it is a short walk westward to the reedbed pool (SJ 5986).

From Lapwing Lane footpaths lead westward past the arable fields of reclaimed Norton Marsh and along a rough track parallel to the Ship Canal. After 1.5–2 km the mudbanks of the Mersey can be viewed.

Calendar
All year: common waterfowl including Little Grebe; resident woodland species including Willow Tit, woodpeckers.

December–February: Wildfowl include few Gadwall, Teal, Wigeon, Pochard, Tufted Duck. Finch and sparrow flocks in weedy areas. Possibility of Peregrine, Short-eared or Long-eared Owl. Cormorants, Lapwings and Golden Plovers on Mersey, where loafing gulls may include rarer species.

March–May: Sand Martins arrive along ship canal and Mersey, with passage Wheatears on sandy areas; breeding warblers arrive, and passage birds visit the woodlands and scrub.

June–July: Breeding warblers include Reed, Sedge and Grasshopper

Warbler, Whitethroat and Willow Warbler; Little Grebes and other waterfowl with young.

August–November: Wildfowl return, including Shoveler; warblers mingle with tit flocks in scrub. Lapwing flocks build up on the Mersey, where there is a greater likelihood of additional wader species.

61 LOWER WEAVER VALLEY: ACTON BRIDGE TO KINGSLEY

OS Map 117
SJ 57

Habitat

The River Weaver was canalised to facilitate the export of salt from the Cheshire wiches. It is still used on a small scale in association with the chemical industry, and increasingly by pleasure craft. Continuous dredging is necessary to keep the canal open, the silt being pumped into large riverside lagoons to drain. Such sludge tanks at Acton Bridge and Kingsley are both excellent bird habitats, showing quite different stages of vegetational succession. At Acton Bridge recent pumping has left areas of open mud and small pools with low, marshy vegetation, although nettles and coarse grasses are spreading rapidly. At Kingsley, where the lagoon has been unused for some years, a *Phragmites* reedbed has developed with scrubby margins and a sizeable, shallow pool. The Weaver itself is fringed by reeds in places, notably by the side channel to Dutton locks, and there are further reedy cut-off pools between here and Kingsley. The valley bottom is intensively farmed, both for arable and dairying, but there are a number of ancient woods on the steeper valley sides. Warburton's Wood, at Kingsley, is a particularly good example, being a reserve of the Cheshire Wildlife Trust. In May the blossom on the wild cherry trees can be spectacular. Small-leaved lime and wild service tree are present, both being rare in the county, and many unusual fungi appear in autumn.

Species

In winter small numbers of dabbling ducks feed at the sludge beds, but that at Kingsley is shot over on occasions. Reed Buntings pick seeds from flattened grasses at both sites, and Water Rails lurk in the Kingsley reeds. Tree Sparrows and Yellowhammers flock to stubble fields, and may be joined by Corn Buntings. A wintering Green Sandpiper may feed at Acton Bridge, or rise unexpectedly from the side of the Weaver. Snipe are regular in damp ground, along with a Jack Snipe or two. From mid afternoon parties of gulls call in at Acton Bridge to bathe on their way to roost around the Mersey estuary. April brings passage migrants to the valley. At Acton Bridge White and Yellow Wagtail dart around the pools. Whitethroats dance over the banks and Lesser Whitethroat rattle from cover. Depending on the state of the tanks, Sedge Warblers may settle, and Reed Warblers sing from the Dutton reeds. Common Sandpipers flicker along the river, and may hop over the bank onto the sludge bed perhaps to join a Green Sandpiper or two. In May, wader passage increases, provided that recent pumping has left an expanse of open mud. Dunlin are more likely and parties of arctic Ringed Plover drop in. Other species, such as Greenshank, may call in. Cuckoos may occur in small migrant parties, calling noisily from the telephone wires above the riverbank, and gliding down to snap up caterpillars.

Meanwhile at Kingsley, Reed and Sedge Warblers have taken up territories in the reedbed, and a Grasshopper Warbler or two may sing from bramble patches. Cuckoos often enter the reeds and may lay in Reed Warbler nests—unusual behaviour in the region. Towards dusk a Water Rail may start its eerie calling. Various scrubland birds breeds around the lagoon. On the open water look for broods of Mallard, Coot, Little Grebe and other waterfowl.

Great and Lesser Spotted Woodpeckers are resident in the woodlands, along with other typical woodland species. Marsh Tits remain numerous along the Weaver valley.

Autumn brings Shoveler, Teal and perhaps a Garganey to the sludge beds. Green Sandpipers are of regular occurrence, and a few other waders visit. Small passerines feed in the muddy tanks following pumping, especially pipits, wagtails and Reed Buntings. Stock Doves join Yellowhammers in stubble fields.

Timing

Early morning visits are likely to be most productive at Acton Bridge, but any time of day will do, provided that recent pumping has left muddy pools to attract wildfowl and waders. Unless shooting is taking place, the Kingsley lagoons are less prone to disturbance.

Access

For Kingsley lagoon, head east from Kingsley village (southeast of Frodsham) along the B5153, turning left into Ball Lane after 0.5 km. There is space to park at the right-angled bend where the track to Hall o'th' Hey farm branches off to the north (SJ 557758). Walk up to the farm and a cart track continues down to the river. At the riverbank turn

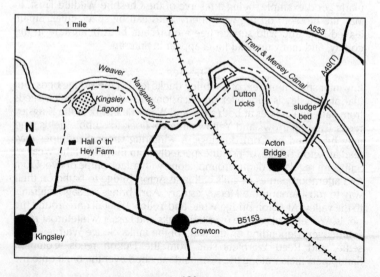

right for the lagoon, which may be viewed by climbing the bank, or turn left to follow the bottom of Warburton's Wood. Members of the Cheshire Wildlife Trust can obtain further access to the wood.

From Kingsley it is possible to walk through to Acton Bridge, following the riverbank for much of the way. Alternatively park on the side road off the A49 beside the Weaver swing bridge (SJ 601761). A private road and public path follow the Weaver westward past the lagoon, which again may be viewed over the fence by climbing the bank. Be careful when first topping the bank, or birds may be flushed by your sudden appearance. Continue along the riverside to the Dutton locks. Here a path skirts the reedbed. Cross the river and continue downstream for further reedy pools.

Calendar

All year: Marsh Tit, woodpeckers, Stock Dove, Corn Bunting and Tree Sparrow.

December–February: Small numbers of waterfowl, Green Sandpiper, Water Rail, Reed Bunting.

March–May: Waders such as Ringed Plover, Little Ringed Plover, Green Sandpiper, Common Sandpiper, Dunlin may occur at Acton Bridge when the tank is wet. Warblers here and at Kingsley include Reed, Sedge and Grasshopper. Cuckoo often conspicuous.

June-July: A quiet time, but waterbirds have young, and families of Marsh Tits may be seen in the woodlands. Wader passage resumes in July.

August–November: Wader passage continues. Dabbling ducks gather in eclipse plumage. Stock Doves, buntings and other seed-eaters in stubble fields or weedy tanks.

62 FRODSHAM MARSH AND THE WEAVER BEND

OS Map 117
SJ 47, 57

Habitat

The Mersey estuary supports wildfowl and wader populations of international importance but, unfortunately, is for the most part inaccessible to the casual birdwatcher. However, the Frodsham Marshes, a stretch of flat grazing marsh between the M56 motorway and Manchester Ship Canal, together with the 'estuary' of the river Weaver which flows into the canal, provide opportunities to see most if not all the estuarine species, and others too.

Frodsham Score lies to the north of the Ship Canal and consists of an area of closely-cropped turf bordering the tidal mudflats of the Mersey. The estuary is severely polluted by the various chemical works in the vicinity. Nevertheless, considerable numbers of Shelduck and waders feed out on the mud.

Much of Frodsham Marsh is taken up by huge sludge tanks into which dredgings from the Ship Canal are pumped to drain. Ultimately the tanks revert to pasture, but while still wet they may form habitats of outstanding value for wildfowl and waders. The new No.6 tank contains drowned hedgerows and stands of *Phragmites* reed which have grown out from the drainage ditches of the embanked, former farmland. Bulldozing during construction work on the retaining banks of the tanks often results in a good crop of weed-seed on the disturbed ground. Established banks develop a cover of scrub and rough grassland.

The low-lying fields on the remainder of the marsh are bordered by tall berry-bearing thorn hedges and drained by deep ditches which contain stands of reed. Some fields are devoted to cereal crops, the resultant stubble providing winter feeding for many birds.

The Weaver Bend consists of a meander of the river Weaver extending to some 2 miles (3.2 km) between the motorway bridge and the Ship Canal, where it overflows into the estuary through the Weaver Sluice. The Bend contains extensive mudbanks which are exposed at low tide, depending on the operation of locks and sluices on the canal. These banks, and the riversides which are lined with marsh vegetation in places, attract wildfowl and waders.

Species

In winter a wide range of wildfowl visit the Bend. Tufted Duck and Pochard feed near the junction with the Ship Canal and may be joined by a few Scaup, often brown immature birds. Goldeneye are often present in small numbers and one or two 'redhead' Smew are infrequent visitors. Ruddy Duck arrive in severe weather when the flow of the river keeps the Bend open after meres have frozen. Cormorants and Great Crested Grebes are also more likely to appear under such conditions. Scarcer diving ducks, such as Long-tailed and the American Ring-necked, have been recorded. Numbers of surface-feeding ducks fluctuate wildly, not least owing to the early morning visits of wildfowlers. The vast flocks on the Mersey form an enormous reservoir from which birds move into the Weaver. To give some idea of the potential involved, the following figures are the highest species totals on the Mersey Marshes from monthly counts in 1994: Shelduck—4,584; Wigeon—17,650; Teal—12,098; Mallard—1,149; and Pintail—1,636. Much higher numbers are noted in more severe winters. Some of these birds are occasionally seen on the Score, and up to several hundred Teal and a smaller number of Wigeon often visit the Bend. Pintail have been infrequent visitors in recent winters. A flock of Canada Geese has taken up residence. Bewick's and more rarely Whooper Swans are infrequent visitors. Small flocks of grey geese, usually either Pink-footed or White-fronted, occasionally alight on the marsh.

Many other birds inhabit the fields. Up to 1,000 or more Golden Plover roost on the sludge tanks and feed on the fields or Score along with 2–3,000 Lapwing. Several times a day the alarm calls of Lapwing and the excited whistling of Golden Plover signal the approach of a predator. The whole flock rises with a rush of wings which must prove bewildering for the incoming Peregrine, often an inexperienced immature bird, or smaller Merlin, for which these heavy plovers are outside the normal range of prey species. Other waders attach themselves to the plover flocks: Snipe, Redshank and Dunlin, perhaps a Ruff or two, or even a Black-tailed Godwit.

Such waders, and in some winters a few Little Stint, may also be seen on the Weaver Bend. Two hundred or more Snipe and even larger numbers of Dunlin may feed here. The highest tides may flush several thousand Dunlin and other waders off the Mersey to roost on the sludge tanks. Short-eared Owls quarter the embankments on the lookout for small mammals and birds. A few of these pale, long-winged owls hunt here each winter. In good vole years there may be a dozen or more. Hen Harriers are occasional visitors. Stubble fields attract flocks of Woodpigeon, Stock Dove and finches including dozens or hundreds of Chaffinch, Brambling and Greenfinch, with smaller numbers of Linnets and possibly a few Twite. In snowy weather hundreds of Skylarks from further inland gather on the stubbles. Cold weather may drive in thousands of Fieldfares and other thrushes which strip any remaining berries off the tall thorn hedges before being forced to feed on the ground. Coveys of Grey Partridge inhabit most fields. They are as common here as anywhere in the region south of the Mersey and partridge shoots are held in most winters. A few Red-legged Partridge or hybrids are also seen. Many of the winter flocks remain intact during March before dispersing as spring approaches. Golden Plovers may still be present in late April, by now showing the extensive black on the underparts which characterises the northern race. Spring arrives late in high latitudes, so these birds time their departure accordingly. Many Woodpigeons nest late, so there may still be 1,000 or more on the Marsh in early May.

Garganey are recorded in most springs, occasionally in March but more likely in April or May. Oystercatcher, Ringed and Little Ringed Plovers all breed locally in small numbers, and by April they are back in territory. Common Sandpipers pipe as they fly beneath the riverbanks, and other passage waders such as Ruff and Greenshank may occur. Sanderling and northern Ringed Plover move through in May and early June, when there is more chance of a Curlew Sandpiper or perhaps a Temminck's Stint. Other rare waders at this season have included Dotterel, Collared Pratincole, Red-necked Phalarope, Broad-billed and Stilt Sandpiper. The flooded, reedy ditches and tanks have attracted such southern, marshland rarities as Spoonbill, Little Egret, Marsh and Montagu's Harrier and Black-necked Stilt. Common, Arctic and Black Terns may pass along the Weaver, sometimes flying straight on upstream without stopping. Passerine migrants include Wheatear and Reed Bunting in late March, joined by Yellow Wagtail and perhaps a Rock or Water Pipit in April. Goldfinch and Linnet move through in parties, and may fall victim to a lingering Merlin. Short-eared Owl usually remain into April. Reed Warbler appear in stands of *Phragmites* and Sedge Warbler chatter along the ditches. The thin reeling song of the Grasshopper Warbler emanates from bramble clumps on the sides of the tanks, where Whinchats formerly nested—the species is now an uncommon passage migrant. A small nesting population of Meadow Pipits shares the same embankments.

By July return passage is already underway. Often a single adult Little Stint or brick-red Curlew Sandpiper portends the main passage which is due to follow a month later. These are birds which may have lost their eggs or perhaps not bred at all, hence their early arrival. 'Dusky' Spotted Redshank may even appear in late June, with Greenshank and Ruff almost certain to be seen at some time in July. Redshank and Dunlin increase, and Curlew start to build up on the fields where they probe with their long bills for earthworms. Swifts gather in hundreds over the Bend and Grey Herons roost on fields nearby.

Wader passage picks up during August and September. Several hundred Dunlin are often present and high tides may force other species off the Mersey estuary to roost on the sludge tanks. A thousand or more Ringed Plover may appear there with Knot more likely from September, and a few Sanderling or Turnstone in either month. On the Bend a few Curlew Sandpipers in August may increase to dozens in September, although in some years almost none are seen. Redshanks similarly increase into the hundreds. Ruffs find the river to their liking and up to 50 may be present. Black-tailed Godwit are also frequent if erratic in their occurrences. Little Stints are usually late in passing through. Small numbers in August may increase to 50 or more in September and October, with a few remaining later. One hundred and sixty were counted in September 1993.

Green Sandpipers tend to stay further up the Weaver towards the motorway bridge, where Snipe become more numerous in late autumn, by which time the plover flocks have returned to the fields and several hundred Curlew may be present. In addition to species mentioned above, most waders that occur regularly in Britain are noted from time to time. Frodsham offers a better chance of seeing truly rare waders than anywhere else in the region. These have included Buff-breasted, White-rumped, Pectoral, Baird's, Sharp-tailed and Stilt Sandpipers, Wilson's and Red-necked Phalaropes amongst others. In August 1990 a Long-billed Dowitcher arrived in breeding plumage.

By August increasing numbers of ducks feed on the marsh: Teal, Wigeon and Shoveler in drab, eclipse plumages. Small numbers of Garganey often consort with the much more numerous Teal. Little Grebes feed on small fish which they pursue beneath the algal blanket on the Weaver or flooded tanks. Terns pass through in autumn as well as spring. Black Tern and Little Gull are now more likely to linger for a few days, picking flies off the water. White-winged Black Tern have occurred several times. Swarms of House Martin gather over the river before leaving for the south, and hundreds or even thousands of Swallows roost with Sand Martin by night in reedbeds by the Ship Canal and elsewhere. A Hobby or two now appear annually, scything in at dusk and perhaps at dawn also to cut down hirundines. Another rarity that turns up with some regularity is the Spotted Crake, a short-billed relative of the rather more numerous Water Rail. During August and early September parties of Yellow Wagtail feed in damp fields, and loose groups of Sedge Warblers, up to 20 strong, move through the reedy ditches. Goldfinch and Linnet form noisy flocks, including many young birds, to feed on the ripening seed of thistles and ragworts. Many of these birds have moved on by October when Rock or scarcer Water Pipit appear briefly beside the Weaver. On overcast days with an easterly breeze southward passage of pipits and Skylark may be heavy, and small parties alight to feed beside the tanks. Reed Bunting may also be prevalent at such times.

Timing

Dawn or dusk visits may coincide with wildfowlers' activities. Otherwise there are good birds to be seen at almost any time, and plenty of habitat to cover apart from the Bend itself and the No. 6 sludge tank. The highest tides are likely to flush waders off the Mersey, and at such times the sludge beds should be checked carefully. Consult tide tables for the predicted height of tides. In severe weather wildfowl may concentrate on the river which remains unfrozen. Thrushes and larks also gather, having been driven west by snow.

Access

Leave the M56 at Junction 12 and follow signs into Frodsham. After passing beneath a footbridge the road descends towards a set of traffic lights. To reach the Weaver Bend, turn right shortly before the lights into Ship Street and follow this lane round until a bridge over the motorway is seen on the left (SJ 520785). Turn left, pass over the bridge, and continue along the unmade road until a gate bars the way. A footpath continues from here up to the Bend. Once the motorway is crossed, the roads on the marsh are private, and while many visitors drive as close to the Bend as practicable, this is a potential cause of friction with landowners and tenants, so is left to the conscience of the individual. For the main marsh and sludge tanks, continue through the lights in Frodsham and pass along the main shopping street before turning right down Marsh Lane. This lane passes over the motorway where, now a private road, it forks (SJ 512779). Take the right-hand fork to reach the Bend. This track runs alongside then climbs the bank of No. 5 tank. From here the path to the Bend is obvious. The left-hand fork leads along the southern side of the embankment of No. 5 Bed, but a fork which climbs the bank to the right skirts the newer No. 6 tank. This is a single-track road with passing places. Take care not to cause obstructions.

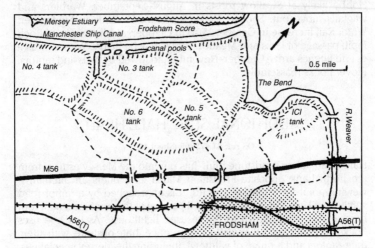

Calendar

All year: Lapwing, Redshank and Dunlin at almost any time; Grey Partridge; Peregrine; Little Grebe, Canada Goose and Shelduck usually present.

December–February: Wigeon, Teal and perhaps Pintail; Pochard, Tufted Duck and Goldeneye, perhaps Smew and Scaup; Ruddy Duck and scarcer waterfowl in frosty weather; wild geese and swans may visit.

Peregrine, Merlin and Short-eared Owl hunt the marshes, with perhaps a Hen Harrier or Long-eared Owl. Flocks of Lapwing and Golden Plover often joined by Ruff, Black-tailed Godwit or other waders; Snipe and Curlew on damper ground. Stubble fields hold large numbers of pigeons, finches and, after snow, Skylark, Fieldfare and Redwing in fields and hedgerows. Water Rails in reedbeds.

March–May: Winter flocks disperse and raptors move back to breeding haunts in March and April, when Wheatear, pipits, wagtails and Reed Bunting appear, with other incoming migrants. Northern Golden Plover remain into May in breeding plumage. Breeding Ringed and Little Ringed Plovers arrive. Passage waders include more Ringed Plover, Sanderling, Common Sandpiper, Ruff, perhaps Greenshank and others. Terns move through quickly. Garganey likely from March onward.

June–July: Meadow Pipit and Grasshopper Warbler around tanks; Sedge and Reed Warblers in reeds. Large feeding concentrations of Swift over river. Return wader passage begins in July: Curlew Sandpiper, Spotted Redshank, Greenshank, Ruff. Dunlin, Redshank and Curlew increase. Diurnal roost of Grey Herons.

August–November: Wader passage most marked August to early October, with Dunlin, Ruff, Redshank, Black-tailed Godwit, Curlew Sandpiper, Little Stint, occasional Turnstone, Sanderling or rarer species. Estuarine waders such as Ringed Plover, Knot on tanks at high tides. Garganey regular amongst Teal and other ducks during August and September. Black and other terns pass through, perhaps Little Gull. Hobby likely at Swallow roosts in August–September. Warblers and wagtails move out. Spotted Crake may lurk in reeds in September; Water Rail increase in October. Also in October, small passage of Rock Pipit; passage of larks and Meadow Pipits may be heavy. Winter thrushes and finches arrive October–November, followed by owls and raptors. Plover flocks reassemble.

ADDITIONAL SITE: HALE HEAD

OS ref: SJ 473809 (Sheet 108)

Hale Head, a low sandstone bluff, juts out into the Mersey estuary from the north bank opposite Frodsham Marsh, and offers an alternative viewing point for estuarine species. It is approached by a minor road south from Hale Village, with limited parking at the southern end. From here a track leads down to the disused lighthouse. As the tide rises flocks of Dunlin and other waders may concentrate offshore, with attendant raptors and a range of wildfowl, including the Mersey specialities, Teal, Wigeon and Pintail. Corn Bunting and Yellow Wagtail breed in the arable fields. Footpaths follow the shoreline to east and west. Pickerings Pasture, 2.5 kilometres to the east, is a reclaimed rubbish tip, landscaped to attract wildlife, and boasting a wader scrape. To the west of Hale Head, Oglet Shore provides further viewing of estuary birds. More direct access is available down Dungeon Lane which skirts Speke airfield.

63 DELAMERE FOREST

Habitat

Delamere Forest derives its name from the medieval hunting forest of Mara, this definition being legal rather than physical. Indeed until recently the character of the forest was one of dry heathland on sandy soils with boggy, sphagnum-filled hollows and odd stands of pine trees. Now much of the area has been ploughed for arable farming, and almost all the heathland has been lost under conifers. Abbots Moss is a floating bog—a mat of sphagnum moss floating over several metres of liquid peat and water. It is noted for its bog plants, such as cranberry and bog rosemary, and for dragonflies, notably the white-faced dragonfly and downy emerald. Green hairstreak butterflies and orange underwing moths flutter around the birch trees, grass snakes and lizards are sometimes seen. The various sand quarries in the area are of some ornithological importance, and not only for aquatic and waterside species. Bulldozing of topsoil and 'overburden' allows the germination of arable weeds whose seeds attract finches and doves. These pits are worked 'wet', that is they are allowed to flood while still operational and sand is pumped out through hoses. Silt draining back in from the stock-piles forms shallow beaches which attract gulls and waders and which eventually develop a covering of reedmace.

Species

The mature plantations support rather few species of birds. Crossbills are seen annually and breed in some years, but flocks of any size are unusual. Siskins may breed in very small numbers but proof is seldom forthcoming. They are far more numerous in winter and especially in spring. The high-pitched squeaks of Goldcrests and Coal Tits, feeding in the tops of conifers, can be heard at all seasons. Wrens nest amongst the ferns beneath the pines, where Chaffinch and Treecreeper sing, in summer they are joined by Blackcap, Chiffchaff and Spotted Flycatcher. A few pairs of Sparrowhawk are also present, and Kestrel hunt the cleared areas. Tawny Owl are common, but the smaller Long-eared Owl has become rare and elusive, it should be sought in winter, roosting in willow scrub. Nightjar formerly bred in some numbers but there are no recent records, although much habitat remains suitable. In some springs Brambling extract seeds from ripening cones in the flat crowns of pines. Green Woodpecker seek out ants in open, sandy areas, and bound away when disturbed on whirring wings, their yellow rumps flashing. In June the noisy young of this species or the Great Spotted Woodpecker may be heard shouting for food from a nest in a shattered conifer or bogside alder. Willow Tits frequent these same alders and birches, and wander into the plantations to feed, as do numerous Nuthatch which nest in roadside oaks and chestnuts. Other birds which favour broadleaved trees around the edges of the conifers are Wood Warbler, Pied Flycatcher and Redstart—all present in very small numbers.

Recent plantations, with trees between six and twelve feet (2–4 m) tall, are quiet in winter but alive with nesting passerines in summer. Tree Pipits have become scarce recently, but a few sing from the tops of isolated birches or in parachuting display flight, and Whitethroats warble scratchy phrases during their briefer, low-level display. The fluty cadences of Willow Warblers mingle with the ringing songs of Yellowhammers and the stammer of Reed Buntings, here nesting in unusually dry habitat. Redpoll and Linnet fly out into surrounding fields in small groups to feed, while Dunnock and Long-tailed Tit are much less conspicuous. Toward dusk a Grasshopper Warbler may sing. Garden Warbler and Bullfinch favour taller, denser stands until such time as the foresters remove the lower branches from the trees.

Seed-eating species attracted to weedy, disturbed ground beside operational sand quarries include Turtle Dove and more numerous Stock Doves. Corn Buntings nest in cornfields in the area and also visit the quarries which now offer a richer supply of seed than do sprayed croplands. The largest colonies of Sand Martins in Cheshire are established in recently exposed sand faces. The most conspicuous feature of the quarries is the diurnal gathering of gulls from late summer until spring. Lesser Black-backed Gulls often exceed 1,000 in the autumn, and Common Gulls are even more numerous in winter. Late on winter afternoons large flocks of gulls of all common species gather to drink and bathe before moving out to their roosts by the estuaries.

In spring pairs of Black-headed Gulls take up territory by quarry lakes and may display, and would probably nest if rafts or islets were provided. The Common Terns which appear from time to time in summer might also be encouraged to breed. A few waders occur on passage. Common Sandpiper and Dunlin are the most frequent species in both spring and autumn, with perhaps a Greenshank or Green Sandpiper at the latter season. Whimbrel pass through the area each May and sometimes alight in fields. With luck a small flock may be seen flying low to northward uttering their tittering, multiple whistle, or even pausing to deliver the full, bubbling song. Little Ringed Plovers have bred on the sandy beaches and in winter a few Snipe and Jack Snipe crouch amongst stands of reedmace. Little and Great Crested Grebe nest on the flooded quarries, and Black-necked Grebes have been seen. Shelduck display in April, but only Mallard, Tufted and Ruddy Ducks nest with any regularity. Up to 20 or 30 each of Pochard and Tufted Duck occur in winter, when up to a dozen Goldeneye and a few Teal are usually present.

Timing

That part of the forest closest to Delamere station attracts large numbers of day-trippers, especially on sunny days, but there are always more remote areas relatively free from disturbance. Morning or evening visits in spring are best for birdsong. Dusk visits in summer might reveal some of those nocturnal species of which little is now known in Delamere. Evening visits to the sand quarries in winter may result in a sighting of an unusual gull attending the pre-roost gathering.

Access

The forest area straddles the A54 Chester to Winsford and A49 Warrington to Whitchurch roads. Access to the plantations is generally unrestricted along Forestry Commission rides. Some of the better sites are listed below.

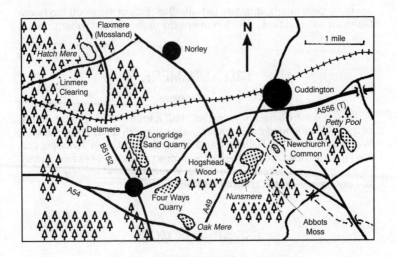

63A DELAMERE SWITCHBACK

Take the B5152 Frodsham road northward from the A556. Pass over the railway bridge and continue for almost a mile (1.5 km) before turning left onto a minor road just before Hatchmere (SJ 552713). Tracks lead north and south from this road into the plantations. Explore this area for woodland birds: Nuthatch, Treecreeper, Green Woodpecker; Siskin in winter and spring, possibly summer; perhaps Crossbill; Redstart, Wood Warbler and Pied Flycatcher. A large peaty area at Blakemere to south of this road has recently been cleared of trees. It is proposed to block drains and allow wet heathland to develop. This should attract uncommon bird species; in time it is hoped that Nightjars may return to the area.

63B FOURWAYS SAND QUARRY

OS ref: SJ 574688

Visible only with difficulty from the A556 half a mile (0.8 km) to the east of B5152 Delamere junction (parking difficult). Tufted Duck and few other wildfowl; Little Ringed Plover and occasional passage waders; large numbers of Common and Lesser Black-backed Gulls; Turtle Dove in summer and Stock Dove all year. Sand Martins nest in banks.

63C HOGSHEAD WOOD

OS ref: SJ 583690

An area of young plantations lying to the west of the A49 opposite Nunsmere. This area tends to be less disturbed than other parts of the forest, and supports good numbers of scrubland species. Bulldozed areas are particularly attractive to butterflies. Part of the wood has been taken for a new quarry, which remains dry at the time of writing.

63D NUNSMERE

OS ref: SJ 590690

A disused quarry adjacent to the A49 half a mile (0.8 km) to the south of the A556 crossroads, with banks overgrown with birch scrub. Garden Warbler, Willow Tit, Bullfinch and Redpoll nest; Green Woodpecker feed in more open areas. Breeding waterfowl include grebes and Tufted Duck despite occasional water-skiing. Winter wildfowl are few in number but have included Long-tailed Duck.

63E ABBOTS MOSS

OS ref: SJ 587685

A forestry track runs eastward from the A49 immediately to the south of Nunsmere. Walk down this, turning left at the end then bear right where a striped pole bars the road. This ride leads between two floating bogs ringed with alder and birch trees, and through conifer plantations. Green Woodpecker, Willow Tit and Tree Pipit nest, with Redstart in some years. Crossbill, Siskin and Sparrowhawk possible at any time of year. Hobby and Goshawk have been seen.

63F PETTY POOL AND PETTYPOOL WOOD

OS ref: SJ 618701

Travel east along the A556 from A49 crossroads and turn right very shortly at another set of lights. After 1.25 miles (2 km), at the end of a line of large houses, a footpath leads into the plantations. Parking is not possible immediately by this entrance, so it will be necessary to park elsewhere and walk back. Rides lead through the plantation to the pool. Breeding waterfowl include Ruddy Duck. Siskin are plentiful in spring; plantation species and few Wood Warbler appear in summer. Rhododendrons by pool hold roosting finches, often including Brambling in winter. Polecats are present in the vicinity.

63G NEWCHURCH COMMON

OS ref: SJ 600688

Continue south along the minor road past Pettypool Wood and take the first right, signposted to Nova Scotia. Turn right at the end and park at the quarry entrance. A bridle-path runs between the two quarries, which are now largely hidden by surrounding trees and scrub which contain nesting Linnets and Yellowhammers. These pools are favoured by Goldeneye, Tufted Duck and Pochard with a few Teal in winter, when Jack Snipe may occur in the reedmace. Large numbers of gulls may be present in winter. Scaup and Common Scoter have occurred. Stubble fields in the vicinity often hold finch flocks. Green Woodpeckers often feed in areas of short grass.

The Whitegate Way, which passes the southern end of the smaller pool, should be followed westward from Newchurch Common to view the Gull Pool, now devoid of nesting gulls, but supporting breeding Little Grebe, Tufted and Ruddy Ducks and rare dragonflies. From here it is possible to follow paths through to Abbots Moss and Nunsmere.

Calendar

All year: Sparrowhawk and Kestrel by day, Tawny and possibly Long-eared Owls by night. Woodland species include Green and Great Spotted Woodpeckers, Nuthatch, Treecreeper, Long-tailed and Willow Tits. Coal Tit and Goldcrest plentiful. Redpoll and often Bullfinch in birches, Crossbill and perhaps Siskin in pines. Stock Dove and Corn Bunting in arable areas. Little Grebe and Tufted Duck on quarries and pools.

December–February: Teal, Pochard and Goldeneye; Snipe and Jack Snipe by quarries. Common Gull abundant. Brambling may feed under beeches.

March–May: Shelduck visit; Ruddy Duck move onto breeding pools. Brambling and plentiful Siskin in mature conifers. Crossbills may have young. Breeding species, including warblers, move into young plantations.

June–July: Grebes, Tufted and Ruddy Ducks may have young. Little Ringed Plover and Sand Martin in quarries. Black-headed Gull may summer and Common Tern appear at times. Turtle Doves feed along weedy banks. Young plantations hold Whitethroat, possibly Grasshopper Warbler, Linnet, Redpoll, Reed Bunting and Yellowhammer. Nightjar formerly bred and might still occur. Crossbill may be augmented by irrupting flocks from further north. Tree Pipit, Redstart, Pied Flycatcher and Wood Warbler locally.

August–November: Summer visitors depart and plantations become quiet. Occasional waders may drop in by quarries where Lesser Black-backed Gull gather in their hundreds.

Habitat

The Peckforton Hills form a ridge of sandstone standing isolated in the middle of the Cheshire Plain, with Beeston Castle surmounting a solitary hill to the north. The tops of the hills are heathy, but most of the summit of Peckforton Hill has been planted with conifers. There are, however, considerable tracts of oak woodland on the steeper slopes, and birch and bracken are spreading extensively across remaining open areas. Cattle have been allowed to browse on Bickerton Hill to stem the loss of heathland to scrub. Bulkeley Hill has numbers of old chestnut and oak trees, but is largely covered by birch woodland. Climbing corydalis is a characteristic plant of the woodlands, with cow-wheat locally plentiful. In summer purple hairstreak butterflies dart around the sunlit crowns of oak trees. Bickerton Hill, and the Larkton Hill property of the National Trust, lie at the south end of the ridge. It is capped by probably the best remaining heathland area in Cheshire. In late summer oak eggar moths fly over the heath, where bilberries fruit in profusion. The deep purple flowers of bell heather, pinker bells of cross-leaved heath, growing in the damper areas, and later flowers of heather attract bees and butterflies to this rich source of nectar. At the highest point of the hill are the Iron Age ramparts of Maiden Castle, now largely overrun by bracken.

Species

The tracts of older oak woodland are particularly rich in woodland species, with a notable concentration of Pied Flycatchers, especially in the Burwardsley woods. Wood Warbler, Marsh Tit and a few Redstart are also present, and all three species of woodpecker breed. Pied Flycatcher and Wood Warbler may also be seen within the grounds of Beeston Castle, along with other more common woodland species. The castle is infiltrated by early Chiffchaffs each March, and the hills in general, as a focus for migrants, would repay much closer attention than they have received to date. Warblers are often attached to mixed flocks of tits in autumn, but

Pied Flycatcher

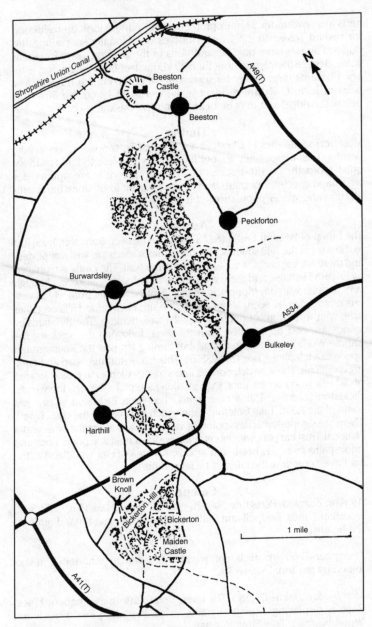

viewing can be difficult in the dense Birch scrub. Siskins have nested in the conifers along the ridge and Crossbills visit. Bramblings sometimes work opening Pine cones during their northward passage in April and May. Bickerton Hill in particular supports a few pairs of Tree Pipit, and Meadow Pipits have also nested recently. Nightjars continue to be reported on passage in May or June, and much habitat remains suitable for this species.

The isolated nature of the hills attracts migrant raptors. Peregrine and Raven both nest, Peregrines having nested here in medieval times. The nests are now under 24-hour protection. A Red Kite took up residence for several weeks in 1994 and Hobbies occasionally soar along the ridges. Fulmars have paid several visits to the Beeston crags in recent years, despite their lying more than 20 kilometres from the nearest estuary. Buzzards can usually be seen somewhere along the ridge. A few pairs of Little Owls are resident in hedgerow Oaks on the farmland below the ridge, and may be heard yelping at dusk.

Timing

Most accessible sites in Cheshire are invaded by trippers at weekends, Beeston Castle especially so, but it is usually possible to find relatively quiet footpaths on the Peckforton Hills. Spring visits are optimal for woodland species, but there is exploratory work to be done here, with autumn and winter populations still poorly known.

Access

The hump of Beeston Castle (SJ 537593) can be seen from afar, lying just to the west of the A49 south of Tarporley. Minor roads are well signposted, and there are car parks at the foot of the outer wall. The castle is managed by English Heritage, and there is an admission charge. The keep, although very popular with day-trippers, is an excellent view point from which various raptors can be seen. Minor roads skirt the Peckforton Hills on either side, with a network of public footpaths well marked. The Burwardsley woods are best approached from the west, following the signs for the Candle Workshops into the village, but turning left past the Pheasant Inn opposite a telephone box (SJ 523565). This is a no-through road and parking is difficult. The lane deteriorates into a track which soon passes an area of old oak wood on the right. Explore along footpaths through the woods. Bickerton (Larkton) Hill is best approached from Bickerton village, just south of the A534. Take Goldford Lane which runs beside the churchyard. There are signposted access points at various points along the lane, and a National Trust car park with its entrance beside a roadside pond. Foot- and bridle-paths cross the heath and woods. An area of oak woodland at the southwest corner of the hill may be rewarding.

Calendar

All year: Buzzard, Peregrine, Raven, woodpeckers, Marsh Tit, Goldcrest, woodland birds. Redpoll and Bullfinch among other scrubland birds on the heaths.

December–February: Resident woodland birds in wandering flocks joined by territorial Marsh Tit.

March–May: Siskin flocks in Larches, Bramblings may frequent Pines. Raptors displaying. Spring migrants arrive, including Pied Flycatcher, Wood Warbler, Tree Pipit, Redstart.

June–July: Breeding species less conspicuous by July, being busy feeding young. Many birds, including Stock Doves, feed on bilberries at Bickerton, where with luck Nightjar may be heard churring at night.

August–November: Woodland quiet, migrant warblers join Tit flocks. Hobby more likely to appear.

65 THE RIVER DEE

Habitat

The meandering River Dee forms the Welsh boundary from the south-western corner of Cheshire at Shocklach northward to Aldford where the boundary swings westward around Eaton Park. The river is over-hung by Willows, but sandy banks are exposed on the inside of bends and it is here that the nymphs of club-tailed dragonflies crawl from the water to begin their aerial life. Banded demoiselle damselflies may be very abundant around riverside herbage in summer. Otters have been seen in recent years. The river is prone to flooding following prolonged rain or rapid snow melt from the Welsh hills during the winter months, and then flooded arable land and pasture attracts wildfowl inland from the estuary. Hybrid lime, hybrid poplar and other trees beside the lake in Eaton Park support a wild population of regionally rare mistletoe, curiously so since the park is a noted haunt of Mandarin Duck, an oriental symbol of fidelity. Small-leaved lime trees, a rarity in Cheshire, are present on the river banks between the Iron Bridge and Eccleston. The village of Eccleston lies on the west bank of the river Dee. It is characterised by lichen-rich sandstone walls and a mixture of mature evergreen and broadleaved trees. Hawfinches frequent the village, moving both southward into Eaton Park and northward into the outskirts of suburban Chester.

Species

The mature timber of Eaton Park houses many hole-nesting birds: Stock Dove, Jackdaw and Little Owl at the larger end of the scale, Nuthatch, Marsh Tit and Tree Sparrow at the smaller end. A few pairs of Redstart still nest in old ash trees in the southern part of the valley. Of special interest are the few pairs of Mandarin which also nest in hollow trees. Feral Greylag Geese are frequent visitors to Cheshire, but the flocks are very mobile, wandering into Wales as well as further east across the county. Good numbers often consort with Canada Geese beside the park lake, but the latter species continues to flourish, nesting even beside small field ponds, and has displaced the Greylag as a breeding species.

From autumn until early spring, the lakeside trees at Eaton hold one of the county's main inland Cormorant roosts, with several dozen birds regularly present. A smaller roost is established in riverside trees near Churton. Towards spring some birds show characteristics of the continental race—the origin of inland Cormorant continues to arouse speculation. Many Cormorants fly out to the Dee estuary to feed and can be seen commuting over Chester, where tamer birds fish on the weir and are blamed for the decline of Salmon in the river. Other winter waterfowl include small numbers of Goldeneye, parties of Teal and the occasional Goosander. Mandarins may be seen in winter on tree-lined stretches of river, particularly northwards from Farndon. When the river floods following heavy rain or a rapid thaw of snow off the Welsh hills, flocks of up to several hundred Pintail and other ducks fly in from the estuaries to flooded farmland upstream of Farndon or along Aldford Brook.

Mandarin

As the days lengthen, warblers and other migrants appear in riverside trees, and itinerant Common Sandpiper skim low across the river. In the early morning Nuthatch pipe from the tree-tops and woodpeckers drum on hollow branches, the rattle of Lesser Spotteds being in longer bursts than those of the Great. As morning wears on, their display becomes less frequent as do the laughing calls of Green Woodpecker. It is in March and April that Hawfinch may become conspicuous. Listen for their explosive, vaguely Robin-like 'tick' from the tops of trees near the river, or in Eccleston village where birds may be seen in song flight.

There is a large heronry in the secluded woods of Eaton Park, from which birds radiate to feed in marl-pits, by rivers, or beside the salt-marshes of the Dee estuary. Mandarin may be seen with ducklings along quieter reaches of the river. Kingfisher too breed locally and may be seen at any season. From about the middle of June, Hawfinches may bring their offspring to feed in cherry trees near Eccleston Church. By mid-August, when the cherries are finished, the Hawfinches turn to ripening Hawthorn and Yew berries and may be seen around the Overleigh cemetery. Look for the scatter of split haw or yew kernels beneath bushes, even under those at roadsides, but beware the similar but rougher work of grey squirrels.

Careful observation along the banks of the Dee, a large river with north-south orientation, might produce surprises at migration time. Common and Green Sandpipers appear, following the riverbanks, and with the onset of autumn parties of Siskins appear in the alders.

Several pairs of Buzzards are now resident in the area, feeding on a flourishing population of rabbits. Ravens are also seen with increasing frequency, having nested on Chester Town Hall in 1996. A Peregrine is sometimes seen in winter, roosting on electricity pylons.

Timing

Hawfinch are most reliably present in March–April and June–August, but with luck may be encountered at other seasons. The riverbank foot-path at Eccleston attracts its share of visitors, so Mandarin are most like-ly to be seen in the early morning, before disturbance drives them away. This is, however, a pleasant walk at all seasons. The riverside path

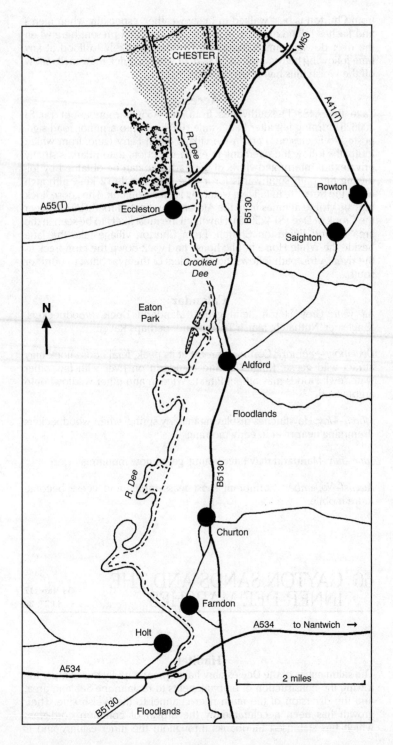

from Churton is best walked in frosty weather, especially when meres and flashes inland are frozen. Mandarins are often present here when the river downstream is disturbed. Farmland is likely to flood at any time following heavy, prolonged rain, or when a quick thaw melts snow off the Welsh hills higher up the catchment.

Access
Take the A483(T) southwards from the A55(T) roundabout (at SJ 390625) turning left after half a mile (0.8 km) onto a minor road signposted to Eccleston. Park in the village or on Ferry Lane, from which footpaths follow the riverbank in either direction. Eaton Park is strictly private, but interrupted views of the park lake can be obtained by following the path southwards for a little over a mile (2 km), although when the trees are in full leaf watching is more difficult. The goose flock may be visible at times from the Aldford/Huntington road (B5130) near the Crook of Dee (SJ 425615). Hawfinch are most likely to be seen in the area around Eccleston Church. From Churton village take the lane beside the White Horse public house and walk down the farm track to the river. A footpath follows the meanders of the river bank to north or south.

Calendar
All year: Grey Heron, feral geese, Mandarin Duck, woodpeckers, Kingfisher, Nuthatch, Marsh Tit, Buzzard; perhaps Raven.

December–February: Cormorant roost at its peak; feral goose flock may attract wild geese. Kingfisher and Mandarin on river with few other waterfowl. Floods may attract Pintail, Wigeon and other wildfowl onto arable land.

March–May: Hawfinches displaying in early spring, when woodpeckers drumming near river in early morning.

June–July: Mandarin may have young; geese now moulting.

August–November: Cormorant roost reassembles and geese become more mobile.

66 GAYTON SANDS AND THE INNER DEE MARSHES

OS Map 117
SJ 27, 28

Habitat
The saltmarshes of the Dee estuary have spread rapidly this century following the construction of embankments to reclaim the Sealand area, and the diversion of the main river channel to the Welsh side. Their growth has been accelerated by the arrival of common cord-grass which has stabilised mudbanks throughout the inner estuary and is

now threatening to cover the beaches at West Kirby and Hoylake in the Dee mouth, despite attempts to curb its spread. Within the saltings tidal creeks and gutters persist, and in places shallow, brackish pools have formed. Upper parts of the marshes are heavily grazed by sheep but elsewhere such saltmarsh plants as sea aster, scurvy-grass and sea purslane flourish. The marshes now extend from beyond the Cheshire border at Burton Point seaward as far as Heswall. Off Denhall Lane at Burton a part of the grazing marsh is managed as a refuge by the Dee Wildfowlers Club. Pools here and below the Decca station towards Neston attract marshland waders. At Neston the character of the marsh changes since it is not grazed, and from here past Parkgate to Gayton it is owned by the RSPB. The reserve extends to 5000 acres (2040 hectares) and includes a small reedbed near to the sewage works at Neston.

The Wirral Way, a disused railway track, runs parallel to the coastline from Neston northwestward. It is lined with scrub and passes through farmland, which includes stubble fields in winter. To the south of the Burton Marshes and separated from the estuary by the Wallasey–Wrexham railway embankment lies an area of flat fields. Formerly saltmarsh, these Shotwick fields now attract plovers and occasionally geese. A reserve has been purchased at Inner Marsh Farm by the RSPB, and excavation of scrapes and pools has attracted many wildfowl, waders and other birds, but it will be some time yet before large-scale visiting will be possible to what seems destined to be an outstanding birdwatching site.

Species

The Dee was once famous for its wild geese, but excessive disturbance early this century drove away the already dwindling remnants of the former flocks. Since the establishment of Gayton Sands RSPB reserve, however, numbers of wildfowl wintering in the estuary have risen markedly. The Pintail is well adapted to the open, estuarine environment, its long neck enabling it to detect approaching predators from considerable distances. Several thousand are present on the edge of the saltmarsh from October until February. Hundreds of Shelduck feed in the channel off Gayton; and hundreds of Mallard and Teal, and thousands of Wigeon frequent the outer edge of the marsh in the same area. Red-breasted Mergansers may be seen way out on the river channel. Teal and Wigeon also feed in the wildfowl refuge off Denhall Lane. In recent winters small parties of Pink-footed and White-fronted Geese have been seen with some regularity on Burton Marsh. Family groups of Bewick's Swan may also take up residence, roosting at Inner Marsh Farm. Whooper Swans are less frequent in occurrence.

Farmland, marshland and estuarine waders meet in the inner Dee in winter. Several hundred Golden Plover and Lapwing may feed on the Shotwick fields or Burton Marsh. Spotted Redshank and Greenshank are occasionally present at the Decca pools or elsewhere, and at high tide estuarine species gather to roost on the marshes. A roost on the pasture at Burton will hold several thousand birds: Oystercatcher, Knot and Dunlin, Curlew and Redshank. The last two species also roost well out on the marsh at Parkgate.

The saltmarsh plants produce vast quantities of seeds which are floated up the various creeks by the tide and deposited in masses along the tideline. This abundance of seed draws vast flocks of finches to the edge of the marsh. Between Parkgate and Gayton the top outer edge of the sandstone seawall is yellow with lichens, encouraged to grow by the droppings of the winter finches. These may include hundreds of Chaffinch and Greenfinch, although these have been less numerous of late. Brambling are erratic in their appearances but may number 1,000 or even 5,000 when other food is scarce. Linnet are most numerous in autumn, but dozens are present in winter. A few Twite winter further out on the marsh, but at times move to the landward edge where their distinctive twanging calls help to separate them from Linnets. Where there are thistles, as in the rougher pastures bordering the marsh, Goldfinches may gather. House and Tree Sparrows also form flocks, and a few Corn Buntings occur. Skylark feed out on the marsh, as do many Reed Buntings, although these birds are less prone to flocking than finches. Lapland Buntings are reported in most winters. Usually these dumpy, short-tailed bunting are seen only in flight when their call, 'ticatic', followed by a whistled 'teu', betrays their presence to those familiar with the species.

Bramblings

Rock Pipits move into the Dee in October, remaining until April. They feed along the gutters and forage amongst the debris at the high-water mark. While counts of 1–200 Rock Pipits are possible, a few Water Pipits may also be seen below the car park at Parkgate and around the Neston reedbed. Towards spring they become greyer above and develop a pink flush on the breast which loses its streaking. In late March and April a few such birds may be seen either at Neston or Burton, frequenting the grazing marsh.

The profusion of birds feeding on the marsh and the mudflats beyond attracts predators, and this is one of the best sites in the region to see raptors. Kestrels hover in search of small mammals, and Sparrowhawks steal in low from the landward side hoping to snatch an unwary finch. One or two Hen Harriers may quarter the marsh systematically, gliding along just above the ground with their wings held in a shallow V. When prey is spotted the wings are folded back abruptly and the hawk drops from sight. A Merlin may sometimes be seen in the air simultaneously, apparently taking advantage of the harrier's flushing of larks or small waders which the falcon then pursues. Peregrines also hunt the area, and can generally be seen during a morning's watch. Another characteristic predator of the marshes from autumn to spring is the Short-eared Owl. Numbers fluctuate in response to vole populations, and in some winters almost none are seen. In a good year, however, ten or more may be present, with several in the air at once. Marauding Ravens, which have infiltrated the area in recent winters from their Welsh mountain strongholds, are now often seen.

One final feature of winter birdwatching, but one that happens infrequently now as the marsh continues to grow and the open water becomes more distant, is the flooding of the marshes by the highest tides. As normally dry parts of the marsh are inundated, small mammals must break cover and swim for higher ground. Shrews, voles, mice and rats all fall victim to the owls and harriers, or to the more numerous gulls, or to the Grey Herons which line the advancing tide. Water Rails too are driven out of the cord-grass, and if the marsh floods completely they fly up onto the seawall and take cover under parked cars, in fields, or in gardens. Not all the rails make it to safety, for some are eaten by Grey Herons. Finches, larks and buntings are also displaced from the marsh and move to coastal fields, as do Snipe and a few short-billed Jack Snipe.

Wheatears appear along the seawall from March when Meadow Pipits pass over in large numbers, and in April White Wagtails may be numerous, although Yellow Wagtails have declined greatly. April and May bring a light passage of marshland waders, some of which have attained smart plumage by the latter month. If a high pressure system becomes established over the continent at this time, southeasterly winds may bring Marsh Harrier in place of the departing Hen Harriers. These migrant birds seldom stay for more than a day or two. A Garganey or two may appear at this season.

A few pairs of Mallard and Shelduck nest on the marshes, and small numbers of Teal, Shoveler and other duck species may spend the summer at Inner Marsh Farm. Redshank and Oystercatcher nest in small numbers, while several hundred pairs of Black-headed Gulls inhabit Inner Marsh Farm. Common Terns nest just over the border in Clwyd and often fish in the Dee or the pools on the marsh. The reedbed at Neston holds breeding Reed and Sedge Warblers, with further pairs of the latter species and a few Grasshopper Warblers in scrub elsewhere along the edges of the marsh. Stonechats increase in numbers given mild winters and may then nest along the landward edge of the marsh. Reed Bunting and Skylark nest commonly. Quails have been heard in most recent summers uttering their trisyllabic call from the marsh or nearby cornfields, and there is a history of evening sightings of Hobby in the area.

Marshland waders are rather more conspicuous on spring passage than in winter, but much larger numbers may occur in autumn. Maximum counts of Greenshank roosting off Parkgate or at Inner Marsh Farm at this season have varied between 30 and 70 and up to a dozen or so Spotted Redshank may be seen—in the 1970s counts in excess of 100 off Burton were not exceptional. Black-tailed Godwits may be present in hundreds in almost any month. Curlew Sandpiper and Little Stint are noted annually in small numbers, and Ruff occur more reliably with up to 40 in good years. Scarce or rare species are found from time to time, with Wood and Pectoral Sandpipers, Grey, Red-necked and Wilson's Phalaropes, Black-winged Stilt, Temminck's Stint and Long-billed Dowitcher in recent years. Spoonbill and Spotted Crake have occurred on a number of occasions, and Purple Heron and Crane more rarely. Little Egrets were seen in several recent years, and a Great White Egret in 1996.

As at Red Rocks and Hilbre diurnal movements of thrushes and finches may be heavy given east winds in late autumn.

Timing

The marshes may appear quiet between tides, but activity increases as the river channel floods and waders are forced onto the marsh to roost. Raptors and owls then become more active. Only the very highest tides (33 feet (10–11 m) or more) are now likely to flood the marsh as well. A following wind on the day of the highest tides might still have the same effect. On high tide days the car park at Parkgate fills up with birdwatchers very quickly, so it is advisable to take up a good position an hour or two before the tide. Evening visits give views of harriers entering the roost as the light fades. Prolonged east or southeast winds in May are a sign that passage harriers may occur, or perhaps even some overshooting southern heron. Similar winds in September or October may bring Eurasian waders to the pools.

Access

Access is essentially restricted to a series of lanes and footpaths which run the length of the landward side of the marshes from Burton northwestward to Gayton. The whole area lies to the west of the A540 Chester to Hoylake road. To view Burton Marshes, take Denhall Lane westward from Burton village until the marshes, here grazed by sheep, appear in front (SJ 302736). Pools here may hold waders at any time, Wigeon and Teal in winter. An unmade road runs north from here to Neston, with birdwatching all the way. The Decca pools, beyond Denhall House Farm, are particularly productive and can be viewed by climbing the bank opposite. The other main vantage point is the site of the old baths at Parkgate, now a car park. From Parkgate village take the road along the front northwestward until it swings away from the marsh. Here fork left along a side road with speed ramps which leads to the car park (SJ 273791). Watch from here for raptors and possibly rails. Walk northwards along the seawall for further views of finches and perhaps Water Pipit. A path which leads inland from the car park connects to the Wirral Way.

Walk southwards from Parkgate along the edge of the marsh to reach

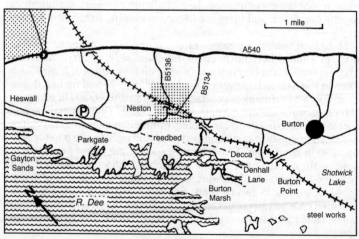

Neston reedbed. Raptors may also be seen here in winter, Water Pipit in spring and warblers in summer. The Shotwick fields are viewed by taking the industrial estate road westward off the A550(T) south of Shotwick village (SJ 338708).

Calendar

All year: Shelduck, Oystercatcher, Redshank and Lapwing breed; Black-headed Gull always present and many pairs nest; Black-tailed Godwits usually present. Reed Bunting and Skylark nest commonly, with perhaps Stonechat. Grey Herons stalk along the shoreline. Raven and Peregrine often seen.

December–February: Flocks of finches gather along edge of marsh; Chaffinch, Brambling, Greenfinch, Linnet, fewer Twite and Goldfinch, joined by House and Tree Sparrow, perhaps Corn Bunting. Hundreds of Skylark and Reed Bunting out on marsh, with Rock and a few Water Pipits in creeks. Lapland Bunting annual. Snipe, Jack Snipe and Water Rail may be flushed into view by high tide. Lapwing and Golden Plover at Burton or Shotwick, where perhaps joined in severe weather by grey geese or wild swans. Pintail, Teal and Wigeon in thousands out on marsh, and Shelduck on flats. Spotted Redshank and Greenshank occasional. Merlin, Hen Harrier and Short-eared Owl hunt marshes, with commoner Kestrel and Sparrowhawk.

March–May: Wildfowl mostly depart in March. Wader flocks disperse a little later; a sprinkling of stints or 'shanks' may pass through in April or May. Raptors still regular to early April, then progressively scarcer. Marsh Harrier possible in May. Pink-breasted Water Pipit in March and April.

June–July: A few Pintail, Teal, Shoveler may linger along with small numbers of non-breeding waders such as Bar-tailed Godwit. Common Tern fly out from Shotton (Clwyd) to fish in marsh pools or the Dee. Grasshopper, Reed and Sedge Warblers in Neston reedbed. Quail in some years.

August–November: Wader passage in August may bring Spotted Redshank and Greenshank in large numbers which continue into September when Little Stint and Curlew Sandpiper may also appear. Rarer waders more likely in September or October, when raptors also return.

Habitat

Hilbre, at just under 12 acres (5 hectares) and with cliffs rising to 55 ft (17 m) on the exposed western side, is the largest of a group of three islands lying about a mile (1.6 km) to the west of the north-west tip of Wirral in the mouth of the Dee estuary. At low tide the islands are accessible, with caution, across the sands from West Kirby, but at high tide they are cut off from the mainland. All three islands are composed of red sandstone and topped with rough grassland. Apart from a few bushes on Hilbre and some bracken on Middle Eye, there is little cover for birds and, other than an old, roofless lifeboat house and a small, often full seawatching hide, even less shelter for birdwatchers. Since 1957 detailed notes have been kept of the island's birds by members of the Hilbre Bird Observatory. The West Hoyle Bank, a large sandbank to the west of the islands, is regularly used by grey seals which haul themselves out of the water there. At high tide the seals are often seen bobbing below the cliffs of the island. At low tide sands are exposed stretching from Hoylake and West Kirby to Hilbre, but there are a number of deep runnels to trap the unwary. These extensive flats are the feeding grounds for thousands of shorebirds—waders and gulls. Sea-ducks are seen occasionally off Hilbre. Their former haunt in the channel off Caldy is less attractive following progressive silting of the estuary.

Species

In excess of 225 species have been recorded at Hilbre, but few breed because of the restricted habitat. Shelduck are perhaps the most appealing to the casual visitor. Cormorant rest on sandbanks offshore at low tide. Vast flocks of waders winter in the estuary. In late July the first Dunlin, perhaps a thousand or more, return from the tundra. They are joined by flocks of white-bellied Sanderling, on the way to winter quarters on African beaches, which continue to pass through during August and September. Up to 20,000 Oystercatcher, sometimes more, arrive in August and remain in similar or even larger numbers right through the winter. August also sees the peak of Ringed Plover passage; Dunlin, Curlew and Redshanks continue to increase; and early Knot, some of them 'red' summer-plumaged birds, black-bellied Grey Plover and godwits of either species may arrive. Turnstones reach 200–300 on Hilbre in August and September, flicking over seaweed and pebbles in their search for food. Grey Plovers may exceed 1,000 in September as Knot increase, reaching several thousands by October. A speciality of the island is the flock of Purple Sandpiper which builds up from mid October into November, reaching perhaps 40–50 birds in total. Winter Knot flocks have reduced in size in recent winters, but may still exceed 5,000. There may be 10,000–20,000 Dunlins, several hundred Bar-tailed and over 1,000 Black-tailed Godwit, with a similar number of Curlew and several thousand Redshanks. Hundreds of Grey Plover and a smaller number of Ringed Plover will also be present, with several hundred Sanderlings at times, while Oystercatchers remain abundant and highly conspicuous.

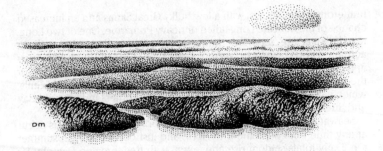

Knot flock

By no means all of these birds will use the outer estuary at any one time, and many commute between the Dee and the Alt or Ribble estuaries. High-tide roosts may gather on the two lesser Hilbre islands, which should be left undisturbed at high tide for this purpose. Quite often the roosts are disturbed by a Peregrine, several of which hunt the estuary daily in winter. Rather less often a Merlin appears. Lacking the burst of speed with which Peregrine take their prey, Merlin rely on persistence instead and may be watched towering and swooping for minutes on end as some unfortunate wader seeks to throw the falcon off its tail.

Numbers of waders in the estuary are falling by March. In April and May the Purple Sandpiper flock returns north, perhaps to Greenland. By June only a few Oystercatcher, Curlew and Redshank remain, with occasional birds of other species.

Shelduck also haunt the outer estuary in moderate numbers. In most winters they are joined by at least one small party of Brent Goose, usually dark-breasted birds. This is a scarce species in the region as a whole. A favourite haunt is around the Tanskey Rocks south of Little Eye, where Wigeon may be seen resting over the high tide. Large numbers of dabbling ducks winter on the marshes of the inner Dee, but few wander this far out. Occasionally parties of Pink-footed Geese fly over from the Southport mosslands and continue up the Dee or into Wales, and Pintail may fly over from Gayton Sands. In March herds of Icelandic Whooper or Siberian Bewick's Swans pass over.

Scaup are seen infrequently now off Hilbre. Up to 400 have been counted, although they can be elusive. At high tide look for the grey-backed drakes bobbing offshore with the chocolate-coloured ducks. Often a few Goldeneye are present also, and perhaps a Merganser or even a Long-tailed Duck. In rough weather the occasional sea-duck shelters on West Kirby Marine Lake. Visitors to Hilbre often go there specifically for the seawatching. Given two or three days of strong north-westerlies in the autumn Leach's Petrels will appear. Ideal conditions are infrequent, and in some years non-existent, but most autumns produce at least a handful of birds. Outstanding among recent years were 1978, when 959 passed by on 27 September, 1980 with 337 on 14 September, 1983 with 265 on 19 October and 243 on 13 September 1987. Most birds beat westward into the wind close by the north end of the island. Exhausted birds may settle for a while on the sea. Storm Petrels occur only rarely among the larger Leach's. The same autumnal storms blow in other exciting seabirds. Arctic Skuas, which occur occasionally in spring and at any time from July to October, are more numerous at such times, with a few bulky Great Skuas and an increased chance of the delicate Long-tailed or heavy Pomarine. One or two Long-tailed Skuas are reported during most prolonged windy spells in autumn. Grey Phalaropes are not seen every year but odd birds may appear under such conditions. As Kittiwakes stream past look out for the tricoloured wing pattern of rare Sabine's Gull. A flock of Little Gulls, which varies greatly in size from year to year, winters in Liverpool Bay and these birds too may be blown inshore.

Seawatching is not limited to autumn storms, however. Divers occur at any time from September to April, and just occasionally in summer too. Daily totals seldom rise above ten, with Red-throated Diver by far the most numerous species. Great Northern Diver are seen on only a handful of days each year, and Black-throated even less often. Up to 20 or more Great Crested Grebe may be counted offshore in late autumn, with 60 or more early in recent winters. The smaller grebes are seldom noted—only three or four a year—with Red-necked more likely than Black-necked or Slavonian.

Fulmars fly within sight of land between March and October when the wind blows from the west or northwest. On windy days more than 50 may be logged. Manx Shearwaters appear under similar conditions between June and September, with seldom more than a dozen even on good days, although 267 were seen on 31 July 1993. Gannets are seen from March to November. Few ducks frequent the open sea off the Dee mouth. Common Scoter may be seen in any month, perhaps least often in late winter and early summer; occasionally rafts of up to 100 bob offshore, but more usually small parties fly past in lines, the black drakes and browner, pale-cheeked ducks easily recognisable by their stocky outline and rapid wingbeats. The heavier Velvet Scoter is rarely seen. Terns occur offshore from April to October. Common Tern are generally the most numerous, and occur throughout the summer. Dozens may be counted on spring days, but from July to September much larger numbers may be seen. Recent reports suggest that the majority of these birds are Common Terns, although Arctic Terns also pass through in small numbers.

The scarcer Little Tern passes the Dee mouth from mid-April to late May with perhaps 15–20 birds on a good day, and again on the return passage. Noisy Sandwich Terns show a similar pattern of occurrence with a predominance of autumn records. Fifty to 100 pass by on better days in late April or May, and several hundreds may be counted in August. A few late birds are seen in October. The Roseate Tern is a very scarce migrant, not reliably seen even once a year; Black Terns are a little more frequent.

Both Guillemot and Razorbill occur offshore with a small moulting flock in Liverpool Bay in summer. These birds may be accompanied by chicks, too young to fly, which have nonetheless swum considerable distances from their breeding colonies, perhaps in North Wales or on the Isle of Man. The browner-backed, shorter-tailed Guillemot is usually the more common of the two species. Only single figures of either are likely on any day from November to June, but larger numbers may come within range given onshore winds in autumn. Other auks—Puffin, Little Auk and Black Guillemot—occur only rarely.

Movements of passerine migrants have been studied intensively at Hilbre. Spring passage begins in March with the first Chiffchaff, Wheatear and perhaps a Ring Ouzel, and the start of a movement of

Meadow Pipits which reaches its peak in the first few days of April, when over a thousand may pass in a day. Migration is at its height in late April or early May when, given suitable conditions, the bushes may be full of migrants shortly after dawn. The Willow Warbler is the principal species involved. Spring passage at Hilbre is in fact more varied than autumn. Sedge and Grasshopper Warblers, Common and Lesser Whitethroats, Redstart and Whinchat are typical spring migrants. Tree Pipits are also frequent. Most summer visitors occur in at least small numbers. A Melodious Warbler passed through in May 1994. The shortage of cover on Hilbre means that migrants are unlikely to stay for more than a few hours. Considerable numbers of Goldfinch and Redpoll pass in April and May, with perhaps 30 or so of either species at Hilbre on some days. Tree Sparrows also pass through.

Emigration of summer visitors picks up in August, when the largest autumn totals of Willow Warblers occur. On occasion over 100 of these dainty birds will descend on Hilbre. Variety on the island on autumn passage is somewhat restricted, but Garden Warblers occur more often at this season than in spring, with perhaps the odd Pied Flycatcher. A few Black Redstarts are noted each year, in either spring or late autumn. Yellow-browed Warblers have appeared several times in late autumn; an Icterine Warbler was seen in September 1993; and a Yellow-breasted Bunting in September 1994. Relatively few diurnal migrants pass over, these preferring to follow the mainland coastline. Immigrant winter thrushes and Starlings fly over the island in large numbers, however, from the end of September onwards, when finch movements may also be heavy. Renewed movement of plovers, larks and thrushes may follow winter frosts. Snow Buntings are seen occasionally.

Timing

For seawatching, strong winds from a northwesterly quarter are ideal, and a persistent blow for two or more days in September or October will bring in petrels, Little Gull and skuas. Tide tables should be consulted and visits timed around the high tide. Particular attention should be paid to the state of the tide when visiting Hilbre (see under Access). In April and May the largest arrivals of warblers and other passerines take place with southwesterly winds curving up from Spain, or on southeasterlies. Birds arrive shortly after dawn, rest and feed briefly then move on. Few remain by mid morning. In autumn east or northeast winds bring in the birds. Severe winter weather may bring large westward movements of birds seeking milder conditions. A thaw following prolonged cold induces return movements.

Access

Permits are no longer necessary to visit the island, except for any group of more than six persons. Such groups should apply to the Visitor Centre, Wirral Country Park, Station Road, Thurstaston, Wirral, L61 0HN. The centre is open daily from 10 am until 5 pm, (tel: 0151 648 4371/3884). The walk across the sands to Hilbre can be tricky and should not be attempted in foggy conditions. From junction 2 of the M53 follow signs for West Kirby, then the brown signs for the Marine Lake which lead to Dee Lane. It is usual to set out from the end of Dee Lane at least three hours before high tide and head for the left-hand side of the southernmost (i.e. left-hand) island, Little Eye, thereby avoiding treacherous gutters. Follow the western side of Little Eye and Middle

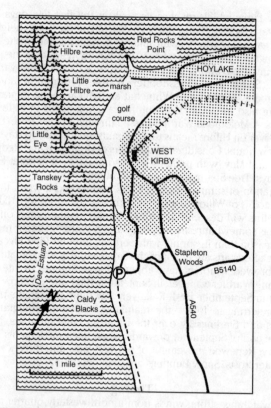

Eye to Hilbre. Visitors must then remain on the island until at least two hours after high tide when it is again possible to return to the mainland. The state of the tide clearly places constraints on those wishing to visit the island at dawn to see migrants. Most early risers will be satisfied with the possibilities offered by the Red Rocks area. The marine lake at West Kirby is obvious from the end of Dee Lane, and should be checked for waterfowl.

Calendar

All year: Few nesting species, but Cormorants and Kestrels present for much of year.

December–February: Vast flocks of estuarine waders including Black-tailed Godwit, Turnstone and Purple Sandpiper on Hilbre. Perhaps a few Brent Goose. Scaup and other sea-ducks. Peregrine and Merlin hunt the waders. Red-throated Diver and Great Crested Grebe on sea; possibly rarer divers or Red-necked Grebe. Severe weather brings westward movement of Lapwing, Golden Plover, Skylark and thrushes, with wandering Pink-footed Goose. Snow Bunting a possibility.

March–May: Winter duck and wader flocks disperse. Spring passage brings Sanderling, perhaps Whimbrel, and other wader species. Purple Sandpiper depart by mid May. Seawatching improves, with possibility of Fulmar, Gannet and Kittiwake from March onwards, and perhaps a skua. Terns appear during April. Passerine migration starts in March; heavy movement of Meadow Pipit in early April. Passage peaks late April–early May with falls of Willow Warbler, with other warblers and chats. White and Yellow Wagtails also regular, with steady passage of hirundines.

June–July: Common Tern offshore, with Fulmar, Gannet and Manx Shearwater in windy weather, Razorbill and Guillemot from July onwards. Small numbers of non-breeding waders summer in the estuary, and by late July Sanderling and other species start to return.

August–November: Wader flocks increase. Early birds may be in breeding plumage. Purple Sandpiper return in October and November. Northwesterly gales in September and October, or even early November, bring Leach's Petrel; Arctic, Great, perhaps Pomarine and possibly Long-tailed Skuas; Kittiwake and Little Gull with the occasional Sabine's Gull. Manx Shearwater until end of September, Fulmar and auks into October, and Gannet until November; Common Scoter throughout the period. Large gathering of terns in early autumn. Falls of warblers in August or September consist mostly of Willow Warbler or Chiffchaff, with the occasional rarity. Diurnal passage in October and November of winter thrushes, Starling, Chaffinch, Linnet and Greenfinch, and buntings (which may include Snow Bunting).

ADDITIONAL SITE: STAPLETON WOODS

A small but varied woodland in which most typical woodland birds may be seen. All three woodpeckers, Wood Warbler, Pied and Spotted Flycatchers are present in season. The woods are well situated to receive migrants at passage seasons.

Access
From West Kirby southwards on the A540. A small car park is situated on the right a short distance after the Grammar School (SJ 236861). The wood is divided into two by the public footpath, with mature beech and oak trees below the path and more open birch woodland above. Numerous paths run through the woods, but the most productive skirts the southern edge, at the boundary with open fields.

68 RED ROCKS, HOYLAKE

Habitat

Red Rocks Point at Hoylake, the northwest tip of Wirral, consists, like Hilbre Island (site 67) of a sandstone outcrop. The farthest point, Bird Rock, is cut off by the tide and is then popular with roosting waders, provided it is not occupied by anglers. Gardens at the point contain a number of bushes attractive to migrants. Around the corner into the estuary a line of mature sand dunes runs south to West Kirby, separating the golf course from the shore. Between the dunes and the beach lies Red Rocks marsh, a reserve of the Cheshire Wildlife Trust, with its reedbed and alder thickets.

Species

In excess of 235 species have been recorded at Red Rocks, making this one of the richest areas for birdwatching in the region. Sedge Warbler and possibly Reed and Grasshopper Warblers are the only breeding birds of note, although Kestrels may hunt the dunes. Many of the Dee's estuarine waders can be seen feeding off the marsh and, as the tide rises, in flight out of the estuary past the point. These birds used to roost on the beach here, but were frequently disturbed by horseriders and dog walkers, so now usually roost elsewhere. Peregrine are frequently seen hunting waders over the estuary. As at Hilbre, movements of passerine migrants have been studied intensively, and there is a great deal of similarity between movements at the two sites. March brings the first spring visitors, and emigrant Goldcrest visit the gardens. Meadow Pipit passage is also heavy in early spring. Westward passage of Collared Doves is a feature of April, with up to 100 or more on the best days. Conditions suitable for a fall are infrequent. Prolonged southerly winds and poor visibility may ground Willow Warblers and small numbers of other migrants at the point soon after dawn. Such days are rare, however, and the vast majority of migrants pass straight through. White Wagtails are seen more regularly on the west coast of Wirral than anywhere else in Cheshire. It seems probable that these pale, slender wagtails are moving up the west coast of Britain towards Icelandic rather than continental breeding grounds. Up to 45 or so may frequent the beach at Red Rocks between mid April and mid May, with 350 the record count. The native Pied Wagtail will often be present alongside for comparison. Spring rarities have included Dartford Warbler, Tawny Pipit, Savi's Warbler, Serin and Red-backed Shrike. Hoopoes have occurred on several occasions. Given the nature of movement through the site, many of the rarities reported are seen by only one or two observers.

Seawatching can be good given onshore winds. Fulmars and Gannets are visible offshore between March and June and again in autumn. Manx Shearwaters pass in small numbers between June and September, with the occasional larger scale movements characteristic of this species. On 31 July 1993 three Mediterranean Shearwaters were seen during a passage of hundreds of Manx. Autumn gales may bring Leach's Petrels, skuas and other exciting species.

Diurnal autumn migrants, following the coastline southwards, start with Swifts in July. Sizeable movements of hirundines may follow as autumn progresses. Tree Pipit may be picked up overhead by their rough 'teez' calls. Notice that their flight undulates more evenly, and lacks the jerky irregularities typical of Meadow Pipit. Easterly winds in autumn, as in spring, may also bring in rarities. These have included Yellow-browed Warbler, Richard's Pipit and Red-throated Pipit. From mid September to mid October parties of Blue Tit fly westward along the north coast of Wirral and either drop into the reeds at Red Rocks or continue westward across the sands past Hilbre into Wales. They are accompanied by smaller numbers of other tits and the occasional Treecreeper or woodpecker. Ringing has shown these to be local birds dispersing after the breeding season. From late September into November immigrant winter visitors fly over the Dee mouth in large numbers. Movement is most concentrated at the point in the second half of October. Hundreds, even thousands of Starling, Redwing, Fieldfare and Chaffinch may be counted in a day, with smaller numbers of Linnet, Greenfinch and other species. Snow Buntings may also join in these movements, and from this season onwards small parties visit the area infrequently until April. Winter frosts may initiate weather movements. With the onset of severe weather Golden Plover, Lapwing, Skylark, thrushes and other birds fly west into Wales, perhaps on the way to Ireland.

Timing

Waders seldom roost these days on West Kirby shore, but birds can be watched feeding from various points as the tide rises and again as it falls.

Spring arrivals of migrant passerines are assisted by winds from a southerly quarter. Dawn visits are advisable at Red Rocks, although a search of the bushes here and along the coast may reveal lingering migrants later in the day. In autumn east or northeast winds bring in the birds. Rarities do not turn up with the same regularity as at some east coast stations, and the casual visitor is unlikely to see anything very special, but persistence will eventually be rewarded.

Dispersal movements may be witnessed at Red Rocks on any fine morning in the autumn, but for diurnal movements of long distance migrants conditions are more critical. Low cloud with a fresh or strong breeze from a southerly quarter will result in heavy, visible passage for the first two hours after dawn especially, although movement may continue throughout the day. There is little passage with strong wind, mist or fog, but with clear skies and light wind the birds will fly too high to be seen.

Access

From the Hoylake roundabout on the A553 turn north onto a minor road then first left into Stanley Road (SJ 214889). Park at the far end and walk right to the point (SJ 203886) for seawatching or to scan the flats, or turn left, when the marsh is soon obvious between the beach and the golf course. Migrants may frequent the reedbed or bushes in the dunes. The best cover is a small poplar plantation at the north end of the marsh.

Calendar

All year: Certain wader species may be present all year with non-breeding birds summering in the estuary.

December–February: Wader flocks and Shelducks offshore, with hunting Peregrine. Severe weather brings westward movement of Lapwing, Golden Plover, Skylark and thrushes, with wandering Pink-footed Goose. Stonechats along the dunes; Snow Bunting a possibility.

March–May: Passerine migration starts in March, peaking late April–early May. Similar species involved as at Hilbre, but White Wagtails along Red Rocks shore, and westerly movement of Collared Dove. Fulmars and Gannets in onshore winds, with Terns from April.

June–July: Common Terns offshore and Manx Shearwaters on passage days. Small numbers of non-breeding waders. Grasshopper Warbler along the coast. Mediterranean Gull seen with some regularity.

August–November: Falls of common warblers in early autumn, with perhaps the odd rarity. Locally bred tits and other species on dispersal. Diurnal passage in October and November of winter thrushes. Starling, Chaffinch, Linnet and Greenfinch, and buntings which may include Snow Bunting. Seawatching may be excellent at this season, with skuas and petrels after strong westerlies.

69 NORTH WIRRAL SHORE

OS Map 108
SJ 29

The north shore of Wirral, running east from Hoylake to New Brighton, is largely given over to market gardens, defended from the sea by a fixed dune system. The whole area may prove attractive to migrants, given the right weather conditions. Rarities have included Great Grey Shrike, Red-breasted Flycatcher, Richard's and Red-throated Pipits, Pallas' Warbler, Yellow-browed Warbler, Savi's Warbler and Britain's fourth Desert Warbler. During onshore gales, the entire coastline offers good seawatching, especially at high tide in autumn. Vehicular access to the top of the seawall is no longer guaranteed, but the car park at Dovepoint is a useful vantage point.

69A DOVE POINT, MEOLS

OS ref: SJ 234907

Reached by driving to the easternmost point of Hoylake promenade. After northwesterly gales in September, petrels, skuas and shearwaters may be seen. Leach's Petrel often come closer to shore here than at any other vantage point along the coast. Dove Point, like New Brighton (site

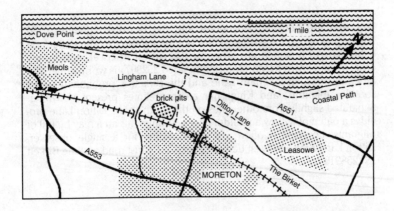

66), allows the luxury of seawatching from a car, an important factor in a gale. However, the state of the tide is critical. Unless the East Hoyle sandbank is completely flooded, passing birds will be too distant for adequate views. On less windy days this sandbank is worth checking, particularly in August, when numerous gulls and terns roost on its easternmost end. In recent years, Mediterranean Gull have been seen regularly between here and Hoylake.

69B MEOLS AND LEASOWE COMMON

OS ref: SJ 250910

In migration periods, the Common, immediately behind the seawall, is particularly good for Wheatear, Whinchat, Ring Ouzel and pipits, whilst Snow Bunting, Twite, Stonechat and Black Redstart are often present in winter. The hedges and ditches are attractive to warblers, and Grasshopper Warblers regularly breed. Access to the market gardens is limited, but they can be viewed from the public footpath and private road (a public right of way). Moreton Brick Pit holds Great Crested Grebe, and is a favourite bathing place for gulls. Mediterranean and Glaucous are regular, and Ring-billed has been seen on a number of occasions.

Leach's Petrel

Access

The area lies between Dovepoint and the Leasowe lighthouse (SJ 262918). Lingham Lane runs south from the lighthouse. The hedges on either side of this lane are probably the easiest to cover, and in any case, a walk down to Moreton Brick Pit (SJ 252907) is worthwhile. The junction between Lingham Lane and the Birkett is probably the best spot for migrants, and Kingfisher are sometimes present in winter. Separated slightly from other sites on the north shore, Ditton Lane provides a patch of willow and alder cover. Though this area may be full of migrants, covering it often proves frustrating for a single observer. Ditton Lane runs east-west between the A551 coast road and the Birkett (SJ 258913).

70 NEW BRIGHTON AND THE OUTER MERSEY ESTUARY

OS Map 108
(See map, p. 125
(site 45))

Habitat

The former holiday resort of New Brighton stands on the corner of the Mersey estuary at the east end of the north Wirral shore. Unusually for the area, the beach here is rocky. A sewage outfall is a further attraction for touring gulls. New Brighton itself has little to offer to birdwatchers, who stand with their backs to the town looking out. The Mersey ferries at Seacombe jetty, to the south, are followed by a mixture of gulls and terns.

Between Rock Ferry oil terminal and New Ferry, 8–10 kilometres up river from the mouth, is another stretch of muddy beach, with some rocky areas and with a developing saltmarsh at its southern end. During autumn and winter there is a small roost of waders by this saltmarsh, while in midwinter up to several hundred Teal and Pintail are regularly present and over 1,000 each of Knot and Dunlin on occasion. There is a rubbish tip to north of Bromborough Pool which attracts large numbers of gulls, many of which rest on the river.

Species

New Brighton is best known for the shelters on its promenade, which provide cover for seawatching during autumn storms. The Irish Sea is largely landlocked, so contains fewer seabird species than more exposed Atlantic or North Sea coasts. Northwesterly gales can produce birds in any month, but the chief attraction is in autumn when hundreds of Leach's Petrel may appear offshore. The Mersey mouth lies in the angle between the Lancashire and North Wales/Wirral coast, so persistent gales, lasting over two or more days, funnel birds into the river. Under such conditions petrels may be seen upriver as far as Seacombe Ferry, and odd birds appear over inland meres and flashes. Many beat out of the river mouth past Fort Perch Rock, some of them being blown back to make further passes. The range of other seabirds involved is similar to those at Hilbre or Seaforth. Pomarine and Long-tailed Skuas and Sabine's Gull are regular in appearance given suitable conditions, which may be less than annual.

From late summer to spring Turnstones frequent the rocky beach, and may be joined in winter by a few Purple Sandpipers. Eider are occasionally seen off Fort Perch Rock. Gulls around the sewage outfall may include uncommon species. Birds following the Mersey ferries at Seacombe have included Little and Mediterranean Gulls as well as Kittiwake. Little Gulls are very often present in the river, although usually on the Liverpool side. The river mouth is at its narrowest here, so watches at passage times allow reasonable views of terns, including Black Terns following easterly winds. Rarer gulls and terns have been recorded.

The New Ferry wader roosts consist chiefly of Redshank, Curlew, Oystercatcher, Knot and Dunlin, but many other estuary species appear from time to time. Teal and Pintail are present along the shore in winter, the latter offering unusually close views at times. Glaucous and other gulls join the scavenging throng at the tip or loafing offshore.

Timing

For seawatching, strong winds from a northwesterly quarter are ideal, and a persistent blow for two or more days in September or October will bring in petrels, Little Gull and skuas. At low tide the sea retreats a considerable distance from the shore, although watching is still practicable from New Brighton, and during the strongest blows petrels may be seen flying over the beach at Leasowe. The shore at New Ferry is narrower although birds are more likely to be driven into view by a rising tide. Roosts are largest here during January and February. Waders also move downriver on the falling tide from roosts further into the estuary to which access is very restricted. Tide tables should be consulted and visits timed around the high tide.

Access

During storms and in winter months, there is seldom any difficulty in parking along the seafront at New Brighton. View from the shelters near to the fort, or from a parked car. The sewage outfall lies towards the southern end of the promenade along the Mersey shore. Traffic is prohibited here, but a walk along the front to check the gulls will also give a chance to scan for waders, possibly including Purple Sandpiper, feeding on the rocky shore. The Seacombe ferries ply across the river from a pierhead some 2 miles (3.2 km) upriver from New Brighton. Watch the boats from vantage points south of the terminal.

To view the New Ferry wader roost and winter wildfowl, take suburban roads eastward from New Ferry village and look down the clay cliffs at SJ 343855.

Calendar

December–February: Purple Sandpiper occasional with regular Turnstones on New Brighton beach. Gulls at sewage outfall, New Ferry rubbish tip and following ferries. Occasional sea-ducks or auks in river. High-tide wader roost at New Ferry of Curlew, Dunlin, Knot, Redshank and other species.

March–July: Tern passage in spring and birds feed offshore in summer. Otherwise quiet except during onshore gales.

August–November: Turnstones return from August, few Purple Sandpiper later. Tern passage along river may bring rarer species. Greater likelihood of uncommon gulls. Petrels and skuas after storms.

SELECT BIBLIOGRAPHY

The authors wish to thank the authors and organisations for a source of information from the following publications.

Books

Cooper, J.H. & Wood, J.C. (1986) *A Checklist of the Birds of Bolton*, Bolton RSPB Group.

Craggs, J.D. (1982) *Hilbre, The Cheshire Island*, Liverpool University Press.

Green, G. & Cade, M. (1989) *Where to watch birds in Dorset, Hampshire and the Isle of Wight*, Christopher Helm.

Guest, J., Elphick, D., Hunter, J.S.A., & Norman, D. (1992) *The Breeding Bird Atlas of Cheshire and Wirral*, Cheshire and Wirral Ornithological Society.

Hardy, E. (1979) *Birdwatching in Lancashire*, Dalesman.

Harrison, R. & Rogers, D.A. (1977) *The Birds of Rostherne Mere*, NCC.

Hutcheson, M. (1985) *Cumbrian Birds*, Frank Peters, Kendal.

Madders, M. (1985) *Birdwatching in the Lake District*, Bartholomew guides.

Madders, M. & Welstead, J. (1989) *Where to watch birds in Scotland*, Christopher Helm.

Mitchell, W.R. & Robson, R.W. (1973) *Pennine Birds*, Dalesman

—— (1974) *Lakeland Birds*, Dalesman.

Prater, A.J. (1981) *Estuary Birds of Britain and Ireland*, Poyser.

Sharrock, J.T.R. *et al.* (1976) *Rare Birds in Britain and Ireland*, Poyser.

Spencer, K.G. (1973) *The Status and Distribution of Birds in Lancashire*, Turner & Earnshaw, Burnley.

Wilson, J (1974) *The Birds of Morecambe Bay*, Dalesman.

Wilson, J.D. (1985) *Birds and Birdwatching at Pennington Flash*, Pennington Flash Joint Committee.

Annual Reports

Birds in Cumbria, Cumbria Naturalist Union.

Birds in Greater Manchester, Greater Manchester Bird Club

Cheshire and Wirral Bird Reports, Cheshire and Wirral Ornithological Society.

Fylde Bird Club Reports.

Lancashire Bird Reports, Lancashire and Cheshire Fauna Society.

Lancaster and District Birdwatching Society Annual Reports.

Seaforth Bird Reports, Lancashire Wildlife Trust.

Walney Bird Observatory Annual Reports.

CODE OF CONDUCT FOR BIRDWATCHERS

Today's birdwatchers are a powerful force for nature conservation. The number of those of us interested in birds rises continually and it is vital that we take seriously our responsibility to avoid any harm to birds.

We must also present a responsible image to non-birdwatchers who may be affected by our activities and particularly those on whose sympathy and support the future of birds may rest.

There are 10 points to bear in mind:
1. The welfare of birds must come first.
2. Habitat must be protected.
3. Keep disturbance to birds and their habitat to a minimum.
4. When you find a rare bird think carefully about whom you should tell.
5. Do not harass rare migrants.
6. Abide by the bird protection laws at all times.
7. Respect the rights of landowners.
8. Respect the rights of other people in the countryside.
9. Make your records available to the local bird recorder.
10. Behave abroad as you would when birdwatching at home.

Welfare of birds must come first

Whether your particular interest is photography, ringing, sound recording, scientific study or just birdwatching, remember that the welfare of the bird must always come first.

Habitat protection

Its habitat is vital to a bird and therefore we must ensure that our activities do not cause damage.

Keep disturbance to a minimum

Birds' tolerance of disturbance varies between species and seasons. Therefore, it is safer to keep all disturbance to a minimum. No birds should be disturbed from the nest in case opportunities for predators to take eggs or young are increased. In very cold weather disturbance to birds may cause them to use vital energy at a time when food is difficult to find. Wildfowlers already impose bans during cold weather: birdwatchers should exercise similar discretion.

Rare breeding birds

If you discover a rare bird breeding and feel that protection is necessary, inform the appropriate RSPB Regional Office, or the Species Protection Department at the Lodge. Otherwise it is best in almost all circumstances to keep the record strictly secret in order to avoid disturbance by other birdwatchers and attacks by egg-collectors. Never visit known sites of rare breeding birds unless they are adequately protected. Even your presence may give away the site to others and cause so many other visitors that the birds may fail to breed successfully.

Disturbance at or near the nest of species listed on the First Schedule of the Wildlife and Countryside Act 1981 is a criminal offence.

Copies of Wild Birds and the Law are obtainable from the RSPB, The Lodge, Sandy, Beds. SG19 2DL (send two 2nd class stamps).

Rare migrants

Rare migrants or vagrants must not be harassed. If you discover one, consider the circumstances carefully before telling anyone. Will an influx of birdwatchers disturb the bird or others in the area? Will the habitat be damaged? Will problems be caused with the landowner?

The Law

The bird protection laws (now embodied in the Wildlife and Countryside Act 1981) are the result of hard campaigning by previous generations of birdwatchers. As birdwatchers we must abide by them at all times and not allow them to fall into disrepute.

Respect the rights of landowners

The wishes of landowners and occupiers of land must be respected. Do not enter land without permission. Comply with permit schemes. If you are leading a group, do give advance notice of the visit, even if a formal permit scheme is not in operation. Always obey the Country Code.

Respect the rights of other people

Have proper consideration for other birdwatchers. Try not to disrupt their activities or scare the birds they are watching. There are many other people who also use the countryside. Do not interfere with their activities and, if it seems that what they are doing is causing unnecessary disturbance to birds, do try to take a balanced view. Flushing gulls when walking a dog on a beach may do little harm, while the same dog might be a serious disturbance at a tern colony. When pointing this out to a non-birdwatcher be courteous, but firm. The non-birdwatchers' goodwill towards birds must not be destroyed by the attitudes of birdwatchers.

Keeping records

Much of today's knowledge about birds is the result of meticulous record keeping by our predecessors. Make sure you help to add to tomorrow's knowledge by sending records to your county bird recorder.

Birdwatching abroad

Behave abroad as you would at home. This code should be firmly adhered to when abroad (whatever the local laws). Well behaved birdwatchers can be important ambassadors for bird protection.

This code has been drafted after consultation between The British Ornithologists' Union, British Trust for Ornithology, the Royal Society for the Protection of Birds, the Scottish Ornithologists' Club, the Wildfowl Trust and the Editors of *British Birds*.

Further copies may be obtained from The Royal Society for the Protection of Birds, The Lodge, Sandy, Beds. SG19 2DL.

INDEX OF SPECIES BY SITE NUMBER

Index of Species by Site Number